Race, Education, and Reintegrating Formerly Incarcerated Citizens

Critical Perspectives on Race, Crime, and Justice

Series Editor

Tony Gaskew, University of Pittsburgh, Bradford

This book series seeks interdisciplinary scholars whose work critically addresses the racialization of criminal justice systems. Grounded within the connective space of history, the nuances of race continue to define the standard of how justice is applied throughout policing, courts, and correctional systems. As such, this series is open to examine monographs and edited volumes that critically analyze race from multiple narratives—sociopolitical, cultural, feminist, psychosocial, ecological, critical theory, philosophical—along criminal justice lines. The Critical Perspectives on Race, Crime, and Justice book series speaks to the significant scholarship being produced in an era where race continues to intersect with crime and justice.

Titles in the Series

Race, Education, and Reintegrating Formerly Incarcerated Citizens: Counterstories and Counterspaces, edited by John R. Chaney and Joni Schwartz

Race, Education, and Reintegrating Formerly Incarcerated Citizens

Counterstories and Counterspaces

Edited by
John R. Chaney
Joni Schwartz

LEXINGTON BOOKS
Lanham • Boulder • New York • London

Published by Lexington Books
An imprint of The Rowman & Littlefield Publishing Group, Inc.
4501 Forbes Boulevard, Suite 200, Lanham, Maryland 20706
www.rowman.com

Unit A, Whitacre Mews, 26-34 Stannary Street, London SE11 4AB

British Library Cataloguing in Publication Information Available

Library of Congress Cataloging-in-Publication Data

Names: Chaney, John R., 1951- editor. | Schwartz, Joni, editor.
Title: Race, education, and reintegrating formerly incarcerated citizens : counterstories and counter-
    spaces / edited by John R. Chaney, Joni Schwartz.
Description: Lanham : Lexington Books, 2017. | Series: Critical perspectives on race, crime, and
    justice | Includes bibliographical references and index.
Identifiers: LCCN 2017011825 (print) | LCCN 2017021003 (ebook) | ISBN 9781498540919 (elec-
    tronic) | ISBN 9781498540902 (cloth : alk. paper)
Subjects: LCSH: Prisoners—Education—United States. | Ex-convicts—Education—United States. |
    Criminals—Rehabilitation—United States. | Prisoners—Deinstitutionalization—United States. |
    Education and crime—United States.
Classification: Classification: LCC HV8883.3.U5 (ebook) | LCC HV8883.3.U5 R33 2017 (print) |
    DDC 364.80973—dc23
LC record available at https://lccn.loc.gov/2017011825

Printed in the United States of America

Contents

Foreword

Elliott Dawes

As an interdisciplinary collection of essays written by supporters of higher education reentry programs that enable people with criminal justice histories to access college, *Race, Education, and Reintegrating Formerly Incarcerated Citizens: Counterstories and Counterspaces* represents critical race theory scholarship that bridges the gap between theory and practice. In *Looking to the Bottom: Critical Legal Studies and Reparations*, critical race theorist Mari Matsuda argues that the writings, testimonies, and experiences of marginalized group members should be considered, examined, and incorporated into legal theory and policy making.[1] For Matsuda, "[t]hose who have experienced discrimination speak with a special voice to which we should listen. Looking to the bottom—adopting the perspective of those who have seen and felt the falsity of the liberal promise—can assist critical scholars in the task of fathoming the phenomenology of law and defining the elements of justice. . . . The technique of imagining oneself black and poor in some hypothetical world is less effective than studying the actual experience of black poverty and listening to those who have done so. When notions of right and wrong, justice and injustice, are examined not from an abstract position but from the position of groups who have suffered through history, moral relativism recedes and identifiable normative priorities emerge."[2] Ultimately, as Matsuda argues, "the actual experience, history, culture, and intellectual tradition of people of color in America" is a valuable yet often overlooked resource that should inform our ongoing national public discourse on creating a fair and just participatory democracy.[3]

Matsuda's conception of "bottoms up" inquiry and the exclusion of the voices of people of color in the formulation of legal theory and public policy are much more than "diversity matters" arguments. Of course, understanding diversity does indeed matter in an increasingly multiracial, multicultural, and multilingual nation; but, Matsuda is more concerned about how knowledge and arguments are constructed. For criminal justice reform advocates and practitioners who through their work are attempting to counteract the impact of mass incarceration on communities of color, there must be an internal advocacy within our social movements that demands the inclusion of the voices and perspectives of those who are most impacted by oppressive policies and practices because they are uniquely positioned to share their invaluable insights. As the millennials participating in the Black Lives Matter movement seem to understand already, it makes little sense to advocate for social change without including our best change agents, namely those who have been most directly impacted by criminal justice dysfunction and mass incarceration. Although academics and administrators at community colleges and other open-access institutions often think of themselves as change agents, it cannot be gainsaid, as Colleen P. Eren observes in her chapter, "No Dismantling with the Master's Tools," that the community of criminal justice scholars in the United States does not reflect the demographics of our increasingly diverse nation and therefore often does not include the voices of people of color who are most impacted by criminal justice dysfunction.

With Matsuda's conception of "bottoms up" inquiry in mind, any examination of criminal justice dysfunction, particularly the social costs of mass incarceration, should begin with the perspectives of those who have been most impacted. Because unarmed people of color, particularly young men of color, are often the targets of aggressive policing, the awful reality is that their voices are silenced in the public discourse on policing because so many do not survive encounters with the police. When a victim of police violence is unavailable to speak, however, their family members and allies are often forced to engage in long-protracted struggles to seek justice for their deceased loved ones. However, are they being heard?

For critical race theorists like Matsuda, Anthony Baez, Sean Bell, Ramarley Graham, Eric Garner, Akai Gurley, and Walter Scott, victims of police violence, their family members and allies, and witnesses like Feiden Santana, a Dominican immigrant who had the courage to use his smartphone to record the shooting death of Walter Scott by Officer Michael Slager, are "people at the bottom." In describing people of color and other marginalized groups as "people at the bottom," Matsuda is not only describing a racist social hierarchy in the United States; rather, she is observing a society in which some people are simply not heard. When aggressive law enforcement tactics are constructed, the people of color who are most impacted by dangerous policing are rarely consulted.

At a glacial pace, it is becoming clear to policy makers what critical race theorists like Matsuda have been advocating for decades, that any substantive discussion about criminal justice dysfunction must value the perspectives and experiences of the people of color, including the young men of color, who are most negatively impacted. The academic work assembled in *Race, Education, and Reintegrating Formerly Incarcerated Citizens* represents an enormous step forward in realizing the vision of critical race theorists by presenting model higher education reentry programs and college access programs that are led by practitioners who honor the experiences of the students they serve by first and foremost listening to them. Additionally, as with many of the programs discussed in this text, people with criminal justice histories are not only mere clients of successful higher education reentry efforts but are the leaders, teachers, mentors, and administrators who drive such college access programs.

Similarly, applying Matsuda's conception of "bottoms up" inquiry to an examination of the social costs of incarceration necessarily requires listening to the views of formerly incarcerated people. As many of the writers in this text lament, it is an incontrovertible fact that the United States leads the world in the actual numbers as well as the proportion of its citizens who are incarcerated.[4] African American men, in particular, are subjected to various forms of criminal justice supervision in grossly disproportionate numbers. With well over two million Americans under some form of criminal justice supervision, and an even larger number of people with criminal justice histories, any reparations agenda for black America must consider that the vestiges of slavery and segregation are present in today's society in the form of mass incarceration resulting from the war on drugs.[5]

Critical race theorist Mari Matsuda developed her idea of "bottoms up" inquiry in a 1987 article that, in part, addressed opposition to movements for Japanese American reparations for their internment during World War II, native Hawaiian reparations for the United States military's overthrow of the Hawaiian monarchy in the 1890s, and African American reparations for the enduring vestiges of slavery, segregation, and racism discussed in Michael Holzman's "Schooling for Prison, Incarceration for Poverty," the first essay of this text. Given the enormous impact of mass incarceration on black America, with well over a million people, disproportionately African American, imprisoned for non-violent offenses, particularly non-violent drug offenses, an African American reparations agenda should advocate for returning college education programs to prisons and jails as well as higher education reentry programs. But, since the 1990s, the nation has promoted the complete opposite in its public policy and practices by investing in increased incarceration, defunding higher education in prisons and jails and ignoring access to higher education as an effective reentry strategy despite limited funding opportunities under the federal Second Chance Act of 2008.[6]

In addition to focusing attention on the exclusion of people with criminal justice histories from the discourse on criminal justice dysfunction, *Counterstories and Counterspaces* also features a number of essays that explain the trauma experienced by people of color, particularly young men of color, growing up in communities that are subjected to constant police surveillance and unorthodox policing that make them vulnerable to pipelines to incarceration rather than pipelines to college. Whether reading John R. Chaney's compelling autoethnography, "Epiphany of the Prodigal Son," recounting his struggles with addiction leading to his incarceration or Carlyle Van Thompson and Paul Schwartz's "A New Normal: Young Men of Color: Trauma and Engagement in Learning," it is evident that pronounced trauma can result from being: (1) subjected to aggressive policing, (2) adjudicated through criminal justice systems that are rife with discrimination, and (3) incarcerated in a jail or prison where violence is widespread and even encouraged. For far too many New Yorkers, particularly young men of color incarcerated at Rikers Island, a jail that holds legally innocent people awaiting trial, the trauma associated with surviving pervasive violence can be a lifelong struggle. Despite reform efforts, the campaign to close Rikers Island continues. But, even the most cursory review of recent events at Rikers reveals that the dysfunction at the nation's largest jail is deeply entrenched, and therefore our attention must be focused on the health and well-being of the people, particularly the young men of color, who survive incarceration at Rikers.

On August 4, 2014, the United States Attorney's Office for the Southern District of New York (SDNY) issued a 79-page report stating that the New York City Department of Correction had systematically violated the civil rights of adolescent inmates, defined as male inmates between the ages of 16 and 18, at Rikers Island by failing to protect them from the rampant use of unnecessary and excessive force.[7] In a press conference announcing the release of the report, SDNY U.S. Attorney Preet Bharara referred to "a deep-seated culture of violence at Rikers Island" that harmed inmates, largely African American/black and Latino/Hispanic teenagers.[8] In particular, in a section entitled "Lack of Staff Professionalism," the SDNY report provides:

> A lack of staff professionalism exacerbates the volatile atmosphere in adolescent housing areas and contributes to the high level of violence. Although there are exceptions, the unprofessional demeanor of staff and supervisors is widespread and readily apparent.
>
> During our tours, we observed and heard staff yelling unnecessarily at inmates and using obscenities and abusive language. Supervisors did not react or reprimand the officers in any way. Numerous inmates told our consultant that staff are disrespectful and regularly scream, threaten, berate, and curse at them. Inmates noted that staff frequently insult them and use racial epithets, such as "n----r." The RNDC[9] Grievance Coordinator described the facility as simply a very "hostile" place.
>
> Staff also humiliate and antagonize inmates, which provokes physical altercations. For instance, one EMTC correction officer reported that staff have ordered adolescents to strip down to their underpants and walk down the dormitory hallway (referred to as "walking down Broadway") when they misbehave. Inmates also complain that staff retaliate against them by spitting in

their food, tossing their belongings, and depriving them of food, commissary, and recreational privileges [quotation modified]. [10]

Over the course of the last decade, inmates at Rikers, nearly all men of color, have died horrible deaths due to the actions and inaction of NYC Correction Officers. The cases of Christopher Robinson, [11] Jason Echevarria, [12] Jerome Murdough, [13] Quannell Offley, [14] and Bradley Ballard [15] raise obvious questions as to whether these violent deaths would have occurred had the victims not been young African American/black and Latino/Hispanic men of color from families of limited economic means. Although many of the DOC officers who perpetuated the culture of violence against adolescent inmates were also African American/black and Latino/Hispanic, the race of the perpetrators matters much less than the race of the victims who were impacted by patterns and practices of domination, regulation, and control that are tantamount to torture and rooted in the nation's history of slavery and segregation. [16]

The administration of New York City Mayor Bill DeBlasio has attempted to respond to the federal government's report with long overdue changes such as the prohibition of solitary confinement for adolescents at Rikers Island, particularly after the recent suicide of Kalief Browder. At great personal risk, Browder shared his story with journalists about being held at Rikers Island for three long years without a trial on ridiculous charges that he vehemently denied. A person of limited economic means whose family did not have the resources to post bail, Browder languished at Rikers Island for three long years like so many other young people awaiting trial for no better reason than their inability to afford freedom. Profiled in an article in *The New Yorker* magazine by Jennifer Gonnerman, Browder's three-year confinement brought national attention to the official misconduct and inhumane conditions at Rikers Island. [17] After the charges against him were dismissed and his subsequent release, Browder demonstrated great courage by speaking out and exposing the immoral official and unofficial policies and practices of domination, regulation, and control at Rikers Island that lead to the deaths of Robinson, Echevarria, Murdough, Offley, Ballard, and too many others to name here.

Despite the unjustified seizure of his person and the violence and resulting trauma that he endured at Rikers Island, Browder still had the determination to continue his education after he was released. At the Lehman College Adult Learning Center (LCALC) which receives annual funding from The City University of New York Black Male Infinitive (CUNY BMI), [18] Mr. Browder worked with adult education professionals, under the leadership of former LCALC director Jaye Jones, to earn the high school equivalency credentials that allowed him to enter Bronx Community College (BCC) of The City University of New York (CUNY). While at BCC, Browder participated in Future Now, another CUNY BMI–funded opportunity program led by educator Elizabeth Payamps. Future Now provides support to many young people who have fallen out of traditional K–12 educational pipelines to college including court-involved youth and formerly incarcerated people. After participating in Future Now, a model college access program, Browder thrived.

In a profile of Mr. Browder for the ABC News program *Nightline* entitled "Who Kalief Browder Might Have Been," it was reported that the young man had become a successful 22-year-old college student and was thriving at Bronx Community College where he earned a 3.56 grade point average during his first semester.[19] Despite the progress that he was making, the impact of (1) the unlawful seizure of his person for three years, (2) the violence he survived at the hands of correctional officers and other inmates, and (3) the inhumane conditions at Rikers Island that he endured, all had a profound, indelible negative impact on Browder's mental health. On Saturday, June 12, 2015, Browder committed suicide by hanging himself at his mother's home.[20] Less than a year later, Browder's mother, Venida Browder, his advocate throughout his life and after his death, died of a heart attack.[21]

As we advocate for access to higher education for people with criminal justice histories, we must remember the trauma that Kalief Browder endured during those three long years of unjustified incarceration at Rikers Island that did not destroy his strong desire to continue his education after his release. Despite being traumatized by his unjustified three-year-long incarceration, Kalief Browder willfully seized opportunity after his release from Rikers Island with the assistance of higher education reentry and college access programs. It is this type of admirable resilience that so many formerly incarcerated people demonstrate that deserves our collective attention, support, and study.

As discussed in Terrance Coffie and John R. Chaney's "A College Initiative Success Story" and Dwayne Simpson, Davon Harris, and John Chaney's "Short-Term and Long-Term Incarceration and Educational Reengagement," higher education reentry programs like The College Initiative, that also receives annual funding from CUNY BMI, support the educational aspirations of people with criminal justice histories but also respects the resilience and experiences of the people who they serve. Higher education reentry and college transition programs like the College and Community Fellowship (CCF), a higher education reentry program for women, the College Initiative and Future Now also provide opportunities for their advanced students and recent graduates to demonstrate leadership by mentoring the students who come after them. These communities of support and mentorship empower students to be able to shape the program activity of higher education reentry programs and college access programs. Further, the input of formerly incarcerated college students in the administration, management, and policymaking of higher education reentry programs like the College Initiative represents an essential best practice by empowering current program participants to determine how to best serve future students in need of guidance and direction. In this sense, *Race, Education, and Reintegrating Formerly Incarcerated Citizens* represents the realization of a long-standing concern of critical race theorists to include the perspectives of marginalized people in policy discussions, particularly when the policies and practices might have a negative impact on communities of color. In acknowledging that they have survived the trauma of incarceration and the violence that is all too often associated with it, what is our collective responsibility to listen to the voices of formerly incarcerated people and people with criminal justice histories about the best ways to support reentry through access to college? *Race, Education, and Reintegrating Formerly Incarcerated Citizens: Counterstories and Counterspaces* offers detailed answers to this most salient question with its unprecedented academic review of higher education reentry strategies and college access programs that are conceived, implemented, and managed by people with criminal justice histories, formerly incarcerated people, and their allies.

NOTES

1. Matsuda, Mari, *Looking to the Bottom: Critical Legal Studies and Reparations—Minority Critique of the Critical Legal Studies Movement*, 22 Harv. C.R.-C.L. L. Rev. 323, 324 (1987).
2. Id.
3. Id.
4. Tyjen Tsai, Tyjen, and Scommegna, Paola, *U.S. Has World's Highest Incarceration Rate*, Washington, DC: Population Reference Bureau (August 2012) *citing* Paul Guerino, Paige M. Harrison, and William J. Sabol, *Prisoners in 2010* (Revised) (Washington, DC: Bureau of Justice Statistics, 2011); and Sara Wakefield and Christopher Uggen, "Incarceration and Stratification," *Annual Review of Sociology* 36 (2010): 387–406. Clarification, Oct. 28, 2014; Minton, Todd, *Jail Inmates at Mid-Year 2010—Statistical Tables* (Washington, DC: Bureau of Justice Statistics, 2011)) (http://www.prb.org/Publications/Articles/2012/us-incarceration.aspx).
5. Wing, Nick, "Here Are All Of The Nations That Incarcerate More Of Their Population Than The U.S.," *Huffington Post*, August 13, 2013, and updated August 14, 2013 (http://www.huffingtonpost.com/2013/08/13/incarceration-rate-per-capita_n_3745291.html); For most recent data, see also, International Centre for Prison Studies, *Highest to Lowest: Prison Population Total*, London: International Centre for Prison Studies (ICPS), The Institute for Criminal Policy Research (ICPR), School of Law, Birkbeck, The University of London (2015).
6. Gray, Katti, "The Run-On Sentence: Eddie Ellis On Life After Prison," the *SUN* Interview, the *SUN*, Issue 451, July 2013, quoting Edwin (Eddie) Ellis, Founder and Former Director, Center for NuLeadership (http://thesunmagazine.org/issues/451/the_run_on_sentence?print=all); Weissman, Marsha; Rosenthal, Alan; Warth, Patricia; Wolf, Elaine; Messina-Yauchzy, Michael; Siegel, Loren, *The Use of Criminal History Records in College Admissions Reconsidered*, New York: The Center for Community Alternatives (CCA): Innovative Solutions for Justice (2010), p. 42 (http://communityalternatives.org/pdf/Reconsidered-criminal-hist-recs-in-college-admissions.pdf).

7. Weiser, Benjamin, and Schwirtz, Michael, "U.S. Inquiry Finds a 'Culture of Violence' Against Teenage Inmates at Rikers Island," *New York Times*, August 4, 2014 (http://www.nytimes.com/2014/08/05/nyregion/us-attorneys-office-reveals-civil-rights-investigation-at-rikers-island.html); Report, United States Department of Justice, United States Attorney, Southern District of New York (SDNY), *CRIPA Investigation of the New York City Department of Correction Jails on Rikers Island*, August 4, 2014 (http://www.justice.gov/usao/nys/pressreleases/August14/RikersReportPR/SDNY%20Rikers%20Report.pdf).

8. Id.

9. Robert N. Davoren Center ("RNDC"), a DOC facility located on Rikers Island that houses adolescent male youth. See generally, Yaroshefsky, Ellen (Professor); Berkovits, Melody; Fernando, Dinisha; Jean-Francois, Nadia; Kornblit, Michelle; Melworm, Lindsay; Tolentino, Casandra; and van Ginkel, Karina, *Rethinking Rikers: Moving from a Correctional to a Therapeutic Model for Youth—Proposal For Rule—Making Report for the NYC Board of Correction*, New York: Youth Justice Clinic, Benjamin N. Cardozo School of Law, Yeshiva University (January 2014), p. 8 (https://cardozo.yu.edu/sites/default/files/YJCFeb2_0.pdf).

10. Report, United States Department of Justice, United States Attorney, Southern District of New York (SDNY), *CRIPA Investigation of the New York City Department of Correction Jails on Rikers Island*, August 4, 2014, p. 41 (http://www.justice.gov/usao/nys/pressreleases/August14/RikersReportPR/SDNY%20Rikers%20Report.pdf).

11. In 2008, Christopher Robinson, an African American 18-year-old, held in a Rikers detention unit for teenaged inmates, was fatally beaten to death by two inmates under the supervision of two NYC correction officers, Michael McKie and Khalid Nelson, who later pleaded guilty to assault and attempted assault for their role in the killing. Associated Press, "City Pays $2 Million in Case of Inmate Killed at Rikers," New York Region, *New York Times*, June 8, 2012 (http://www.nytimes.com/2012/06/09/nyregion/city-pays-2-million-to-mother-of-inmate-killed-by-other-rikers-island-inmates.html); Buettner, Russ, "Rikers Extortions Noted Before Death," New York Region, *New York Times*, March 15, 2009 (http://www.nytimes.com/2009/03/16/nyregion/16rikers.html); Moynihan, Colin, "Two Officers Sentenced in Rikers Island Assault Case," New York Region, *New York Times*, January 17, 2012 (http://www.nytimes.com/2012/01/18/nyregion/rikers-island-officers-sentenced-in-assault-case.html); Harrisoct, Elizabeth, A., "Correction Officers Plead Guilty in Assault Case," New York Region, *New York Times*, October 21, 2011 (http://www.nytimes.com/2011/10/22/nyregion/two-officers-at-rikers-island-plead-guilty-in-assault-case.html).

12. On August 19, 2012, during his final hours, Jason Echevarria, a 25-year-old Latino/Hispanic man held in a unit for mentally ill inmates, was in enormous physical pain and distress after swallowing a toxic detergent packet that burned his mouth and esophagus as well as compromised the function of his internal organs. Echevarria's pleas for help and medical attention, over the course of several hours, were ignored by NYC correction officers. Schwirtzmarch, Michael, "Complaint by Fired Correction Officer Adds Details About a Death at Rikers Island," New York Region, *New York Times*, March 25, 2014 (http://www.nytimes.com/2014/03/26/nyregion/complaint-by-fired-correction-officer-adds-details-about-a-death-at-rikers-island.html); Schlossberg, Tatiana, "Ex-Captain at Rikers Is Found Guilty of Civil Rights Violation in Inmate's Death," New York Region, *New York Times*, December 17, 2014 (http://www.nytimes.com/2014/12/18/nyregion/rikers-captain-guilty-of-civil-rights-violation-in-inmates-death.html).

13. On October 31, 2014, the NYC comptroller's office announced a $2.25 million settlement for the Murdough family for the wrongful death of Jerome Murdough, an African American former Marine, due to hyperthermia on February 15, 2014, when his cell in a mental health unit at Rikers overheated to over 100 degrees for several days due to faulty heating equipment. Murdough was left unattended in the overheated heated cell for hours, completely ignored by DOC officers, until he died. Schwitz, Michael, "$2.25 Million Settlement for Family of Rikers Inmate Who Died in Hot Cell," New York Region, *New York Times*, October 31, 2014 (http://www.nytimes.com/2014/11/01/nyregion/settlement-for-family-of-rikers-inmate-who-died-in-overheated-cell.html); Associated Press, "Mom Sues After Suicidal Inmate Son Kills Himself at Rikers," *New York Times*, February 11, 2015 (http://www.nytimes.com/aponline/2015/02/11/nyregion/ap-us-nyc-jail-suicide-lawsuit.html).

14. On February 12, 2015, the family of Quanell Offley filed a $25 million lawsuit in Bronx Supreme Court for his wrongful death; the 31-year-old African American man died in the hospital a few days after hanging himself at Rikers on December 3, 2013. After being convicted on robbery charges and sentenced to four years in state prison, Offley repeatedly told jail guards that he was suicidal when he was placed in solitary confinement. Offley's cries for mental health treatment or to be transferred to the mental health unit were ignored by NYC DOC officers. Associated Press, "Mom Sues After Suicidal Inmate Son Kills Himself at Rikers," *New York Times*, February 11, 2015 (http://www.nytimes.com/aponline/2015/02/11/nyregion/ap-us-nyc-jail-suicide-lawsuit.html).

15. On January 22, 2015, the family of Bradley Ballard, including his mother, Beverly Ann Griffin, and her husband, Curtis Griffin, filed a federal lawsuit against the City of New York for the wrongful death of their loved one. On September 11, 2013, Bradley Ballard, a mentally ill inmate was found dead, naked, and covered in feces after being locked in his cell for six days. Although NYC Correction Officers, medical personnel, and other inmates were aware of the extreme foul stench emanating from Ballard's cell, no one entered his cell in the six days before the young man died or sought medical attention for him. Weiser, Benjamin, and Winerip, Michael, "Family of Rikers Inmate Sues New York City Over His Death," *New York Times*, September 10, 2014 (http://www.nytimes.com/2014/09/11/nyregion/family-of-mentally-ill-rikers-inmate-sues-new-york-city-over-his-death.html).

16. Campbell, James, *Crime and Punishment in African American History*, New York: Palgrave Macmillan/St. Martin's Press (2013); Hadden, Sally, E., *Slave Patrols: Law and Violence in Virginia and the Carolinas*, Cambridge, MA: Harvard University Press (2001).

17. Gonnerman, Jennifer, "A boy was accused of taking a backpack. The courts took the next three years of his life," Before the Law Section, *The New Yorker*, October 6, 2014 (http://www.newyorker.com/magazine/2014/10/06/before-the-law); Ford, Dana "Man jailed as teen without conviction commits suicide," CNN, June 15, 2015 (http://www.cnn.com/2015/06/07/us/kalief-browder-dead/).

18. Based on promising models at Medgar Evers College, the City University of New York Black Male Initiative (CUNY BMI) was created to support projects throughout the CUNY system dedicated to increasing the enrollment and retention rates of underrepresented groups in higher education, including African, African American/black, Caribbean and Latino/Hispanic males. After hearings conducted in 2005 by the New York City Council's Higher Education Committee, chaired by then council member Charles Barron, the NYC Council funded CUNY BMI. Since 2005–2006, with the generous support of annual NYC Council grants, CUNY BMI has funded projects throughout the university. CUNY BMI website, History and Purpose section (http://www1.cuny.edu/sites/bmi/about).

19. Id.

20. Pitts, Byron, *"Who Kalief Browder Might Have Been,"* Nightline, June 18, 2015 (http://abcnews.go.com/Nightline/video/kalief-browders-life-bars-31851874); Pitts, Byron; Yu, Katie; Effron, Lauren, *"Who Kalief Browder Might Have Been If He Hadn't Spent Over 1,000 Days in Jail Without a Conviction,"* (http://abcnews.go.com/US/kalief-browder-spent-1000-days-jail-charges/story?id=31832313).

21. Jacobs, Shayna, and Annese, John, "Mom dies of 'broken heart' after son Kalief Browder killed himself last year," *New York Daily News*, Sunday, October 16, 2016 (http://www.nydailynews.com/new-york/bronx/exclusive-mom-late-kalief-browder-dies-broken-heart-article-1.2833023).

Acknowledgments

We write this text with gratitude to Rowman & Littlefield/Lexington Books, who shared in our mission to create both a scholarly and readable text that was long overdue. We would also like to thank the Justice Studies Association which first introduced us to Tony Gaskew, our series editor, whose support and expertise undergirds this volume. Finally, our academic home, City University of New York–LaGuardia Community College, provided us with the intellectual and creative space to research, write, and collaborate with experts and practitioners across disciplines and institutions.

Neither my contributions to this book nor my ability to gain a modicum of expertise in the ever-growing field of reentry would have been possible without having received inspiration, support, and opportunities afforded me by these amazing mentors and colleagues: Lance Ogiste, Esq. and Charles J. Hynes, Esq. of the Kings County District Attorney's Office; the KCDA ComALERT reentry program Dream Team of Norma Fernandes, Michael Davenport, Fredda Broza, Kim Ray, and Sandra Torres-Brown; Wendy Hersh of NY State Department of Education's ACCES-VR and the Brooklyn Reentry Consortium; Obafemi Wright of the NYS Department of Correction and Community Supervision; Lazetta Duncan-Moore of Brooklyn Plaza Medical Center; and Dr. Jennifer Wynn of City University of New York's LaGuardia Community College. Special thanks to reentry partners NY State Division of Criminal Justice Services; Criminal Justice section of the American Bar Association; Project Liberation; Counseling Services for the Eastern District of New York; and to the thousands of successful reentry graduates who continue to teach and inspire me. Last but not least, my love and thanks to my mother Joyce Chaney and sister Joanne Chaney for believing in me and for showing me through example how to successfully navigate through life with confidence, compassion, and humility.—John

I am grateful to be a part of LaGuardia's Humanities Department with its amazing scholars and artists who inspire me to "think outside the box" and work in interdisciplinary ways toward social justice scholarship; thank you— Michael Rodriguez, Hugo Fernandez, Sandra Dickinson, Louis Lucca, Vera Albrecht, Shaunee Wallace, John Chaffee, Stefanie Sertich, Sumonth Inukonda, Rob Bruno, Erika Heppner, and Jaime Riccio. A special thanks to Brian Miller, who for me inspired this edited book; to Terry Parker and Bethany Jacobson, who continue to labor on our reentry documentary, and to John Powell, Kareem Smith, Juan Merced, Johnny Davis, Paul Waters, and Stanley Gill—thanks for sharing your lived experiences and friendship with me.Finally, much love and thanks to my son, Matthew. Your support and love mean everything to me.—Joni

We would be remiss if we did not acknowledge Cathy Powell, our copyeditor, who kept us organized during the process of putting this book together. Cathy, your encouragement, support, and expertise in the midst of your own life obstacles is an inspiration on how to live well.

Editors' Introduction

John R. Chaney and Joni Schwartz

Building on the framework of critical race theory (CRT), this book through academic research and analysis engages the voices of formerly incarcerated college students' lived experiences as well as college faculty and administrators' understanding of academia as created spaces for reentry. Through the tools of counterstories and counterspaces, this book examines the intersection of race, post incarceration, agency, trauma, and educational settings.

This edited volume is interdisciplinary in that it intersects the work of adult educators, criminal justice professionals, communication scholars, social scientists, and administrators with the writing of formerly incarcerated faculty and students. This mixture of voices and positionality creates a rich tapestry of perspectives and style. Research studies and personal narrative are interwoven to make this a source book both accessible to student readers but of interest to scholars in criminology, social science, adult education, communications, humanities, and related fields who are interested in moving a social justice agenda forward. As an undergraduate or graduate text, this book is well suited as it can be read straight through or individual chapters can be selected for stand-alone reading assignments.

There are three interrelated goals of the book: (1) to reinforce the argument that education, and the support of opportunity for higher education particularly, is a substantiated solution to the issue of recidivism; (2) to create a forum where the formerly incarcerated can come to voice around issues of race, incarceration, and education through engaged action research and analysis; and (3) finally to highlight learning spaces related to college and high school equivalency which successfully address reentry.

Race, Education, and Reintegrating Formerly Incarcerated Citizens: Counterstories and Counterspaces is a book in the series *Critical Perspectives on Race, Crime, and Justice* edited by Dr. Tony Gaskew. Consistent with the theme of this important book series, *Counterstories and Counter-spaces* demonstrates that particularly for people of color the pursuit of higher education has the potential to be an agent of change.

In the tradition of critical race theory (CRT), this book is divided into three major sections: Part I: Context, Critical Race Theory, and College Reentry, Part II: Counterstories, and Part III: Counterspaces. Part I opens with Holzman's chapter, "Schooling for Prison; Incarceration for Poverty," which establishes the context and overview of mass incarceration and education in America; chapters 2 and 4, by Feldman and Eren, lay out critical race theory (CRT), its relationship to reentry, and the role of white privilege, while in chapter 3 Gaskew makes the case that reentry and education must include focus on black cultural privilege. Part I ends with Schwartz's chapter on the role of writing and voice in reentry, leading into the counterstories of Part II.

Part II begins with a phenomenological study by Baston and Miller and uses a military metaphor to describe the experience of incarceration. Bains and Halberstam present the counterstory of a black female returning citizen and her white mentor in chapter 7. Chapter 8 is comparative case study of short- and long-term incarceration narratives by Harris, Simpson, and Chaney followed by another study and documentary examining the intersection of educational trauma and black males by Van Thompson and P. Schwartz. Part II concludes with a powerful autoethnography by Chaney—a college faculty's counterstory.

Part III: Counterspaces, another CRT concept, explores institutions, programs, and classrooms that support post-incarceration transition to school. Chapter 11, written by college students Miller, Mondesir, and Stater with their professor, again returns to the theme of war and incarceration and the supports needed in the classroom to succeed. Conti and Frantz in chapter 12 consider their role of scholar-allies in an inside-out counterspace. Chapter 13 is one man's experience in a college initiative program. The final chapters 14 and 15 take a broader lens looking at GED preparation as counterspace and a college-wide strategic plan for reentry.

We, the editors of this volume, regard the intersections of race, the criminal justice system, and education to be one of the greatest civil rights issues of our day. And as previously stated, this volume attempts to not only present the massive racial incarceration practices that make reentry services on such a large scale necessary, but to give voice to those who have experienced incarceration and exemplify programs and spaces that support successful reentry. Having stated this, we are cognizant and humbled by the words of the late Derrick Bell, the scholar-activist who is primarily credited with the origination of CRT:

I cannot emphasize enough what I see as the potentially dangerous and destructive consequences of words and actions intended to do good . . . it is the most frequently ignored pitfall of those motivated by good intentions, particularly those involved in social change and progressive politics. Without a willingness to continually critique our own policies, question our own motivations, and admit our own mistakes, it is virtually impossible to maintain programs, and practices that are truly ethically related to the real needs of those we wish to serve. (Bell, chapter 6)

As collaborating editors, we took these words to heart reflecting on our own positionalities, a white female and black male. For me, Joni, as a white female, I grappled with my own white privilege, white supremacy, and the CRT concept of interest convergence. This often uncomfortable reflexivity was important as we grappled with chapter writings, author selections, and I engaged in conversation with my coeditor.

For me, John, it was absolutely essential for this text to offer our readers a stimulating array of outstanding CRT-savvy authors in academia and experiential learning, while also incorporating the strong, diversified voices of our citizens who used education as a formidable tool in successfully transitioning from incarceration. It was also important for our book to serve as a responsible and timely contribution to the national discussion that increasingly challenges traditionally accepted social constructs and their impact upon formerly incarcerated persons of color.

Our editors' collaboration has been a rich intellectual and emotional adventure. We hope as you journey through *Race, Education, and Reintegrating Formerly Incarcerated Citizens: Counterstories and Counterspaces*, you will share our adventure and that it will prompt greater reflexivity, classroom and program innovation, and educational policy changes as we each attempt to bring change to our corners of the world.

REFERENCE

Bell, D. (2002). *Ethical ambition: Living a life of meaning and worth.* New York: Bloomsbury.

Part I

Context, Critical Race Theory, and Education's Role in Reentry

Chapter One

Schooling for Prison, Incarceration for Poverty

Michael Holzman

What are the purposes of the American criminal justice and education systems? One way to determine this is to examine their mission statements. The mission of the United States Department of Justice is, among other things, *"to ensure fair and impartial administration of justice for all Americans."* The U.S. Department of Education is *"dedicated to . . . prohibiting discrimination and ensuring equal access to education."*

Another way is to look at the actual effects of the actions of those institutions.

The incarceration rates for Americans vary by race and ethnicity, in spite of the U.S. Department of Justice's mission statement. The incarceration rate for the descendants of enslaved Africans is nearly six times the incarceration rate for white non-Hispanics (Bureau of Justice Statistics, 2010). Keeping in mind the mission of the U.S. Department of Education, we find that in 2015, at grade eight, according to the Department's own National Assessment of Educational Progress (NAEP), 42% of white non-Hispanic students in the public schools read at or above grade level, but just 15% of black students did so.

Such are the professions of governmental institutions in regard to their missions and such are the realities on the ground. They are not in accord. Under those circumstances, all that is left for the U.S. Department of Justice and the U.S. Department of Education would be to say, with Richard Pryor, "Who are you going to believe, me or your lying eyes?"

It is, of course, possible that the U.S. Department of Justice, and the parallel institutions at the state and local levels, despite good faith efforts, simply cannot achieve their mission of "fair and impartial administration of justice," just as it is possible that the federal, state, and local education authorities, despite their best efforts, cannot provide equal access to education. It may also be possible that the descendants of enslaved Africans in this country are six times as likely to commit crimes as the descendants of European immigrants and that white children are nearly three times as good at learning to read as black children. If this were correct, it might be reasonable to propose different missions for the federal departments, more closely aligned with current realities, perhaps missions based on eugenics and other such racist theories which an objective observer might assume, given their outcomes, actually determine the actions of those responsible for the country's educational and criminal justice systems.

THE PERSISTENT HERITAGE OF SLAVERY

The history of the United States has to a large extent been shaped by the history of racial relations, that is, by the history of black oppression. Those who are not oppressed, and even more, the oppressors themselves, rarely allow themselves to understand this situation as in fact it is. They express, and no doubt believe, statements like "Whatever the faults of slavery in the Old South, there was a human relationship, often a deep affection, and slaves were cherished . . ." (*The American Legion Magazine*, 1952, p. 18ff) and such, down to the warm memories, even today, of young white people from Delta planter families for their black nursemaids, how they were "part of the family." The romantic legends of the virtues of the white Old South have been inverted, from the same point of view, as stories about the vices of the black inner city. However, those latter stories are no more realistic, no more objective, than the others. They are both stories told from the viewpoint of oppressive power.

The history of the United States is best understood not from the point of view of "authorities" but from the point of view of those oppressed by their power: African Americans—enslaved Africans and their descendants. "If something is not true in the eyes of the least favored [most oppressed], says Sartre, then it is not true" (Bakewell, 2016, p. 271). Seen from this perspective, various unusual features of American history and society are more intelligible, from our endemic violence to our failure to develop social services typical of other industrialized countries. It becomes evident that the violence of American life manifests most typically as the violence perpetrated on the bodies of black men: by police, by white men, by other black men. And that educational opportunities, for example, are rationed by race, because of race. This latter is accomplished at the elementary and secondary levels, by means of racially differentiated public funding, and at the postsecondary level by a combination of the racially determined outcomes of precollegiate education and the ever-great costs arbitrarily levied on the student, rather than borne by government as a public good, as is done by civilized countries elsewhere.

These differences between the United States and otherwise similar countries, such as those of Western Europe, are puzzling if racism is not considered. Why differentiate basic education opportunities by neighborhood income levels? Why place the burden of paying for a social good like higher education on, say, medical students, rather than on the society that needs physicians? Why structure unemployment insurance as if, as in the days of the poor laws and workhouses, anything other than brief layoffs were a choice of the unemployed, to be discouraged by inadequate allocations, severely time-limited? These matters and others are not solely artifacts of racism, but racism is a major determining component. They are puzzling when considered from a point of view of bureaucratic rationalism, yet perfectly understandable when considered from the point of view of the descendants of enslaved Africans.

This does not mean that police chiefs and prosecutors, judges and school superintendents, get up each morning and ask themselves what they can do to oppress black people. It is the effect that defines racism, as stated by the *Final Report* of the Flint Water Advisory Task Force in regard to environmental injustice: "Environmental injustice is not about malevolent intent or deliberate attacks on specific populations, nor does it come in measures that overtly violate civil rights. Environmental injustices as often occur when parties charged with the responsibility to protect public health fail to do so in the context of environmental considerations" (p. 54). Racist effects, such as environmental injustice, manifest when those in authority *do not* get up each morning and ask themselves what they can do to *end* the oppression of black people and others at the lower end of the power distribution. The situation is similar in regard to the criminal justice and education systems. The American criminal justice and education systems, as they have evolved and as they function today, are, among other things, themselves instruments for the oppression of African Americans. They keep black people in their place. It is astonishing how blandly it is accepted that half of those incarcerated are black, when the black population is just 13 or 14% of the total, that the high school graduation rates for young black men are, in many places, below what sheer chance would bring about.

BLACK STUDENTS AND THE SCHOOLS

What, from the point of view of their black students, is the actual mission of America's school systems? Surely not to educate young black men for college or careers, as professed, but, more honestly, to set many of them on the path to incarceration. Although incarceration rates are not entirely an artifact of educational attainment, there is a very strong correlation. The probability of a black male who has not received a high school diploma serving time behind bars is ten times that of a black man with a college degree. More than two-thirds (68%) of the former will spend some years incarcerated (Western & Pettit, 2010). If the percentage of black men who complete high school were raised to that of white, non-Hispanic, men, the number of black men at risk of incarceration would drop by one-third, all other factors (such as police behavior) being equal. But why is it that the percentage of black men without high school diplomas is half again as great as that of white men? There are various stories about this, generally having to do with supposed characteristics of black families, but, in fact, the key variable is the quality of schools available to black children and those schools are markedly inferior to most schools available to white children. The qualitative inferiority of the schools attended by most black children overwhelms all other factors (Palardy, 2013).

This can be illustrated by an example from the nation's largest school system. The New York City Department of Education annually performs a natural experiment in regard to the differing quality of education it offers to the city's students. That school system has eight specialized high schools, admission to which are based on an examination, which is basically a mathematics test. The most prestigious of these schools is Stuyvesant High School. For the 2016–2017 school year, Stuyvesant accepted 883 students, 1.2% of the city's students entering grade nine. There were 682 Asian students (including both East and South Asian students), 178 white, non-Hispanic students, 9 black students, and 14 Hispanic students (Christ, 2016). Relatively few black or Hispanic students even bothered to apply. Some did not identify themselves as suitable; some came from families that could not afford the requisite tutoring. Of course, both those factors are themselves filters of educational opportunity, having to do with home environments and income, rather than the democratic ideal.

It was one-third as likely that a white, non-Hispanic student would apply and be accepted by Stuyvesant as an Asian student and approximately one-fortieth as likely that a black or Hispanic student would apply and be accepted by the school as a white, non-Hispanic student. Which seems more reasonable: that black students in New York are at most one-fortieth as capable of benefitting from the elite education offered by Stuyvesant as white students or that the chances of a black student receiving an education in New York City preparing them for the Specialized High School Test are one-fortieth that of a white student?

Who are you going to believe, the New York City Department of Education or your lying eyes?

This brings us to the question of *why* the schools attended by most black children offer inferior educations to that of those attended by most white, non-Hispanic children.

That *why* leads in two directions: one ideological, the other instrumental. Ideologically, as the Stuyvesant example makes clear, the schools attended by most black students offer inferior educations *because* their students are black. Racial/ethnic classifications in New York City and certain other areas are complicated by the presence of groups identifying as Hispanic/Latino who are of African descent and therefore "seen," and treated as, black. With educational injustice, as with environmental injustice, this is not to say that the responsible officials meet, say, weekly, to decide how to restrict educational opportunities for black students. It is simply that they do not ensure that equal educational opportunities are provided in schools predominately attended by black students. Instrumentally, those schools are inferior because they are inadequately funded and therefore not fit for purpose.

School finance is one of the ways in which American institutions differ from those in other developed countries. Few other countries base school funding on local property taxes. The usual response of Europeans to learning that this is the case in the United States is to ask why anyone would want to do that? The answer would require two parts. One is historical. The provision of education in the United States was originally a local responsibility and local revenue was—and is—often based on property tax. But that is not always the case, there are local sales and income taxes, for example, and the definition of "local" is neither uniform nor invariant. Local government on Long Island, New York, for example, consists of two counties, on the one hand, and on the other 127 school districts, the latter with boundaries drawn with obvious racial gerrymandering intent.

The well-known *effects* of local tax-based school financing are better understood as its *purpose*, its intention, rather than as unfortunate consequences of random political decisions. School finance is locally based because of its class and racial effects. Locally based school finance provides more funding for the children of wealthy families (typically living in neighborhoods with other wealthy families) and less for the children of families living in poverty. According to an oft-cited study by Bruce J. Biddle and David C. Berliner, "Public school funding in the United States . . . generates large funding differences between wealthy and impoverished communities. Such differences exist among states, among school districts within each state, and even among schools within specific districts" (Biddle & Berliner, 2002, p. 50).

As poverty rates increase, per student expenditure decreases, and vice versa. This is a minimal effect, derived from absolute expenditures. The curve would be even more extreme if the calculation were based on expenditures in relation to need. Students living in poverty simply need more public educational support than students from more prosperous families, as the latter typically receive significant supplementary educational support from their families. (This includes both financial expenditures and cultural capital, e.g., books and computers in the home, the educational level of adults, etc.)

In almost every state, public schools are organized into districts with differing resources. Financing most of school expenses from local, district-specific taxes and the related practice of providing less experienced, less effective teachers to schools serving more impoverished students ensures that schools serving the children of higher income families have larger per student budgets than those serving the children of lower income families. Differences in funding determine educational opportunities. Sociologist Mark Robert Rank wrote that the schemas utilized to fund public education at both the elementary and secondary levels affect greatly the quality of schools and education, and this quality is based on the wealth of the community in which one lives (Rank, 2004).

Poverty has an African American face, as President Reagan often implied. African Americans have been condemned to live in poverty for generations, first by the institution of slavery, then by Jim Crow, and now through the operations of the education and criminal justice systems. Much has been heard of late, and rightfully so, of the increasing poverty of white non-Hispanic Americans, but according to the Pew Research Center, there are still more black children than white, non-Hispanic children living in poverty, even though there are vastly more white, non-Hispanic than black children in the general population (Patten & Krogstad, 2015). Twice the proportion of children living in poverty are black as would be expected if poverty were evenly distributed by race. It is true that there are other groups with low household incomes, especially Hispanics and American Indians, but many of the former are in a transitory situation, typical of first- and second-generation immigrants, and the latter, tragically continuing to suffer the consequences of centuries of genocidal governmental actions and policies, are a very small minority.

Unsatisfactory educational outcomes in America are associated with race, which is associated with poverty and both are associated with inadequate school funding. It is not coincidental that the East St. Louis, Illinois, schools, with their unsatisfactory teacher/pupil ratio, are almost entirely black and 44% of East St. Louis residents have incomes below the poverty level, while the schools of White Plains, with their superior teacher/pupil ratios, are only 15% black, in a city where the poverty rate is just 7%.

The U.S. Department of Education is *"dedicated to . . . prohibiting discrimination and ensuring equal access to education."* And the Illinois State Board of Education's mission is *"achieve excellence across all Illinois districts . . . and ensure equitable outcomes for all students."*

Those responsible for the education of the nation's most vulnerable students fail to ensure equal access to education and excellence and equitable outcomes. This failure results in the vast majority of the nation's black students reaching adulthood with inadequate skills and knowledge, unprepared for college and the rapidly diminishing careers available for those without a college education. This situation is worsened by the efforts of the criminal justice system to which we now turn.

RACE AND THE CRIMINAL JUSTICE SYSTEM

The incarceration rate of the United States in 2012–2013 was more than four times that of the United Kingdom and seven times that of the European average. The difference can be attributed to their differing implicit purposes. Incarceration in other countries is part of a juridical system meant to deter and punish crime and, in some cases, to reform those committing crimes. So it is claimed for the American criminal justice system, and it may be in part, but the surplus rate of incarcerations of the American system over that of comparable countries, say, 500 or the 700 prisoners per 100,000 population, functions, in fact, to maintain a system of limited opportunities for the descendants of enslaved Africans.

Bruce Western and Becky Pettit have calculated the cumulative risk of imprisonment, in percentages, for white, non-Hispanic, and black men, who were young adults in 2010, by educational attainment. They found that just over a quarter of the comparatively small percentage (13%) of white young adults without high school diplomas can expect to spend some time in jail or prison. On the other hand, most, more than two-thirds, of young adult black men without high school diplomas or the equivalent (21%) can expect to experience time in jail or prison during their "life-course," to use Pettit's and Western's phrase. These expectations decline steeply with education, but are profoundly racially differentiated. Ninety-four percent of white young adult men with high school diplomas or equivalencies will avoid incarceration. The percentage of black men with high school diplomas or equivalencies who will have been incarcerated is similar to the percentage of white young men without that qualification. A college degree is virtually a get-out-of-jail-free card for young adult white men. A college degree for black men is merely equivalent in its efficacy to a high school degree for white men.

Summing the risks of incarceration at each education level, we can estimate that 34% of young adult black men will experience incarceration by age 34. Two-thirds of that group will have not completed high school; nearly all the rest will have either a high school diploma or the equivalent. Just 3% will have completed college. Given that perhaps as many as half of black males reporting high school completion received a GED or other equivalency, rather than a regular high school diploma, it would not be surprising if more than three-quarters of those black males at risk of incarceration by age 34 either did not complete high school at all or did so through some lower-standard alternative (Harlow, 2003).

When we compare the risk of incarceration between that of black and white men, we find that the risk for those without a high school diploma is twice as high for black as for white men and the difference increases with further education, to triple for those with a high school diploma or GED and six times as great for college graduates. In other words, race is increasingly determinate as education increases, which implies that the rate of incarceration of black men includes, as it were, a black "handicap": the risk of incarceration for simply being a descendant of an enslaved African.

INCARCERATION AND DRUG ARRESTS

Crime statistics to a great extent record the actions of the criminal justice system, rather than those of residents. Drug arrests, prosecutions, and convictions are a very important example of this. It is well-known that drug use is approximately equal across racial and ethnic groups and particularly prevalent among young people. And yet it is common knowledge that arrests for drug use and sales are concentrated in segregated neighborhoods and most unusual on college campuses and the surrounding streets. For example, the overall crime rate in Central Harlem, New York's 28th Precinct, is 21 per thousand residents, while that in neighboring Morningside Heights, the location of Columbia University, is reported as 12 per 1,000 residents. The crime rate of Manhattan's Upper East Side, with its concentration of Yuppie singles bars, is just 9 per 1,000 (NYC Crime Map, 2016). In Chicago, drug arrests are overwhelmingly concentrated in the black, and extraordinarily poor, neighborhood of Garfield Park. If these data are to be believed, the wealthy—white—neighborhoods along the Lake, like those of New York's Upper West Side and California's Beverly Hills, are nearly completely free of drug use: no marijuana, no cocaine. In general, throughout the country, law offices and advertising agencies are rarely the subject of police raids; young white bankers and models have little to fear from police attention to their fashionable restaurants and clubs; college dormitories are virtually sacrosanct, no matter how blatant the drug use to be found there. As the hyper-segregation of many American cities forces comparatively prosperous, well-educated, black families to live in neighborhoods of concentrated poverty, even they are more likely to be targeted by police activity than their white suburban peers.

The National Research Council of the National Academies report of April 2014, entitled "The Growth of Incarceration in the United States: Exploring

Causes and Consequences," states: "After four decades of stability from the 1920s to the early 1970s, the rate of incarceration in the United States more than quadrupled in the past four decades." The researchers found that this increase in incarceration was not caused by an increase in general crime rates. While rates for most types of crimes were falling, incarceration rates rose steadily and precipitously. Drug arrests in particular rose, and rose in a racially disparate fashion, so that by 1989 drug arrests for African Americans, which already had been taking place at double the rate for whites, increased to four times the white rate (Travis & Western, 2014). The report's authors found that "The unprecedented rise in incarceration rates can be attributed to an increasingly punitive political climate . . . that significantly increased sentence lengths, required prison time for minor offenses, and intensified punishment for drug crimes." They trace this to the Nixon administration, with its "war on crime" consciously arising from its Southern Strategy (Travis & Western, 2014, p. 116). In other words, in order to win elections in the South, the Nixon administration decided to criminalize African Americans, joining Southern politicians such as George Wallace in a revival of Jim Crow. Therefore, the authors of the report conclude that "High rates of incarceration in the United States and the great numbers of people held in U.S. prisons and jails result substantially from decisions by policy makers to increase the use and severity of prison sentences . . ." (Travis & Western, 2014, p. 70).

MASS INCARCERATION AND THE BLACK COMMUNITY

Three hundred sixty thousand of the four million African-American males between ages 20 and 34 are incarcerated. They are the products of racially skewed school systems interlocking with a criminal justice system operated in an objectively racist manner. In Western and Pettit's famous phrase, "For these men with very little schooling, serving time in state or federal prison had become a normal life event" (Travis & Western, 2014, p. 68). This applies to approximately two million men between the ages of 18 and 54, with the highest concentration in urban areas. It is, of course, worse than that. Not all those under the control of the criminal justice system are behind bars. Michael Katz found that "Every day one of three black men in their twenties 'is under some form of criminal justice supervision . . . either in prison or jail or on probation or parole.' By and large, they exit prison lacking job skills, unattractive to employers, and headed for poverty, the irregular labor market, and, too often, crime and repeat incarceration" (Katz, 2013). This latter is usually deplored as "recidivism," apparently, the propensity of the formerly incarcerated to decide to return to actions that led to their incarceration in the first place. The solution to recidivism, then, would be, perhaps, some form of counseling. However, the solution to recidivism, it seems to me, is to end mass incarceration, which in turn means to end the educational and policing policies leading to it.

We can estimate that in many African American communities half or more of the men will have spent time in prison, unable to contribute to the support of their children while incarcerated, being able to do so only with difficulty if at all afterwards: under-educated, virtually unemployable, disfranchised. It also should be noted that a large percentage of prisoners are incarcerated for parole violations, which can be something as trivial as going to a late movie (or as serious as voting with a felony conviction). In this way repeated incarcerations, recidivism, is built into the system. What is the effect of this on the hypersegregated black community?

The 2010 Census found that 72% of working-age (20 to 64) African American males were then in the workforce, as compared to 85% of white males. In other words, 13% more African American men were out of the workforce than would be the case if their situation were similar to those for white males. They were neither employed nor in the unemployment accounting system. That would be 1.4 million men. Some of these are "discouraged workers," others are not in the general economy at all. They are incarcerated or living outside the system—"on the run"—as described by Alice Goffman (Goffman, 2014).

Seventy-eight percent of white males were employed in 2010, as compared to 61% of black males; the unemployment rate for black males (10% in 2010) was twice that of white males. Combining the 13% excess "out of the workforce" and the 5% excess over the white unemployment percentage, we approach 20% of the working-age male black population not in a position to contribute to the income of the black community, who would have been able to do so if they had the same employment profile as white men.

This calculation can be extended by noting that the median income for African Americans of male full-time, year-round workers is $37,271 and that for white Americans is 33% more: $49,616. Part of the reason for this difference is to be found in the incarceration rate and all that entails. Wakefield and Wildeman found that "A criminal record imposes a drop in earnings of about 10 percent to 30 percent . . . some of which is attributable to the stigma employers attach to a criminal record . . ." (Wakefield & Wildeman, 2010, p. 17). The mass incarceration of young adult African American men affects equally remarkable numbers of the next generation in the black community, contributing to the reproduction of caste status from generation to generation. The NRC report states that "According to the most recent estimates from the Bureau of Justice Statistics, 53 percent of those in prison in 2007 had minor children. In that year, an estimated 1.7 million children under age 18 had a parent in state or federal prison. . . . In 2007, black . . . children in the United States were 7.5 . . . times more likely . . . than white children to have a parent in prison" (Travis & Western, 2014, p. 260). Sixty-two percent of black children in 2009 whose parents had not completed high school experienced parental imprisonment by age 17 (Travis & Western, 2014, p. 262). For white children born in 1990 the risk of paternal imprisonment was 7.8% for children of high school dropouts; 4.8% for children of high school graduates, 1.1% for children of college graduates. On the other hand, "Over half (50.5%) of black children born in 1990 to high school dropouts had their father imprisoned. . . . About 13 [sic: 13.8%] percent of black children of college-educated parents had a parent sent to prison," as did 20% of high school graduates (Wakefield & Wildeman, 2010, pp. 36–38). It is striking that the percentage of black children of incarcerated college-educated parents is nearly twice that of white children of incarcerated high school dropouts. Again, for the descendants of enslaved Africans, even a college education does not provide adequate protection against state policies of mass incarceration.

Black poverty is not a static condition, a pathology, but an outcome to be expected from inadequate schools and inequitable mass incarceration. It is a product of the criminal justice system, of actions continuously undertaken and accomplished, of decisions taken about criminal justice system policies and practices by specific individuals, from the President of the United States to the cop on the beat. For an example at the local level, in New York City, "the Vera Institute of Justice found that race was a significant factor at nearly every stage of criminal prosecutions in Manhattan, from setting bail to negotiating a plea deal to sentencing" (*New York Times*, 2014). Similarly, it is an outcome of the education system, of action continuously undertaken and accomplished, of decisions taken about school policies and practices by specific individuals, from governors to members of state and local boards of education and mayors to superintendents and principals. Mass incarceration leads to the impoverishment of black communities. Inadequate educational opportunities in impoverished communities limits financial mobility. Generation after generation of the descendants of enslaved Africans are policed into this closed system. It is the predominant civil rights issue of our time.

REFERENCES

Bakewell, S. (2016). *At the existentialist café: Freedom, being, and apricot cocktails with Jean-Paul Sartre, Simone de Beauvoir, Albert Camus, Martin Heidegger, Maurice Merleau-Ponty and others*. New York: Other Press.

Biddle, B. J., & Berliner, D. C. (2002). A research synthesis/unequal school funding in the United States, *Educational Leadership*, 59(8), 50.

Bureau of Justice Statistics—Prison Policy Organization (2010). Correctional Population in the United States, 20110 & U.S. Census 2010 Summary File 1. http://www.prisonpolicy.org/graphs/raceinc.html, accessed March 7, 2016.

Christ, L. (2016). Number of Black, Hispanic students offered seats at city's specialized high schools drops again. (2016, March 4). NY1. http://www.ny1.com/nyc/all-boroughs/education/2016/03/4/number-of-black--hispanic-students-offered-seats-at-city-s-specialized-high-schools-drops-again.html.

Flint Water Advisory Task Force. (2016). *Final report.*

Goffman, A. (2014). *On the run: Fugitive life in an American city.* Chicago: University of Chicago Press.

Harlow, C. (2003). *Education and correctional populations.* Bureau of Justice Statistics, Special Report, January.

Katz, M. (2013). *The undeserving poor: America's enduring confrontation with poverty.* (2nd ed.). Oxford: Oxford University Press. 227–28.

New York Times, July 8, citing Kutateladze, B., & Andiloro, N. "Prosecution and racial justice in New York County" (2014). Technical Report. New York: Vera Institute of Justice, January 31.

NYC Crime Map. Maps.nyc.gov/crime, accessed May 5, 2016.

Palardy, G. J. (2013). "High school socioeconomic segregation and student attainment." *American Educational Research Journal*, 50(4), 714–54.

Patten, E., & Krogstad, J. M. (2015). Black child poverty rate holds steady, even as other groups see declines. Fact Tank: Pew Research Center, July 14, 2015. http://www.pewresearch.org/fact-tank/2015/07/14/black-child-poverty-rate-holds-steady-even-as-other-groups-see-declines/. Accessed March 12, 2016.

Rank, M. R. (2004). *One nation, underprivileged: Why American poverty affects us all.* Oxford: Oxford University Press.

The American Legion Magazine, December 1952, p. 18ff.

Travis, J., & Western, B. (2014). *The Growth of Incarceration in the United States: Exploring Causes and Consequences.* Washington, DC: National Academies Press.

Wakefield, S., & Wildeman, C. (2010). *Children of the prison boom: mass incarceration and the future of American inequality.* Oxford: Oxford University Press.

Western, B., & Pettit, B. (2010). *Incarceration & social inequality.* Daeulus–American Academy of Arts & Sciences, pp. 8–19. http://www.amacad.org/publications/daedalus/10_summer_western.pdf.

Chapter Two

Education Outside of the Box

Cory Feldman

This chapter aims to introduce critical race theory (CRT) as a systematic map for creating a successful college reentry program (CRP) for black students returning from prison. The engagement of formerly incarcerated black students in higher education has been shown to provide avenues for employment and societal reintegration (Davis, Bozick, Steele, Saunders, & Miles, 2013; State of New York Department of Correctional Services, 2010). Therefore, exploring potential models for the engagement of formerly incarcerated students in higher education is on the forefront of concern for program designers and educators alike.

Research indicates that if recent reentrants enroll in an educational program, they are less likely to be rearrested and returned to prison (Solomon, Waul, Van Ness, Travis, & Ravitz, 2004), yet there is a paucity of research to offer direction around the best way to attract and retain black students in higher education after prison. One consensus that has emerged out of the literature, however, is that community college campuses are particularly well suited for CRP because they are replete with resources that can be conducive to the reintegration of people coming home from prison (Mellow & Heelan, 2014; Spycher, Shkodriani, & Lee, 2012; Belfield & Bailey, 2011). More so than competitive four-year institutions, community colleges tailor their academic and social support services to non-traditional learners: parenting students, students with disabilities, and students who need financial resources to name a few (Mellow & Heelan, 2014).

While reentry programs for the formerly incarcerated proliferate (Solomon, 2004; Jonson & Cullen, 2015), there seems to be an absence around the role of race for many of these programs, despite the large numbers of black students returning from prison. Many of these black students who are returning from prison are entering society destitute. An education is not only beneficial to these students in terms of their academic skills, but also increases their statistical likelihood of obtaining employment and remaining free (Brazzell, Crayton, Mukamal et al., 2009). A recent study by Ford and Schroeder shows higher education to also have a crime-reducing effect (Ford & Schroeder, 2010). Their study used data from the National Youth Survey to examine the impact of college both in and out of prison. Their findings indicate that college attendance and investment in higher education decreases criminal offending in adulthood (Ford & Schroeder, 2010). The assumption has been that school works as a major agent of socialization by facilitating bonds that promote socially conforming behavior while increasing access to employment and people with social capital (Ford & Schroeder, 2010). Ford and Schroeder's study also provides some evidence that the simple decision to attend college has the potential to change the offending trajectories of some individuals, especially those who were high-rate juvenile offenders (Ford & Schroeder, 2010).

Community colleges can be particularly useful to black students whose education has been interrupted by their incarceration, if their unique position on the community college campus is considered by community college faculty (Roach, 2001). Given that almost 80% of the 2.2 million people in prison and jail have never seen a college classroom, and that nearly half of that same population is comprised of black men, pedagogically speaking, race does matter (Gaskew, 2015). Black people returning from prison need to enter institutions where black people are valued, in leadership positions, and the experience of incarceration is understood.

THE PIPELINE

There is a great deal of discourse surrounding the "public school-to-prison pipeline," which explores how black students who are poor are funneled from underfunded schools with zero-tolerance tactics of hyperdiscipline to upstate correctional institutions (Archer, 2009; Christle, Jolivette, & Nelson, 2005; Cole & Heilig, 2011; Cooc, Currie-Rubin, Kuttner, & Ng, 2012; Darensbourg, Perez, & Blake, 2010; Feierman, Levick, & Mody, 2009; Fowler, 2011; Kim, Losen, & Hewitt, 2010; Skiba et al., 2003; Tuzzolo & Hewitt, 2006; Smith, 2009; Wald & Losen, 2003; Winn, 2011; Winn & Behizadeh, 2011). Understanding and accepting that people are drawn into the prison system as a form of oppression can help liberate thinking about how critical race theory (CRT) can be applied to CRP. This is a particularly useful framework as it shifts the focus from an individualistic approach, where formerly incarcerated students are cast as lacking skills, to an exploration of how community colleges can ease the transition from prison to the free world.

While the school-to-prison pipeline has received scholarly attention, research on how to engage these same black students in continuing their education after prison is just beginning to grow (Rose, 2015). This burgeoning scholarship identified college, or a "prison-to-college pipeline" as a possible solution to the reentry problem (Halkovic, Fine, Bae et al., 2013; Sturm, Skolnick, & Wu, 2010); the problem with reentry being that nearly all people incarcerated in U.S. prisons will return to their communities at some point and over half of these individuals will be sent back to prison within a few years of their release (Travis, 2005).

CRITICAL RACE THEORY AND POST-PRISON EDUCATION

In the mid-1970s, in response to the inequalities of racism evident in the U.S. legal system as applied to black Americans, Derrick Bell (1992) developed what is known today as critical race theory (CRT). Bell suggested that "we use a number of different voices, but all recognize that racial subordination maintains and perpetuates the American social order" (Delgado & Stefancic, 2001, p. 83). Critical race theory scholars argue that:

> CRT, as an analytical framework for addressing issues of social inequity, can be utilized as a way in which to uncover the racism embedded within American social structures and practices. More importantly, critical race theorists seek to reveal the hidden curriculum of racial domination and talk about the ways in which it is central to the maintenance of white supremacy. (Lynn, 2005, 129)

As a critical race paradigm, this perspective does not question the existence of racism but instead explores where, how, and why racism is performed. Critical race scholarship is anti-essentialist, predicated on the belief that there is no singular experience or attribute that is ascribed to or may define any group of people (Harris, 1990; Museus & Iftikar, 2013). It is still important, however, to acknowledge shared experiences, particularly in the form of diminished civil rights, discrimination, and blocked opportunity. With black students returning from prison, acknowledging a shared history and recent experience of racial oppression can be an empowering tool toward reimaging their new identity and contextualizing their experience.

Critical race theory as applied to college after prison analyzes the racial and ethnic subordination in the classroom and incorporates the perceptions, experiences, and counterhegemonic practices of educators and students of color. A critical race pedagogy is constructed by including the reflections of African American practitioners/intellectuals who are committed to the ideals and principles found in CRT. For example, critical race pedagogues are concerned with the persistence of racial discrimination in schools and in the wider society, maintaining cultural identities, and the ways in which race, class, and the criminal justice system collude to make the lives of the black poor perilous. This "liberatory pedagogy" is expressed through dialogical engagement in the classroom as well as engaging in daily acts of self-affir-mation and challenging hegemonic administrators (Lynn, 1999).

As it applies to education, CRT is barely 30 years old (Delgado & Stefan-cic, 2001). Critical pedagogy, with its foundation in Marxist critiques of schooling and society, has traditionally focused on issues of social class more than race (Ellsworth, 1989; Gordon, 1995; McCarthy, 1988; Lynn, 2005). CRT, however, moves away from examining class and examines the ways in which theories of race can and should be visible in the teaching and learning taking place in diverse classrooms. CRT links race, culture, and schooling in an effort to advocate for the creation of spaces where black students, who can also be seen as encompassing all marginalized groups, can feel empowered and represented (Irvine, 1990; Scheurich & Young, 1997). In terms of edu-cating former prisoners, CRT "moves beyond an individualistic focus, is respectful of the sociopolitical realities of marginalized groups, and does not reinforce the power structures in society" (Patton et al., 2007, p. 48). Using the anti-essentialist paradigm proposed by CRT, the college community can question the experiences and perspectives of students who have been incar-cerated, rather than concocting remedies for the imagined deficits they carry.

Black students returning from prison must be given the space and re-sources to inspire an "intellectual revolution" among themselves (Gaskew, 2015). Community colleges are poised to invert the power dynamic that prison impresses on its captives and emancipate the black student experience from the barriers that have kept the classroom culture chained to the tradi-tional and often discriminatory canon. One way that community college cam-puses have the ability to disrupt the systemic oppression is by channeling access to the social capital and avenues to self-determination offered by higher education. In the community college campus context, scholars and practitioner–educators are positioned to create inclusive and engaging spaces in support of formerly incarcerated students (Gaskew, 2015). This can be achieved by creating race-specific clubs that are housed in cultural centers and contain the much needed resources that black students returning from prison need.

Using a critical race lens means shifting pedagogical practice to create relevant courses of study that include race and oppression as well as prison and punishment. Space could be dedicated for discussion and resource ex-change between black students and black faculty. People who are returning from prison can be compensated for sharing their expertise as scholars and speakers. These are just some examples of the ways that community colleges can take a critical race approach to recognizing the value of the black male student returning from prison, and look to encourage their successful reintegration into college.

Two ways that CRT can be used to encourage and engage black students who are returning from prison is by creating space and legitimacy for their voices (Gillborn, 2008). CRT explains that through counterspace and counterstory, community college campuses have the ability to build community where people of color, and in this instance, those with criminal histories, can come together and share their lived experiences. Counterstory presses for the voices of formerly incarcerated people to articulate their experiences and in doing so, challenge the prevailing notions about what it means to be released from prison and now in college.

COUNTERSTORY

Strategic Storytelling can be a highly effective tool in challenging the dominant discourse that frequently ignores the reality of students who have been incarcerated. Sharing experiential knowledge and empowering marginalized voices through storytelling, formerly incarcerated students refute the notion that their experiences are invisible. Indeed, their counterstories challenge the narratives of the majority, and they frame minorities' experiences in a manner that inspires empathy and allows others to stand more easily in the shoes of the oppressed. A fledgling body of research shows that other stigmatized groups resist marginalization by contesting deficit societal ascriptions concerning their identities through a process called narrative identity work (Leisenring, 2006; Opsal, 2011; Riessman, 2000; Rosenfeld, 1999; Snow & Anderson, 1987). Identity work, as defined by Snow and Anderson (1987), refers to a "range of activities individuals engage in to create, present, and sustain personal identities congruent with and supportive of the self-concept" (p. 1348). Those activities that enhance identities through the crafting and supporting of narratives have been historically referred to as identity talk (Snow & Anderson, 1987) and more recently as "narrative identity work" (Case & Hunter, 2012; Ibarra & Barbulescu, 2010; Opsal, 2011).

STORYTELLING EVENTS

Events that involve an open-stage, talent display or spoken word related to incarceration have the ability to invite students from a range of backgrounds to share on a theme. Students who may feel stigmatized by their incarceration are able to attend cultural, strength-based events without disclosing their status. Organizing intentional activities for students with a history of incarceration to express themselves is another way community colleges have been able to offer countervoices to students who go on to produce podcasts, film, storytelling-without-notes events; outsider art exhibits; hip-hop showcases; and theatrical productions. Often these are to the acclaim of all involved and attract the interest and attention of students who have not been in prison. Building on the strengths of formerly incarcerated students in a public way shifts the campus culture toward inclusion without stigmatizing these students as vulnerable.

MENTORSHIP OPPORTUNITIES

Many former prisoners have recently been released from hostile environments with minimal social interaction beyond their prison quarters. To ease the transition from this type of environment to community college, campuses could create paid mentorship programs with formerly incarcerated black students serving as mentors to recently released black students. Black mentors with a history of incarceration understand and help offset the social pressures of reentering the free world. Family life and college campuses can easily become overwhelming for recently released prisoners who have not done many of the things outside of the redundant tasks of prison. Mentors with firsthand experience could connect formerly incarcerated students in activities that can be viewed as restoring power that was taken from them in prison. For example, many formerly incarcerated black students have been incarcerated in facilities where the people in power tend to be white, but the people in prison are more likely to be people of color. This can lead to a skewed view of power and work. One way a community college mentoring program can help restore this balance is by connecting mentorship programs and mentees to black faculty to exchange resources and ideas. Regular weekly meetings, where mentors, mentees, willing faculty and students can also host weekly rotating guests who have successfully reentered society and completed their education. These meetings can create a forum for discussing various issues pertaining to black students reentering society after prison. These issues can include reversing some of the effects of being disempowered.

Regardless of the degree of criminal justice experience, the racism black and Latino students experience is further exacerbated by the chorus of denial from white people when students of color share the reality of their lived experience. For people with histories of incarceration, finding avenues to tell their stories in a meaningful way can challenge how they are viewed but also the way they see themselves. It is by encouraging the telling of this counter-story that community colleges can change the narrative, empowering formerly incarcerated students to derive the full benefit of college. CRT uses the pervasive nature of racism that is experienced in a deep existential way by people of color in the United States as a starting point for program design. By acknowledging the real effects of under-education, over-incarceration, and racism, program designs can be relevant to black students who are returning from prison.

COUNTERSPACES

The counterspaces framework offers a useful conceptual frame for exploring how setting involvement may give rise to and support personal and group identities (Case & Hunter, 2014). A counterspace is a social setting in which two or more people interact in ways that challenge deficit notions concerning a marginalized identity and that creates an identity-affirming environment (Case & Hunter, 2014; Solórzano, Ceja, & Yosso, 2000). Counterspace is a term in critical race theory that is used to describe an educational space that provides marginalized students with an alternative to racist institutionalized spaces (Schwartz, 2014). Black and Latino empowerment clubs have historically afforded their respective constituents an opportunity to position their "marginality as a site for resistance" (hooks, 1990, p. 153) rather than one in need of emancipation. Critical race theory correlates these spatial practices with the experiences of formerly incarcerated students. Creating meaningful space to share, self-disclose, seek assistance, and provide service are qualities that could enhance the experience of black college students who have been incarcerated. The creation of counterspaces within community colleges offers a key area of potential growth for research. Educators are positioned to be architects for these counterspaces that not only cultivate a tenacious resilience in historically disadvantaged students but also foster a "critical" resistance to interrupt hegemonic discourse within student development work.

RACE-SPECIFIC ORGANIZING

One example from LaGuardia Community College's campus is the Black Male Empowerment Cooperative (BMEC). This race-specific organization is able to invert the power structure by having people of color, formerly incarcerated, and historically disenfranchised black students comprise the leadership (Miller & Schwartz, 2016). At the same time, BMEC is also open to people of all races and genders, and affords all constituents a sense of ownership, hence, "Cooperative." The Black Male Empowerment Cooperative is an organization that includes all people invested in the well-being of black men. The cooperative is empowering, using Federal Work Study money to endorse the students who become "BMECers" making presentations to classes, organizing conferences, and mentoring one another. Their space also reflects a great investment of institutional support: a large workspace, refreshments, computers, with black men in visible leadership positions. This type of race-defined club exists in various iterations across community college campuses; it represents the celebration of diversity that traditional four-year campuses often lack.

VIRTUAL COUNTERSPACE

At community colleges, physical space is often at a premium, therefore, programmatic interventions to support and cultivate a sense of belonging among black formerly incarcerated students can be virtual as well as physical. The mobilization of social media such as Facebook, Twitter, and Instagram can enhance the "virtual" counterspace and support formerly incarcerated students anonymously. This virtual realm as a valuable terrain of counterspaces remains underused and under-researched and perhaps still inaccessible to some students without computers or Internet access (Sudbury, 2004), but there is a need for balance in establishing and sustaining such spaces (Benitez Jr., 2010). A critical race lens necessitates that although such spaces centralize the needs of marginalized students like black students with a history of incarceration, and celebrating their narratives, they must also simultaneously address the manifestations of power and privilege rooted in hegemonic discourse (Rothenberg, 2007).

RECOMMENDATIONS AND CONCLUSIONS

Formerly incarcerated black students are typically not targeted for or included in opportunities where they are providing instead of receiving instruction. White faculty who teach criminal justice, provide advisement, wellness services, or even financial aid counseling, could all be targeted for retraining activities that focus on the realities facing black students who have been incarcerated. Black formerly incarcerated students could provide insight into the administration of college programs, curriculum, and classroom management which could help white faculty create more inclusive environments for formerly incarcerated students. Rather than targeting formerly incarcerated black students to receive support, CRT advises that the strengths of black students who have been in prison be recognized in the form of an ongoing income from the college they attend.

Even as community colleges become more accommodating of, and sensitive to the needs of formerly incarcerated black students, the dominant discourse is still one of choice and personal responsibility when it comes to education. The sanitized discourse of the prison to college pipeline is found in its underlying message: that crime is committed by those who lack education and, by learning, these students will cease offending. Replacing this discourse with one that acknowledges the role of intentional and institutional racism can reframe these same students as survivors of trauma and examples of human resilience. Storytelling events, mentorship opportunities and race-specific clubs on campus and online can all be implemented on a community college campus to empower black students who have been incarcerated. This way, black students with a history of incarceration can be heralded for their achievements both in and since prison. To be clear, community college can be restorative for black students who have been to prison, but it is the incarceration that needs to be remediated, not the fictitious intellectual or cultural deficiency that is the smoke and mirrors of racist criminal justice practices (Berliner & Biddle, 1995). It is not the critical-thinking skills that former prisoners lack, it is the social capital and pathways to employment that community colleges can pave.

This chapter offers insights on how colleges, and in particular community colleges which accept large numbers of the formerly incarcerated, can be positioned to create avenues for countervoices and counterspaces that will encourage black students with a history of incarceration to graduate at higher rates and self-actualize after prison. As CRT emphasizes, the structure and outcome of these efforts must originate with the people most directly affected (Delgado & Stefancic, 2001). While caucuses have been assembled to uncover what risk and need factors are, colleges are wise to empower leadership from the increasingly growing pool of students who have been to prison and are now college students.

REFERENCES

Abdul-Adil, J. K., & Farmer, A. D. (2006). Inner-city African American parental involvement in elementary schools: Getting beyond urban legends of apathy. *School Psychology Quarterly, 21*(1), 1–12.

Alexander M. (2010). *The New Jim Crow*. New York: New Press.

Archer, D. N. (2009). Introduction: Challenging the school-to-prison pipeline. *New York Law School Law Review, 54*, 867.

Belfield, C. R., & Bailey, T. (2011). The benefits of attending community college: A review of the evidence. *Community College Review, 39*(1), 46–68.

Bell, D. (1992). Racial realism. *Connecticut Law Review, 24*, 363–79.

Bell, D. A., Delgado, R., & Stefancic, J. (2005). *The derrick bell reader*. New York: NYU Press.

Benitez, M. (2010). Resituating culture centers within a social justice framework: is there room for examining whiteness. In L. Patton (Ed.), *Culture Centers in Higher Education Perspectives on Identity, Theory, and Practice*. Sterling, VA: Stylus Publishers.

Berliner, D. C., & Biddle, B. J. (1995). *The manufactured crisis: Myths, fraud, and the attack on America's public schools*. New York: Addison-Wesley.

Brazzell, D., Crayton, A., Mukamal, D. A., Solomon, A. L., & Lindahl, N. (2009). From the Classroom to the Community: Exploring the Role of Education during Incarceration and Reentry. *Urban Institute (NJI)*.

Case, A., & Hunter, C. (2014). Counterspaces and the narrative identity work of offender-labeled African American youth. *Journal of Community Psychology, 42*(8).

Christle, C. A., Jolivette, K., & Nelson, C. M. (2005). Breaking the school to prison pipeline: Identifying school risk and protective factors for youth delinquency. *Exceptionality, 13,* 69–88.

Cole, H. A., & Heilig, J. V. (2011). Developing a school-based youth court: A potential alternative to the school to prison pipeline. *Journal of Law & Education, 40*(2), 305.

Cooc, N., Currie-Rubin, R., Kuttner, P., & Ng, M. (2012). *Disrupting the school-to-prison pipeline.* Boston, MA: Harvard Education.

Darensbourg, A., Perez, E., & Blake, J. (2010). Overrepresentation of African American males in exclusionary discipline: The role of school-based mental health professionals in dismantling the school to prison pipeline. *Journal of African American Males in Education, 1*(3), 196–211.

Davis, L. M., Bozick, R., Steele, J. L., Saunders, J., & Miles, J. N. (2013). *Evaluating the effectiveness of correctional education: A meta-analysis of programs that provide education to incarcerated adults.* Santa Monica, CA: Rand Corporation.

Delgado, R., & Stefancic, J. (2001). *Critical race theory: An introduction.* New York: New York University Press.

Ellsworth, E. (1989) Why doesn't this feel empowering? Working through the repressive myths of critical pedagogy. *Harvard Educational Review, 59*(3), 297–324.

Fasching-Varner, K. J., & Mitchell, R. (2013). CRT's challenge to educator's articulation of abstract liberal perspectives of purpose. In A. Dixson & M. Lynn (Eds.), *Handbook of critical race theory in education* (pp. 355–67). New York: Routledge.

Feierman, J., Levick, M., & Mody, A. (2009). The school-to-prison pipeline . . . and back: Obstacles and remedies for the re-enrollment of adjudicated youth. *New York University Law School Review, 54,* 1115.

Ford, J. & Schroeder, R. (2010). Higher education and criminal offending over the life course. *Sociological Spectrum, 31*(1).

Fowler, D. (2011). School discipline feeds the "pipeline to prison." *Phi Delta Kappan, 93*(2), 14–19.

Gaes, G. G. (2008). *The impact of prison education programs on post-release outcomes.* Publisher not identified.

Gaskew, T. (2015). Developing a Prison Education Pedagogy. *New Directions For Community Colleges, 2015* (170), 67–78.

Gillborn, D. (2008). *Racism and education: Coincidence or conspiracy?* New York: Routledge.

Gordon, B. M. (1995) Knowledge construction, competing critical theories, and education. In J. A. Banks & C. A. McGee Banks (Eds.), *Handbook of Research on Multicultural Education.* New York: Macmillan.

Halkovic, A., Fine, M., Bae, J., Campbell, D., Campbell, L., Gary, C., Greene, A., Ramirez, M., Riggs, R., Taylor, M., Tebout, R., & Tawaji, A. (2013). *Higher education and reentry: The gifts they bring.* The Prisoner Reentry Institute.

Harris, A. (1990). Race and essentialism in feminist legal theory. *Stanford Law Review, 42*(3).

hooks, b. (1990). *Yearning: Race, gender, and cultural politics,* 1st Edition. Boston, MA: South End Press.

Ibarra, H. & Barbulescu, R. (2010). Identity as narrative: Prevalence, effectiveness, and consequences of narrative identity work in macro work role transitions. *The Academy of Management Review, 35*(1), 135–54.

Irvine, J. (1990). *Black students and school failure: Policies, practices, and prescriptions.* Westport, CT: Praeger Publishers.

Jonson, C. L., & Cullen, F. T. (2015). Prisoner reentry programs. *Crime & Just., 44,* 517–57.

Kim, C. Y., Losen, D. J., & Hewitt, D. T. (2010). *The school-to-prison pipeline: Structuring legal reform.* New York: New York University Press.

Ladson-Billings, G. (2006). From the achievement gap to the education debt: Understanding achievement in US schools. *Educational Researcher, 35*(7), 3–12.

Leisenring, A. (2006). Confronting "victim" discourses: The identity work of battered women. *Symbolic Interaction, 29*(3).

Lynn, M. (1999) Toward a critical race pedagogy: A research note. *Urban Education, 33*(5), 606–26.

Lynn, M. (2005). Critical race theory, Afrocentricity, and their relationship to critical pedagogy. *Critical pedagogy and race*, 127–39.

McCarthy, C. (1988) Rethinking liberal and radical perspectives on racial inequality in schooling: Making the case for nonsynchrony. *Harvard Educational Review, 58*(3), 265–79.

Mellow, G. O., & Heelan, C. M. (2014). *Minding the dream: The process and practice of the American community college*. Lanham, MD: Rowman & Littlefield.

Miller, B., & Schwartz, J. (2016). The Intersection of Black Lives Matter and Adult Education: One Community College Initiative. *New Directions for Adult and Continuing Education, 2016* (150), 13–23.

Museus, S. D., & Iftikar, J. (2013). AsianCrit: Toward an Asian critical theory in education. In *Annual Meeting of the American Educational Research Association, San Francisco, CA*.

Opsal, T. (2011). Women disrupting a marginalized identity: Subverting the parolee identity through narrative. *Journal of Contemporary Ethnography, 40*(2), 135–67.

Patton, L. D., McEwen, M., Rendón, L., & Howard-Hamilton, M. F. (2007). Critical race perspectives on theory in student affairs. In S. R. Harper & L. D. Patton (Eds.), Responding to the realities of race on campus. *New Directions for Student Services* (No. 120, pp. 39–53). San Francisco: Jossey-Bass.

Riessman, C. (2000) Analysis of personal narratives. Boston University (unpublished paper). alumni.media.mit.edu/~brooks/storybiz/riessman.pdf.

Roach, R. (2001). Where are the Black men on campus? *Diverse Issues in Higher Education, 18*(6), 18.

Rose, L. H. (2015). Community College Students With Criminal Justice Histories and Human Services Education: Glass Ceiling, Brick Wall, or a Pathway to Success. *Community College Journal of Research and Practice, 39*(6), 584–87.

Rosenfeld, D. (1999) Identity work among lesbian and gay elderly. *Journal of Aging Studies, 13*(2), 121–38.

Rothenberg, P. (2007). *Race, class, and gender in the United States*, 7th Edition. New York: Worth Publishers, Inc.

Scheurich, J. & Young, M. (1997). Coloring epistemologies: Are our research epistemologies racially biased? *Educational Researcher, 26*(4), 4–16.

Schwartz, J. (2014). Classrooms of spatial justice: Counter-spaces and young men of color in a GED program. *Adult Education Quarterly, 64*, 110–27.

Shajahan, R. (2013). Coloniality and global testing regime in higher education: Unpacking the OECD's AHELO initiative. *Journal of Education Policy, 28*(5), 676–94.

Skiba, R. J., Simmons, A., Staudinger, L., Rausch, M., Dow, G., & Feggins, R. (2003, May). Consistent removal: Contributions of school discipline to the school-prison pipeline. Boston, MA: School to Prison Pipeline Conference.

Smith, C. D. (2009). Deconstructing the pipeline: Evaluating school-to-prison pipeline equal protection cases through a structural racism framework. *Fordham Urban Law Journal, 36*(5), 1009.

Snow, D. A., & Anderson, L. (1987). Identity work among the homeless: The verbal construction and avowal of personal identities. *American Journal of Sociology, 92*, 1336–71.

Solomon, A. L., Waul, M., Van Ness, A., and Travis, J. (2004). Outside the walls: A national snapshot of community-based prisoner reentry programs. Urban Institute.

Solorzano, D., Ceja, M., & Yosso, T. (2000). Critical race theory, racial microaggressions, and campus racial climate: The experiences of African American college students. *Journal of Negro Education, 69*(1/2), 60.

Sturm, S., Skolnick, K., & Wu, T. (2010). Building pathways of possibility from criminal justice to college: College initiative as a catalyst linking individual and systemic change. Retrieved from http://www.changecenter.org/ research-publications/case-studies/Building%20Pathways%20of%20Possibility%20from%20Criminal%20Justice%20to%20 College.pdf/view.

Sudbury, J. (2004). A world without prisons: Resisting militarism, globalized punishment, and empire. *Social Justice, 31*(1–2), 9–30.

Spycher, D. M., Shkodriani, G. M., & Lee, J. B. (2012). The Other Pipeline: From Prison to Diploma Community Colleges and Correctional Education Programs. *College Board Advocacy & Policy Center*.

Travis, J. (2005). *But they all come home*. New York: Urban Institute Press.

Tuzzolo, E., & Hewitt, D. T. (2006). Rebuilding inequity: The re-emergence of the school-to-prison pipeline in New Orleans. *High School Journal, 90*(2), 59–68.

Wald, J., & Losen, D. J. (2003). Defining and redirecting a school-to-prison pipeline. *New Directions for Youth Development*, 99, 9–15.

Winn, M. T. (2011). *Girl time: Literacy, justice, and the school-to-prison pipeline: Teaching for social justice*. New York: Teachers College Press.

Winn, M. T., & Behizadeh, N. (2011). The right to be literate: Literacy, education, and the school-to-prison pipeline. *Review of Research in Education, 35,* 147–73.

Chapter Three

Do I Want to Be a 30 Percenter or 70 Percenter?

Black Cultural Privilege

Tony Gaskew

The most difficult life decision a black American will ever have to make is to either own the truth or live the lie; to either be awake or to stay asleep; to either accept their black cultural legacy or to enslave their black cultural potential. You see, Fanon (1961) declared, there is only one true right, "that of demanding human behavior from the other," and one true duty, "that of not renouncing my freedom through my own choices" (pp. 228–29). For far too many years, black people have been making life decisions without fully understanding the truth of their choices, because these choices have been blurred by 400 years of systemic humiliation. That is, a static set of institutionally owned and socially constructed set of rules, customs, and beliefs designed to create and sustain a black American culture that inherits the crippling effects of shame, self-segregation, and transgenerational learned helplessness (Gaskew, 2014; Gaskew, 2015). A set of humiliations designed to strip away any level of black dignity and self-respect.

However, speaking the language of a social scientist, systemic humiliation is not the root cause of this protracted human genocide but the insidious side effect of an invisible history of micro- and macroaggressions against blackness. Born from the womb of our nation's *original sin* of chattel enslavement and the black American Holocaust, the mental illness of white supremacy is the fundamental "cause" in this social experiment of human suffering and continues to sit at the core of how black spaces are "effected" through oppression, marginalization, and humiliation (Gaskew, 2014; 2015). The psychosis of white superiority and black inferiority has saturated the poisons of greed, anger, and ignorance (Williams, 2000) into every single American social institution. This mental illness has created an alternate American reality, a white American idealism, where all the universal virtues of blackness and everything that encompasses being nature's first human beings has been systemically erased from the minds of those who suffer from this infliction. This supernatural *evil* has served as the root killer of black American choices, and has resulted in the mass incarceration of tens of millions of black bodies across four centuries of zero tolerance policing on black spaces. Truth to power, attempting to place blackness, our world's greatest natural resource, into a cage, has been America's greatest legacy and ultimately it's karmic demise.

Since the systemic humiliations inherited by the black American experience are metaphysical in nature, scope, and understanding, it's only logical that a black ontological lens be used to examine solutions. In the brief space of this essay, using an autoethnographic methodology, I will attempt to synergize the thousands of interviews and group discussions I've had as an active participant observer in the black American experience and my 30-year study of race, crime, and justice. My findings suggest that in order for formerly incarcerated black people to transform humiliation into humility and liberate themselves from the mass incarceration poisons of greed, anger, and ignorance as well as the psychosis of white supremacy, the reawakening of a black consciousness must take root. Inspired from the applied concepts contained within my book *Rethinking Prison Reentry: Transforming Humiliation into Humility,* this reawakened black consciousness is known as *black cultural privilege* (BCP) (Gaskew, 2014). BCP applies the essence of *black fearlessness, truth, accountability, empowerment,* and *healing* to nurture formerly incarcerated black people to address the pain and suffering of white superiority and black inferiority, and to make a life choice to either become a 30 percenter or a 70 percenter.

THE SEARCH FOR BLACKNESS IN AN
AGE OF MASS INCARCERATION

Arguably, there is no greater by-product of this psychosis than the criminal justice system, and the direct and structural violence it has inflicted on black bodies. During my 30-year odyssey in the corporately constructed matrix of the criminal justice system, which includes working as a police-detective at M.P.D. assigned as a member of the DOJ's Organized Crime Drug Enforcement Task Force, and now as a tenured associate professor of criminal justice and founding director of a nationally recognized prison education program at the University of Pittsburgh (Bradford), there is very little that I have not seen, heard, or done in the business of crime and justice. Without any doubt, there is clearly an explicit and implicit systemic process in place to criminally define and enslave the black American experience. Today, despite making up less than 5% of the adult population, black bodies occupy nearly 40% of our nation's prison cells (The Sentencing Project, 2015). Black people are more likely to be stopped, more likely to be arrested, and more likely to be incarcerated. As a result, today a police officer can walk into any maternity ward in America, and with an almost statistical certainty, place handcuffs on one out of every three nameless newborn black American infants.

When Tom Burrell (2010) noted, "Black people are not dark-skinned white people," it was not meant to be a disparaging slight on white America (p. xi). In fact, the inherent beauty behind his words is that the true essence of American "blackness" and its incredible historic cultural diaspora is not based on any socially constructed standard of American "whiteness." Blackness stands on its own two feet and defines itself, in whatever limitless shapes, sounds, or shades that are determined by the people who own and occupy its essence. Blackness is not homogenous. It crosses macro- and microlevel social perspectives of religion, politics, class, ethnicity, language, and music, infusing itself into the multifaceted identities of the lived black American experience. At its roots, the unifying component of blackness in America resonates in the collective pride of a people that is so culturally rich, diverse, and powerful, that 400 years of systemically supported humiliations only served to strengthen its inner core (Gaskew, 2014).

However, the reality of black America today is collectively being able to navigate through the political campaign of systemic shame, self-segregation, and transgenerational learned helplessness that started with chattel enslavement in 1619, and continues today with the mass incarceration of black bodies, without leaving blackness feeling spiritually, physically, emotionally mentally, and culturally raped. I've discovered that one of the secrets for successfully navigating humiliation into humility for incarcerated black students is by focusing on the Humiliation to Humility Perspective (HHP). That is black truths. Black truths about history; black truths about crime and justice; black truths about victimization; and black truths about life choices and decisions (Gaskew, 2014). In essence, liberation through the knowledge blackness. Knowing and understanding the truths behind the who, what, where, when, and how of blackness. Nurturing a *sustainable whole person by black truth* (Gaskew, 2014). This self-awareness strips humiliation of its negative powers that create self-hate and nihilism among black bodies, and gives birth to a humility-filled realization where pride, self-worth, and karmic success become part of the black consciousness.

For nearly a decade as the founding director of the UPB Prison Education Program (UPBPEP), I have been discussing the concept of *blackness* with incarcerated black students at Bureau of Prisons (BOP) Federal Correctional Institution (FCI) McKean. In fact, some of the most dynamic dialogues on the essence of blackness have been led by a vanguard set of incarcerated black educators serving as professors for two University of Pittsburgh courses: *ADMJ 1447: The United States of America vs. The United States of America* and *PEP 0250: Just Mercy: A Transformative Criminal Justice Journey to Expose and Uproot White Supremacy* (Thompson & Connors, 2015; Thompson, Boyd, & Colon, 2016). These two postsecondary courses uncovered another layer of radical pedagogical genius, one of incarcerated black intellectualism, which could only come to the surface from black faces imprisoned at the bottom of the well (Bell, 1992). Although these two courses will be the subject of another critical essay in the future, I would only add that these educational spaces provided me with a better understanding of my own blackness and the blackness of every incarcerated black educator and student participating in those radical experiments in pedagogy.

As one of the very few black American male tenured university professors working as a postsecondary volunteer at a federal correctional facility, which by itself is problematic and a direct reflection of the ongoing systemic humiliations present within the paradigm of prison higher education nationwide, I have spent the majority of time and energy cultivating an HBCU-like culture at FCI McKean, which like the majority of BOP facilities across the country houses a majority black American male population. In fact, the UPB Prison Education Program commonly refers to the prison facility as the *University of Pittsburgh at FCI McKean,* and just as Malcolm X discovered many years ago, the search for blackness in an age of mass incarceration must start at the center of institutional liberation: the prison library. As noted by Williams (2000) when living beings seek refuge from pain and suffering, they turn to teachers, teachings, and community. Recognizing the dearth of black teachers, black teachings, and a supportive black community behind the walls of mass incarceration, the UPB Prison Education Program has provided access to hundreds of *teachers* and from hundreds of *teachings,* ranging from the liberating works of Clarke, Frazier, Garvey, Du Bois, Woodson, Diop, Williams, Baldwin, Malcolm X, Douglass, Asante, Hughes, Fanon, Bell, Karenga, and Bennet just to name a few. We have nurtured the continued growth and evolution of a *community* of incarcerated black scholars who actively serve as life coaches, mentors, and college educators, creating a metaphysical place of refuge and reawakening for incarcerated black American students.

However, the epic journey from humiliation to humility is not an easy one. The road to *black fearlessness, truth, accountability, empowerment,* and *healing* (Gaskew, 2014) for incarcerated black people returning home is paved with temptations, disappointments, and failures. When black spaces seek refuge, unemployment will still be high. The educational system will still be broken for black people. There will still be more liquor stores than schools in black American neighborhoods. A war to humiliate black bodies will continue to be waged by the *Great White Shark* (Gaskew, 2014) of policing, courts, and corrections. Black Americans will still have the greatest opportunity to be victimized by a person within their own community due to the mental illness of white supremacy. You see, for incarcerated black students returning home, they must first be able to make a clear choice and ask themselves: Do I want t be a 30 percenter or 70 percenter?

ARE YOU A 30 PERCENTER OR A 70 PERCENTER?

The absolute worst environment for incarcerated black students to find themselves in, specifically those who are nearing an end to their criminal justice enslavement, is an environment where their blackness goes uneducated, unchallenged, and unused. Whether it be the prison politics of racialized segregation or racialized criminalization, each provides a dangerous *cultural safety cushion* for incarcerated black people, where refuge is presented in territorial cliques, street hustlers, and lessons on criminal enslavement. These safety cushions are present in all prison settings from low to high, and normally consist of the following: free meals, free recreation, free medical/health services, no bill collectors, no parenting or family responsibilities, and the continued ability to use violence, intimidation, and gangsterism to foster black enslavement. They are structurally inspired delusions that allow incarcerated black bodies to embrace their criminalization as an extension of their blackness. All of these safety cushions are built into the prison environment, and every single incarcerated black student has to fight off the addiction to them before being released, an impossible task if one doesn't stay mentally and spiritually focused on the true essence of one's blackness.

Over the past 10 years one of the most intellectually vibrant conversations that I've ever witnessed has taken place between incarcerated black educators and their mostly white non-incarcerated college students, in the presence of incarcerated black students, under the academic umbrella of explaining the nuances of so-called *black-on-black* crime. There is absolutely no critical engagement in academia that challenges white supremacy, white fragility, and white privilege within the construction of race, crime, and justice that is more scholarly profound than when communicated by unapologetic, fearless, and awoken incarcerated black educators (Thompson & Connors, 2015; Thompson, Boyd, & Colon, 2016). As subject-matter experts using a cause and effect methodology, incarcerated educators explain how the mental illness of white superiority and black inferiority has saturated black American minds over the past 400 years and acknowledge that this psychosis has created a *black counterculture of crime* (Gaskew, 2014) in America that "lives in the darkness of Whiteness" educators (Thompson & Connors, 2015) and in its blindness, destroys the essence of blackness. You see, these incarcerated black scholars set the tone for a reawakening in black consciousness, by explaining that in order to transform humiliation into humility, incarcerated black students must make a choice of whether to be a 30 percenter or 70 percenter.

A "70 percenter" is an incarcerated black student who has made the *choice* to never leave the lifestyle and humiliations created by a black counterculture of crime. A "30 percenter" is an incarcerated black student who has made the *choice* of fearlessness, truth, accountability, empowerment, and healing, in order to take back the universal legacy of blackness (Gaskew, 2014). Incarcerated black students must make a *decision* to be committed to the reawakening of their black consciousness, physically, mentally, and spiritually. Incarcerated black educators explain to their non-incarcerated white students that they will either be passive observers for a socially constructed lie that encourages *70 percenters*, white supremacy, direct, and structural violence toward blackness or active participants for universal truths that encourages *30 percenters* to reclaim the universal tenets of mercy, compassion, and respect toward blackness. These incarcerated black scholars explain to their incarcerated black students that they will either be passive observers enslaved in a black counterculture of crime that encourages *70 percenters* to destroy the essence of blackness or active participants as the founders of humanity in making choices as *30 percenters*, enriching the legacy of blackness. The final decision for all stakeholders belong to them once they embrace truth.

During my 30 years of being a participant observer in the study of race, crime, and justice, one of the most profound exchanges I have ever witnessed regarding *decisions* and *choices* made by incarcerated black students preparing to transition away from incarceration and trying to escape the clutches of the black counterculture of crime, took place between an incarcerated black student and a non-incarcerated white student. While looking directly at a non-incarcerated white student, the incarcerated black educator stated:

Now . . . the most important thing I learned about myself over the past twenty years of living behind these prison walls . . . is that I am never coming back. Now . . . I don't mean that I don't think I'm coming back, or I hope that I'm not coming back, but I can guarantee that I'm never coming back. You see, I possess some skills and family support that I believe will allow me to make a *choice*. I don't ever plan on going back into crime . . . but . . . if I ever made the *decision* of going back into this culture . . . I want you to know if we come face-to-face . . . and you're a police officer . . . and your job, which I respect, is to put me back into one of these cages . . . I want you to know right now that you're not gonna make it. One of us is not going to walk away from that meeting, and since the innocence of taking a person's life is already on my résumé, I will not hesitate a bit on doing what I have to do. Since you don't have that experience, I can guarantee that you will not win and just because we know each other in this class does not mean anything to me. I know that ultimately your people [other police officers] are going to eventually get me, but either way, I'm never coming back to prison. So, you better be 100% positive that this is the career field you want because I'm not alone in my thinking . . . there are other black men just like me and you might meet them . . . but I really hope not.

The non-incarcerated white student sat there motionless with a glazed look, as the remaining white students echoed his appearance. Nothing more was ever discussed in public about this exchange by either part. I never spoke to the incarcerated black student about the exchange but I understood every-thing he said. He would never allow the shame, self-subjugation, and trans-generational learned helplessness of the criminal justice system to enslave him again. He would separate himself physically from this world if that became his reality. It was clear that he possessed the fearlessness of a re-awakening and life would never be the same again. He was later moved to another facility to prepare for his release and I never heard from him again. The non-incarcerated white student went on to graduate and successfully enter the policing component of the criminal justice system. Although we do not see each other very often due to our busy and conflicting schedules, I've occasionally run into him during an alumni event and he never fails to ac-knowledge how this exchange has always remained on his mind. He told me the conversation changed his life and for a very brief moment, he felt what it might be like to be *awake* as an incarcerated black student. I agreed and told him that this incarcerated black student had been liberated by acquiring the truth of his *black cultural privilege* (BCP).

THE REAWAKENING OF BLACK CONSCIOUSNESS: BLACK CULTURAL PRIVILEGE

James Baldwin (2010) believed that black Americans are the conscience of America, and to be black and conscious in America is to be in a constant state of rage. You see, a strong and vibrant black consciousness has always been the moral compass of saving America from itself. It has been at the forefront of fighting the war against the mental illness of white supremacy for nearly four centuries in America. It has successfully won the physical, psychological, and spiritual battles of the holocaust of enslavement, the Black Codes, and Jim Crow. As a black American man born in the early 1960s, I saw firsthand the incredible life force of black consciousness with the awakening of the *Black Power Movement*, giving birth to a generation of revolutionaries who immersed themselves in the collective goals echoed by Karenga (2010): to solve pressing problems within the black American com-munity, and to continue the revolutionary struggle being waged to end white supremacy, racism, and oppression against black spaces. Today, black consciousness needs a reawakening—a reawakening I describe as *black cultural privilege* (BCP). Black cultural privilege is the physical, mental, and spiritual awareness that connects the rich diverse history of an African past with the ever-evolving journey into the legacy of the collective lived black American experience. It's an unconscious bond that exists among a people whose roots share an indestructible cultural DNA that has only been strengthened by 400 years of direct and structural violence, enslavement, the Black Codes, and Jim Crow. BCP defines the essence of blackness.

Without a doubt, we, as an entire universe of living beings, are one. Everything in it, around it, and shaped by it is alive, always in motion, and connected to everything else. We know this for a fact because our common senses are designed for the sole purpose of this synergy. When the sun shines, the wind blows, or the rain falls, it brings with it the same window of life to all beings. Nothing in the universe is spared. However, the human connection to this vast universe is only between 6,000 and 150,000 years old, depending on which story—science or faith—you enjoy. Regardless of the version, the human connection with the universe began in the rich cultural soil of Africa, the original Garden of Eden, and through the DNA of its black African people, the original Adam and Eve. Black bodies were the first human students of the universe and black Americans are their living testament. Black bodies were the first human voices, created the first human languages, and the first human civilizations. Black bodies were the first *Bodhisattva*; the first human beings to be taught the gifts of truth, humility, and forgiveness; that we all share the same duty of preserving life; that we are all connected under the universal principle that if one living being suffers, all living beings suffer; they were the first to absorb the life lessons of compassion, mercy, pride, empathy, righteousness, courage, unity, compromise, and love; the first to apply the gift of the *fourth eye.* Black bodies were the first scholars of metaphysics, the ethnosphere, spirituality, enlightenment, faith, and karma (Karenga, 2010; Williams, 2000); the first to apply the philosophical concepts of awareness, morality, and wisdom (Williams, 2000); the first to be taught about the poisons of greed, anger, and ignorance (p. 46); the first to use the family building blocks of teachers, teachings, and communities (pp. 33–35); the first to understand the universal rule of cause and effect, that pain and happiness, along with life and death, are all part of the interconnected cycle of life. Black bodies were the first to apply the principles of fearlessness (p. 166) as a life road map; the first to recognize the duty of not contributing to evil, doing good, and doing good for others (p. 91). The universe taught the world's first human beings, black people, *the art of life* (p. 7).

Just to be clear, this reawakening is not just another layer of Afrocentricity (Asante, 2003). Black Americans are no longer negotiating from a position of social, political, or economic weakness. Those days are over. We have the resources to frame and define the concepts of crime and justice. Kwame Ture (1967) once noted that "confusion is the greatest enemy of the revolution" (p. viii). There is no longer any confusion in our revolution. We know exactly what to do. We now simply have to do it. This reawakening is the natural evolution of the black American conscience. It's a visionary consciousness that filters, deconstructs, and eliminates the by-products of shame, self-segregation, and transgenerational learned helplessness (Gaskew, 2014) inherited by 400 years of white supremacy. It empowers black spaces in the ideological war against white superiority and black inferiority. It produces a cultural fearlessness that challenges the legitimacy of any social construct in America that attempts to criminalize blackness. It confronts the systemic actors of direct and structural violence that use the mask of "law and order" to conspire against the black American diaspora. It compels truth and demands accountability, holding institutional stakeholders responsible for maintaining justice to standards established and owned by black American voices. As the founders of humanity, black people must take responsibility for their own destiny. Black Americans must make peace with their own historical legacy. Black Americans must take ownership of either transforming or disposing of the current criminal justice system. Black Americans must wake up each morning and take full responsibility for the changes that we want to make in *our* lives and in *our* world (Williams, 2000, p. 178). The reawakening of a twenty-first-century black American conscience will end the life cycle of white supremacy and place the moral compass back into the hands of the universe's first human beings. For formerly incarcerated black people, black cultural privilege serves as the bridge between humiliation and humility.

FINAL THOUGHTS

For incarcerated black people returning home, the road is paved with temptations, disappointments, and failures. Without a life map as guide, making sense of the pain and suffering that has been socially constructed into the black American experience can leave black people seeking comfort in the mass incarcerated poisons of greed, anger, and ignorance. As Williams (2000) noted, "you can't sign up for enlightenment" (p. 29) and "if you have to go someplace to find a better you and you're going any farther than the mirror, don't take another step" (p. 32). Black cultural privilege can serve as the life map for formerly incarcerated black people who seek refuge, are stuck in fear, and aspire to the answer to the world's oldest question: what is my individual role in this collective universe? Black people are not the center of the universe but we are the first *Bodhisattva*. The reawakening of our black consciousness fills the empty spaces left by 400 years of socially constructed lies, direct and structural violence, and the mental illness of white supremacy. Black people were born with a certain set of metaphysical traits that were given at birth. The fact of the matter is, sometimes it is necessary to understand pain, to be intimate with it, in order to heal it (p. 8). Black people, the first human beings on the planet, are the healers of the world.

REFERENCES

Asante, M. (2003). *Afrocentricity: The Theory of Social Change*. Gilbert, AZ: African American Images.

Baldwin. J. (2010). *The Cross of Redemption: Uncollected Writings*. R. Kenan (Ed.). New York: Pantheon Books.

Bell, D. (1992). *Faces at the Bottom of the Well*. New York: Basic Books.

Bureau of Justice Statistics. (2015). *Employment and Expenditure*. Retrieved from http://www.bjs.gov/.

Burrell, T. (2010). *Brainwashed: Challenging the Myth of Black Inferiority*. Carlsbad, CA: SmileyBooks.

Du Bois, W.E.B. (1994). *The Souls of Black Folk*. Mineola, NY: Dover Publications.

Fanon, F. (1961). *The Wretched of the Earth*. New York: Penguin.

Gaskew, T. (2014). *Rethinking Prison Reentry: Transforming Humiliation into Humility*. Lanham, MD: Lexington Books.

Gaskew, T. (2015). "Developing a Prison Education Pedagogy." *New Directions for Community Colleges, Special Issue: Bringing College Education into Prisons, 2015*(170), pp. 67–78.

Karenga, M. (2010). *Introduction to Black Studies*. Los Angeles: University of Sankore Press.

The National Institute for Justice. (2015). *Policing for Profit*. Retrieved from http://ij.org/report/policing-for-profit/executive-summary/.

The Sentencing Project. (2015). *Black Lives Matter: Eliminating Racial Inequity in the Criminal Justice System*. Retrieved from http://sentencingproject.org/wp-content/uploads/2015/11/Black-Lives-Matter.pdf.

The United States Department of Justice. (2014). *Investigation of the Ferguson Police Department*. Retrieved from https://www.justice.gov/sites/default/files/opa/press-eleases/attachments/2015/03/04/ferguson_police_department_report.pdf.

The University of Pittsburgh at Bradford Prison Education Program. (2016). *Prison Education Program*. Retrieved from http://www.upb.pitt.edu/PrisonEdProgram/.

Thompson, S. & Connors, S. (2015). *The United States of America vs. The United States of America* [Lecture Notes]. Retrieved from https://courseweb.pitt.edu/webapps/blackboard/content/listContentEditable.jsp?content_id=_20249473_1&course_id=_320452_1&mode=reset.

Thompson, S., Boyd, A., & Colon, C. (2016). *Just Mercy: A Transformative Criminal Justice Journey to Expose and Uproot White Supremacy* [Lecture Notes]. Retrieved from https://courseweb.pitt.edu/webapps/blackboard/content/listContentEditable.jsp?content_id=_21479986_1&course_id=_352616_1 &mode=reset.

Ture, K. (1967). *Black Power: The Politics of Liberation*. New York: Vintage Books.

Williams, A. (2000). *Being Black: Zen and the Art of Living with Fearlessness and Grace*. New York: Penguin Compass Press.

Chapter Four

No Dismantling with the Master's Tools

The Problem of Privilege(s) in Reentry/Criminal Justice Education

Colleen P. Eren

It was 6 am and still predawn dark outside as I entered the ground floor of the Hilton in New Orleans, Louisiana. The American Society of Criminology's (ASC) annual conference was entering its last 24 hours, and I was slated for an early panel presentation. The maintenance staff, comprised exclusively of people of color, was hurrying to clean the marbled floors and tables and escalators in advance of the thousands of participants—almost exclusively white—who shortly emerged in their professional attire, clutching their Starbucks and attachés, hurrying to their talks on all aspects of criminal justice. I stood quietly for a few minutes, profoundly uncomfortable. I have had similar instances of visceral recognition of the institutionalization of whiteness, male dominance, and heteronormativity in academia over my 10 years in the profession. Yet this juxtapositioning of the privileged status of white scholars with the invisibility of people of color whose labor made the conference possible was particularly resonant, symbolic, and jarring. It was even an ironic moment, although I wondered how many were cognizant of that irony: the conference was rather infelicitously titled "The Many Colors of Crime and Justice."

I reflected on the discipline itself of criminal justice and the ways in which the dynamic witnessed at the Hilton that morning was emblematic of a pervasive disconnect. Mass incarceration by every indicator has had a disproportionate effect on communities of color. Of those men in state and federal custody in 2014, for instance, black men were 3.8 to 10.5 more likely to be

imprisoned than their white counterparts. Black women similarly were between 1.6 and 4.1 times more likely to be imprisoned *vis a vis* whites.
(Bureau of Justice Statistics, 2014) Violent crime victimization, both fatal
and non-fatal, likewise disproportionately affects the black community (Harrell, 2007). And yet, those appointed as the authority to analyze and speak
about these phenomena to design curricula in criminal justice/criminology
programs, to determine the bounds of acceptable lines of inquiry, and to
identify canonical readings are overwhelmingly white and male.

The purpose of this chapter is not to probe the multifactorial reasons that
are involved in the dominance within the discipline of criminal justice of the
white, male, straight perspective. However, I do want to give educators and
scholars within the field—particularly those who are involved in educating
about reentry—a snapshot of the lopsidedness that is pervasive. I do so to
suggest that those of us who educate both from a theoretical and vocational
perspective critically consider the influence of such institutionalized/normal-
ized whiteness and use critical race theory and other critical theories to
counteract that bias. How does the white, male, middle-class perspective
affect explanations of crime? How does it affect discussion of the prison
experience and reintegration into the community? How does it affect textbooks' coverage of policing and corrections? Of the "system"? In what ways
does it limit discussion, to privilege already extant racial hierarchies and
outmoded ideas about criminality and criminal "cultures?" And how do we
move beyond this narrow perspective without resorting to tokenism or fetish-
izing direct experiences of the criminal justice system in ways that leave
current systems of inequality fully intact?

The current status of criminal justice education in U.S. colleges is—if we
are judging by enrollment, graduation, and program expansion—robust.
Bachelor's degrees in criminal justice are among the top 10 most awarded
degrees in the country (Sloan III & Buchwalter, 2016), with over 125,000
students in the major in the United States. Robinson, in his critique of the
discipline, goes so far as to call criminal justice a "cash cow" for many
campuses (Robinson, 2001). With more than three million people working
directly in criminal justice fields ("Top 10 bachelor level criminal justice
jobs") and many more in fields tangentially impacted by criminal justice,
with positive growth predicted by the Bureau of Labor Statistics across the
board in criminal justice jobs ("Is a criminal justice degree worth it?"), with a
recommitment to Nixonian "Law and Order" by President Trump, and with
private prison stocks soaring in the wake of the 2016 election (Lurie, 2016);
there is nothing to suggest a decline in the expansion of the criminal justice
discipline in the near future. The cultural logic and ineluctability of mass
incarceration has normalized the pursuance of criminal justice degrees and
employment. Furthermore, larger-than-life TV and film representations of
law enforcement or the criminal justice system (*CSI*, *Law & Order* and *Law*

& *Order SVU, Cold Case, Criminal Minds*, among many others) have ensured that criminal justice professions are not only normalized, but glorified, guaranteeing the continuance of high student enrollment.

Given the importance of criminal justice as a discipline and its potential to influence the millions who enter careers made possible by mass incarceration, it is likewise critical to know who you are *teaching* these criminal justice majors. Who are the ones designing curricula and courses? Obtaining data on the demographics of all part-time and full-time faculty of all criminal justice programs across the United States is difficult. There is no central database of the programs, for instance, with lists of full-time faculty and their demographic characteristics. Also, part-time faculty, which make up nearly 75% of all teaching faculty in some institutions, are often not listed on department websites. Nevertheless, we can glean relevant information from other sources. The Association of Doctoral Programs in Criminal Justice and Criminology (ADPCJJ)'s 2013 survey report revealed that the criminal justice and criminology faculty (from programs offering doctoral degrees in the discipline) are overwhelmingly comprised of non-Hispanic whites, and primarily males. In 2013 over 80% of the faculty were whites, and 62% were males. Only 8% were black or Latino. The racial demographics of those who are current Master's and doctoral students demonstrated similar trends. In this group, whites comprised 66% of current doctoral students, however, 57% were female (Association of Doctoral Programs in Criminology and Criminal Justice, 2013).

Another source of demographic data for those likely to be teaching in criminal justice or criminology programs is the American Society of Criminology (ASC), the chief professional academic organization within the discipline, and the organization that sponsored the Hilton conference referenced at the beginning of this chapter. The ASC, "an international organization whose members pursue scholarly, scientific, and professional knowledge concerning the measurement, etiology, consequences, prevention, control, and treatment of crime and delinquency" (About ASC) has a membership comprised overwhelmingly of white scholars and teachers—a paltry 5% self-identified as black, and only 5% as Hispanic (Miller & Brunson, 2011). This same report noted that among the six schools ranked as the top 5 in criminal justice/criminology, only 5% of the faculty were minorities of any race/ethnicity, with two of those schools having no minorities in their tenure-track faculty *at all*. This rather breathtaking homogeneity is unsurprisingly mirrored in the even more exclusive (or exclusionary) criminal justice canon of theorists most referenced and discussed in criminology and criminal justice textbooks. Richard Wright, in his "Recent Changes in the most-cited scholars in criminology" (Wright, 2000), reported on the 59 most cited scholars in 22 introductory criminology textbooks. Of these 59, only five were women. And all 59—including the five women—are white.

One of the hallmark characteristics of privilege of any kind—be it male, white, heteronormative, ableist (or any interlocking/intersectional combination thereof)—is the taken-for-granted nature of its hegemony. Wildman and Davis describe two elements of privilege. The first, most important to our discussion, is that the "characteristics of the privileged group define the societal norm" (Wildman & Davis, 2002). In other words, privilege carries with it a seeming neutrality, its status claimed subconsciously or consciously as the default against which other lived realities, bodies, epistemologies become "Other" and relegated to the periphery. bell hooks in "Representations of Whiteness in the Black Imagination" argues powerfully, "an effective strategy of white supremacist terror and dehumanization during slavery centered around white control of the black gaze. Black slaves, and later manumitted servants, could be brutally punished for looking, for appearing to observe the whites they were serving, as only a subject can observe, or see. To be fully an object then was to lack the capacity to see or recognize reality" (hooks, 2002).

The "gaze" of criminology and criminal justice, as evidenced above, has been trained primarily on black and brown bodies in the search of the structural or cultural or environmental reasons for their "deviance" by white men. Their "findings" then become the basis for instruction not only of other researchers, but inform policy and modes of thought for criminal justice professionals. This gaze is made so "obvious" that the thought of, say, a black ethnographer entering white spaces known for deviance (such as major banks, all of which have long records of wrongdoing. One recent example HSBC's laundering of billions of dollars in drug cartel and terrorist money) to record behavior has an almost humorous impact.

The degree to which patriarchy and whiteness has been institutionalized and other points of view made other within the discipline is made furthermore evident by the "divisions" found within the ASC, which represent "major professional interests that lie *within* the scope of the society" (emphasis mine). Of the 10 divisions, currently active are the "Division on People of Color and Crime," and the "Division on Women and Crime." The word "division" here is not only figurative. Although both divisions are not intended exclusively for people of color or women (respectively) but rather to promote inquiry around issues *related* to these groups, they also *de facto* have become almost as linked to the *identity of the researcher* as to the researcher's particular mode of inquiry. So, the Division on People of Color and Crime includes an actual directory of minority PhD members, and the Division on Women and Crime's membership list reveals that the vast majority of its members are women. Notice, there is no "Division on White People and Crime" or "Division on Men and Crime" (American Society of Criminology, 2017b). The social scientific gaze turned back upon white men by women and people of color, while certainly present, is still on the periphery.

The impact on criminal justice students of giving voice almost exclusively to white males in higher education can be readily found. Brian Jay Frederick argues in his study of the discipline: "Within the core curricula of most academic criminal justice programs, there is a preference for courses that examine the administrative facets of the criminal justice system, as well as the theories and methods associated with mainstream criminological research. Unfortunately, this predilection for 'cops, courts, and corrections' (also known as the 'Three C's') leaves little room for the addition of core courses devoted to other topics or theoretical perspectives, especially those which might be critical of the criminal justice system's handling of issues related to race, class, gender or culture" (Frederick, 2012). The City University of New York's "CUNY Justice Academy" (CJA) exemplifies this predilection. The CJA is a transfer-focused program for community college students across six CUNY campuses majoring in criminal justice. These students take five to six required core courses for the Associate's Degree comprised largely of the "Three C's." Among the six campuses, we find Policing, Corrections and Sentencing, Introduction to Criminal Justice, Criminal Law, Criminology, and Crime and Justice in Urban Society are the standard menu, with some minor variation. This is the norm, not the exception, with most criminal justice majors across the country.

Beyond the limited, "administrative" nature of many criminal justice core courses, additional concerns exist with curricula. There has been the steady exclusion beginning in the 1980s of "outside" social sciences from the required repertoire for undergraduate students. Southerland notes, "Criminal justice initially drew its faculty from the disciplines of sociology, psychology, and political science. These disciplines provided the interdisciplinary foundation for the field." In the study, however, only 12% of the more current programs sampled required courses in these social science disciplines (Southerland, 1991).

There must be deliberate, methodical efforts by those in the academy to reduce the myopia of curricula reflective of a singular hegemonic perspective that reproduces current normative understandings of the criminal justice system, which presents this system as largely ahistorical and avoids contextualization and comparative exploration. Robinson, in arguing for reform within the discipline, emphasizes the urgency of such a project: "Some may argue that we can still have a great impact on criminal justice practice by turning out thousands of informed students each year who go to work in the criminal justice system. Perhaps these students can promote positive change from within. It is unlikely, however, that these students will cause changes in the get tough policies that created their jobs. Creating positive change within the system to achieve social justice depends on those criminologists and criminal justicians in the academy. It is up to us to bring about these changes" (Robinson, 2001).

How to achieve such change? Merely injecting more scholars of color or women into the equation and stirring is not sufficient, so far as they adopt the same dominant theoretical and ideological frames. This would be tantamount to suggesting that the "cure" to the problem of excessive use of force by police is to diversify the force. The infamous live-streamed shooting of Philando Castile, a black man, by Jeronimo Yanez, a Latino in front of Castile's four-year-old daughter and girlfriend ("Philando Castile has been pulled over at least 52 times. Racial profiling?") and the case of Freddy Gray, also a black man, who died while being transported in a police van with six officers, three of whom were persons of color, make the point (Bult & Schapiro, 2016). Institutional systems premised on hierarchical, discriminatory frameworks are stalwartly resistant to change from within that same system. "Criminal justice as an academic discipline is inherently pro status quo and serves as a portal to a larger and more destructive criminal justice system—more law enforcement and more prisons," Robinson writes (Bult & Schapiro, 2016). Audre Lorde perhaps provided the best-known expression of this sentiment when she wrote, "The master's tools will never dismantle the master's house. They may allow us to temporarily beat him at his own game, but they will never enable us to bring about genuine change" (Lorde, 1983).

Here is a strong case, then, for a complete overhaul and radical revision to curricula among those scholars and educators who believe in transformative approaches that will disrupt the perpetuation of a failed system.

Sociological and criminological theory *has* produced "voices from the outside" that incorporate a new pedagogical agenda for criminal justice, critical voices such as those who have argued for intersectional approaches. A conceptual tool for analysis first posited by black lesbian feminists like Barbara Smith (2000) and her Combahee River Collective (1977), intersectional writings initially pointed out the dearth of discussion and appreciation of the doubly marginalized position of women of color. Since the 1990s, intersectionality attracted attention from scholars working from a variety of disciplines. It looked at the multilayered and simultaneous ways in which oppressions (or privileges) exist based on gender orientation, race, sex, and class, rather than treating each as separate objects of inquiry. Intersectional research, therefore is "a purposed/intended and integrated exploration of the simultaneous operation and/or effects of two or more categories of inequality" (Hill Collins, 1998). The complex relationships of power (Hess, 2012) that arise from the simultaneous operation of these categories present scholars with the task of pushing past the male/female, black/white, poor/rich binaries, both in their writing, but also in the classroom context. The experiences of black women, for example—under a system that incarcerates one in three black men in his lifetime and disproportionately incarcerates black women themselves—should be studied, as well as their role in the movements against mass incarceration and its consequences (Davis, 1981). And, particularly in the wake of a presidential election that was largely decided by "whitelash" (This is a phrase adopted by former Obama advisor Van Jones following the election of Donald Trump. See http://www.cnn.com/2016/11/09/politics/van-jones-results-disappointment-cnntv/), the experiences and lived realities of whites who feel marginalized or left out by class and who engage in hate crimes should also be a subject of serious discussion in the classroom and scholarship (Lichtblau, 2016).

Critical race theory (CRT) is strongly correlated with the intersectional heuristic approach described (and, as Anderson & McCormack point out, the boundaries between the two are blurred and largely inconsequential) (Anderson, & McCormack, 2010). In many ways, CRT provides an ideal lens through which we can begin to rethink criminal justice education, including education that involves talking about reentry. Indeed, critical race theory has its origins as an intellectual movement in the law and legal studies specifically (the key leaders in this push were law professors Derrick Bell of New York University and Alan Freeman of SUNY Buffalo) (Delgado & Stefancic, 2012) lending it a kind of natural affinity for movements in criminal justice. In their brief but seminal *Critical Race Theory: An Introduction,* Richard Delgado and Jean Stefancic note that critical race theory also has an explicitly activist component that attempts to connect theory and praxis—it is not a mere mental exercise, in other words. It is intended to produce actual change and to achieve social justice (Delgado & Stefancic, 2012). It is pointed out that there is no "'canonical set of doctrines or methodologies to which [CRT scholars] all subscribe . . . but these scholars are unified by two common interests—to understand how a regime of white supremacy and its subordination of people of color have been created and maintained in America and to *change* the bond that exists between law and racial power" (emphasis mine; Ladson-Billings, 1998a).

Critical race theorists thus often encourage the use of story and voice, bringing in the perspectives of those who would be silenced, bringing in experience as a legitimate form of knowing, of witness to lived reality. Ladson-Billings notes "Critical race theorists . . . integrate their *experiential knowledge* (emphasis added), drawn from a shared history as 'other' with their ongoing struggles to transform a world deteriorating under the albatross of racial hegemony" (Ladson-Billings, 1998b).

For Solórzano and Yosso in their "Critical race methodology: Counter-storytelling as an analytical framework for education research" (2002), this methodology be used "to identify, analyze and transform those structural and cultural aspects of education that maintain subordinate and dominant racial positions in and out of the classroom."

One can begin to imagine how educators and scholars in criminal justice programs might begin the crucial work of deconstructing curricula premised on white male privilege, guided by these methodological insights. Our project is not about reinventing the wheel or calling for new, uncharted modes of inquiry, but to move to the center of curricula critical race/ intersectional/ feminist/ and critical thought that has been peripheral and/or cosmetic and thus devalued to this point—even increasingly devalued as criminal justice as a discipline "comes of age." Importantly, this thought must be given "play" in the classroom setting. This means in practice not approaching students as *tabula rasas*. They are themselves intertwined in systems of privilege and oppression and come with deep, carnal understandings of these systems. They are living everyday entrenched in a culture that has normalized not only whiteness and male dominance and systems of wealth inequality, but has normalized the idea of mass incarceration as a legitimate way of dealing with social problems and public health issues.

For example, within my own college, the City University of New York's LaGuardia Community College, a conservative estimate of the number of students who are formerly incarcerated is double the national rate (1 in 50 versus 1 in 100) (LaGuardia Community College Correctional Education Initiatives Working Group, 2016).

As one of the most diverse campuses in the nation (LaGuardia Community College Office of Research and Assessment, 2016), our students have been affected by the long reach of the criminal justice system—from their communities being under near constant surveillance by law enforcement, to being frisked and slammed up against police vehicles, to being issued summons for a variety of low-level offenses from walking between train cars to selling cold bottles of water on the subway to walking in a park after dark, to having their close friends incarcerated. Only 13% of LaGuardia students are white, and only 23% of those living away from their parents had a household income above $25,000 (LaGuardia Community College Office of Research and Assessment, 2016). To tap into these students' experiential, embodied knowledges while challenging them to deep self-reflexivity about how cultural imperatives and their positionality have played into their own life goals, and to help them understand the origins of their taken-for-granted assumptions about the "way things are" (which is often reifying of the status quo) is a difficult, but essential pedagogical challenge. The same task exists for professors who teach in majority white colleges or colleges with primarily affluent students.

As much as I have contended that change in criminal justice as a discipline cannot adopt a "add people of color and stir" approach to theory and pedagogy, one additional point must be argued which at first glance may appear paradoxical: Embodied semiotics does matter. And because embodied semiotics matters, there must be active progress toward diversifying criminal justice within the academy. When only 10% of the American Society of Criminology are black or Latino, when only 5 out of 59 of the most-cited criminologists are women, the distinction between symbolic exclusion and *actual* exclusion is a matter of semantics. Any number of steps can be taken to remedy this problem, but until it is recognized *as* a problem by the society and by the many top tier criminal justice journals that continue to promote positivistic, "quant-heavy" scholarship that is dominated by white male scholars, concrete plans are unlikely to emerge.

I have been made acutely aware, by my day-to-day teaching in a majority-minority college, of the way in which I am as a white person an embodied signifier. As typically the only non-minority in the room, I visually represent a racialized criminal justice educational project that validates the status quo, however much I ideologically reject that project. My positionality is *felt* in these moments, in the same way I felt it in the lobby of the Hilton watching my colleagues' breeze past the maintenance staff. As always, with any privilege comes responsibility. To move our students away from "Three C's" curricula emphasizing the administrative, "there is no alternative" aspects of criminal justice, toward critical race, intersectional, and feminist approaches is the responsibility of all who believe in the centrality of social justice. We will then have the tools with which to dismantle the master's house.

REFERENCES

American Society of Criminology. (2017a). "About ASC." https://www.asc41.com/about.htm.

American Society of Criminology. (2017b). "Divisions." https://www.asc41.com/divisions.htm.

Anderson, E., & McCormack, M. (2010). "Intersectionality, critical race theory, and American sporting oppression: Examining Black and gay male athletes." *Journal of Homosexuality*, 57(8), 949–67.

Association of Doctoral Programs in Criminology and Criminal Justice, "2013 Survey Report," http://www.adpccj.com/documents/2013survey.pdf.

Bult, L., & Schapiro, R. "Prosecutors drop charges against three remaining Baltimore officers charged in Freddie Gray's death due to 'dismal likelihood of conviction.'" *New York Daily News*, July 27, 2016.

Bureau of Justice Statistics (2014). https://www.bjs.gov/.

Combahee River Collective (1977). "The Combahee River Collective Statement," http://americanstudies.yale.edu/sites/default/files/files/Keyword%20Coalition_Readings.pdf.

Criminal Justice Degree Schools, "Is a criminal justice degree worth it?" http://www.criminaljusticedegreeschools.com/criminal-justice-degrees/worth-it/.

Davis, A. (1981). *Women, race, and class*. New York: Random House.

Delgado, R., & Stefancic, J. (2012). *Critical race theory: An introduction*. New York: New York University Press.

Frederick, B. J. (2012). "Marginalization of Critical Perspectives in Public Justice Core Curricula," *W. Criminology Rev.*, 13, 21–33.

Harrell, E. (2007). "Black Victims of Violent Crime." Bureau of Justice Statistics Special Report. Available: https://www.bjs.gov/content/pub/pdf/bvvc.pdf.

Hess, L. (2012). Intersectionality: A Systematic Review and Application to Explore the Complexity of Teen Pregnancy Involvement. Columbia University, Dissertation.

Hill Collins, P. (1998). "It's all in the family: Intersections of gender, race, and nation." *Hypatia*, 13, 33, 62–82.

hooks, b. (2002). "Representations of Whiteness in the Black Imagination." In Rothenberg, P. (ed.), *White Privilege*. New York: Worth Publishers, pp. 19–24.

Ladson-Billings, G. (1998a). "Just what is critical race theory and what's it doing in a nice field like education?" *International Journal of Qualitative Studies in Education*, 11(1), 7–24. Ladson-Billings quotes Crenshaw et al (1995) in this reference.

Ladson-Billings, G. (1998b). "Just what is critical race theory and what's it doing in a nice field like education?" *International Journal of Qualitative Studies in Education*, 11(1), 7–24.

LaGuardia Community College Correctional Education Initiative. Estimate provided by the LaGuardia Community College Correctional Education Initiatives Working Group, June 30, 2016.

LaGuardia Community College Office of Research and Assessment (2016).

Lichtblau, E. (2016, November 14). "Hate Crimes surge 6%, fueled by attacks on Muslims," *New York Times*.

Lorde, A. (1983). "The Master's Tools Will Never Dismantle the Master's House," in Moraga, C., & Anzaldua, G. (eds), *This Bridge Called My Back: Writings by Radical Women of Color*. New York: Kitchen Table Press, pp. 94–101.

Lurie, J. (2016). "Private Prison stocks are shooting up after a Trump win." *Mother Jones*, November 9, 2016.

Miller, J., and Brunson, R. K. (2011). "'Minority candidates are strongly encouraged to apply': Making diversity matter in Criminology and Criminal Justice." *The Criminologist* 36, 4: 1–7.

"Philando Castile has been pulled over at least 52 times. Racial profiling?" *The Times Picayune*, June 9, 2016.

Robinson, M. B. (2001). "Wither Criminal Justice? An argument for a reformed discipline." Critical Criminology 10: 97–106.

Sloan III, J. J., & Buchwalter, J. W. (2016). "The State of Criminal Justice Bachelor's Degree Programs in the United States: Institutional, Departmental, and Curricula Features." *Journal of Criminal Justice Education*, 1–28.

Smith, B. (2000). *The Truth That Never Hurts: Writings on Race, Gender, and Freedom*. Camden, NJ: Rutgers University Press.

Solórzano, D. G., & Yosso, T. J. (2002). "Critical race methodology: Counter-storytelling as an analytical framework for education research." *Qualitative Inquiry*, 8(1), 23–44.

Southerland, M. D. (1991). "Criminal justice curricula in the United States: An examination of baccalaureate programs, 1988–1989." *Journal of Criminal Justice Education*, 2(1), 45–68.

"Top 10 bachelor level criminal justice jobs," Criminal Justice Degree Hub, http://www.criminaljusticedegreehub.com/top-10-bachelor-level-criminal-justice-jobs/.

Wildman, S., and Davis, A. (2002). "Making the systems of privilege visible." In Rothenberg, P. (ed), *White Privilege*. New York: Worth Publishers, pp. 89–96.

Wright, R. A. (2000). "Recent changes in the most-cited scholars in criminology: A comparison of textbooks and journals." *Journal of Criminal Justice*, 28(2), 117–28.

Chapter Five

Writing Into Being and Post Incarceration

Joni Schwartz

Mass incarceration and unequal educational opportunity are intersecting civil rights issues. America's current prison population is stratified by race and class, and a disproportionate number of the incarcerated and formerly incarcerated are black or Hispanic and high school non-completers (National Research Council, 2014). This phenomenon has significant implications for adult learning settings, specifically high school equivalency (HSE) and early college, as engagement in adult education for the formerly incarcerated has proven to decrease recidivism by providing avenues for employment and societal reintegration (Davis, Bozick, Steele, Saunders, & Miles, 2013; New York State Department of Correctional Services, 2010). Therefore, the exploration of potential models for the engagement of the formerly incarcerated, particularly black and Hispanic males, in adult learning is expedient.

From my faculty/instructor perspective, this article describes a community college collaborative inquiry project that focused on how formerly incarcerated students might engage in HSE programs and college. Although not contributing directly to this article, students were the co-researchers and writers of the project being described: designing the research, writing, publishing a book chapter, and disseminating findings to the public. Three students also read a draft of this article before publication and gave me feedback.

Beginning with discussion of the conceptual framework which is comprised of two theories, this article describes the project design through five stages of collaborative inquiry and concludes with final reflections, lessons learned, and future action. The purposes of this article are twofold: to suggest a collaborative inquiry model of engagement for use in HSE or college settings, and to bring initial awareness to the unique reengagement issues of the formerly incarcerated.

CRITICAL RACE THEORY AND COLLABORATIVE INQUIRY

The conceptual framework for the project design and this paper was comprised of critical race theory (CRT) and collaborative inquiry. CRT originated in legal studies, but is sometimes applied by adult educators to examine the endemic nature of racism in America (Dixson, 2007) and issues of race and racism pervading our educational institutions (Ladson-Billings, 2005; Closson, 2010). One way critical race theorists address educational inequity is through the telling of people of colors' lived experiences. These counterstories challenge pervading American narratives that inform majority perceptions about racial minorities (Solórzano & Yosso, 2002). The telling of counterstories is especially important for black males, and the formerly incarcerated, in addressing omitted perspectives and in countering stereotypes.

In addition, critical race theorists use the term *counterspaces*, which are corollaries of counterstorytelling. These counterspaces provide room for marginalized individuals, often in white universities, to counteract racial microaggressions (Solórzano, Ceja, & Yosso, 2000), ideally embodying four dimensions. The first dimension, *place*, is the proxemics or physical spaces where the group meets. The second dimension, *temporal*, is mental space and the connection between personal conflict and global issues. The third dimension, *intrapersonal*, is interior or self-reflection. Last, the *interpersonal* dimension is the community space (Schwartz, 2014).

Drawing on CRT's counterstories and counterspaces, this project incorporates collaborative inquiry between students and instructor. Specifically, Chevalier and Buckles' (2013) participatory action research model of collaborative inquiry directed the project through five stages: mediating, grounding, navigating, scaling, and sense-making—combining both quantitative and qualitative data collection and analysis in the service of action learning. This approach contrasts with traditional inquiry, not so much in the actual data collection (navigating) and analysis (scaling) methods, but in how knowledge is constructed (grounding), by whom (mediating), and for what expressed purpose (sense-making) (Kasl & Yorks, 2010). *Who* collects and analyzes the data, the community members or, in this case, student co-researchers, is central to the inquiry. In addition, the research purpose is to explicitly affect change or move to action (Brooks & Watkins, 1994).

COLLABORATIVE INQUIRY WRITING PROJECT

This project began in the classroom where important adventures often begin. As the instructor, I met Brian, Joserichsen, and Timothy in three different community college communication courses. All three self-identified as black, engaged in my courses with fervor, and were developing writers. The project started with four young men, but one disappeared despite our attempts to locate him. We talked about this pattern of disappearing, and sometimes re-appearing, suspecting outside stressors as responsible, including an incarcerated brother, financial constraints, or family problems. However, we can only surmise and, even at the time of this writing, attempt to make contact.

Brian was the impetus for the project. We met in Brian's first semester after he completed a GED and returned from prison. Brian brought the courage of transparency to the classroom—opening up to his classmates about his incarceration and struggle acclimating to an academic culture. Through Brian, I learned that coming from incarceration into academia is no ordinary journey, and I began to be aware of my empathy deficit (Konrath, O'Brien, & Hsing, 2011). As a white female who has never been incarcerated, I was not (and can never be) fully cognizant of resulting post-traumatic stress, daily triggers to past experiences, daily microaggressions (Sue, 2010), and need for new community. I am trying to learn, and Brian is one of my teachers. One of Brian's lessons involved his need for counterspace or a "new family." The inquiry group would begin to serve this role.

> I have expressed my pessimistic belief in family—a concept I struggle with—I have no family. This is an ideology developed over time and through disappointment concluding that family is not necessarily those by birth, but rather those who you are blessed to encounter and *build with—born when there is distress.*

From our reciprocal relationship of student and adult educator, we began an affective and cognitive journey to unearth counterstories of what it is like for black males as they reengage in learning, specifically for males formerly incarcerated. Thus, the collaborative inquiry began with the goal of publishing a chapter in a volume on black males in adult education (Miller, Mondesir, Stater, & Schwartz, 2014). The remainder of this section chronicles how this project progressed through the mediating, navigating, grounding, scaling, and sense-making stages.

Mediating

Mediating is engaging knowledge from different perspectives, initially accomplished by assembling our primary stakeholders (Creswell, 2007). Brian,

Joserichsen, Timothy, and I were positioned differently in regard to race (three blacks, one white), role (three students, one faculty), gender (three males, one female), and age range (19 to 60), and relationships with incarceration (formerly, never, and family/close friends incarcerated). Although most of the stakeholders were black males, their perspectives were similar but different due to a variety of life experiences such as having stayed in or dropped out of high school, growing up in different neighborhoods or neighborhoods changed over time, religious backgrounds, and direct or indirect experiences with police. We discussed our differing positionalities openly in our first meeting, laying implicit and explicit expectations of shared leadership and the validity of everyone's contribution.

The mediating stage also includes the emergent roles of stakeholders (Chevalier & Buckles, 2013). Brian emerged early as our member-checker whose personal experience with incarceration and coming back to school would be the test for authenticity by which we measured our findings (Carlson, 2010; Lincoln & Guba, 1985).

I continually grapple with my positionality as a white female writing about black male issues. One ambiguity is what CRT calls *interest convergence* (Bell, 1980), how my position as a white female faculty privileges me within the inquiry relationship including how I benefit from the writing of this article (Milner, 2007). Whose story is being told? Is it accurate? How does my position influence the process? What are the underlying racial dynamics of which I am unaware? Frequently, these questions are unsettling and uncomfortable but necessary (Pillow, 2003).

Grounding

Particular to *grounding* is the creation of an emotionally safe environment where stakeholders feel free to express ideas (Schwartz, 2014; hooks, 1994). This creation began in the mediating stage through our initial meeting at an Italian restaurant where we lingered over a long meal and began to bond and continued in our early meetings where emotional safety was openly discussed. Grounding also brings awareness to social issues as they relate to personal experience moving the group into a counterspace. So as part of the grounding stage, we talked about the group's own past school experiences as they relate to educational inequality, personal experiences with the police as they relate to racial profiling, and personal experiences with incarceration and America's mass incarceration crisis.

My role in grounding was to facilitate the creation of this safe space (Horsman, 2000; Rosenwasser, 2000) fostering personal transparency and collective decisionmaking. As much as possible, I positioned myself as a collaborative participant rather than leader, trying to listen more and talk less.

Navigating

Navigating is similar to research design and included decisions about additional participants and data collection, and, for us, identifying available resources and how to utilize them (Chevalier & Buckles, 2013). Navigation began at our second meeting, where we decided how to approach *evidence-based inquiry* and *person-based inquiry* (Denzin & Lincoln, 2008). We initially identified four data sources: Wagner Archives, The Fortune Society, formerly incarcerated individuals we knew personally, and ourselves.

Beginning with the archives, a museum curator assisted us in identifying microfilm and hard-copy files of mayoral correspondence and city council minutes that pertained to incarceration and provided us with a list of correspondence, reports, and council minutes to peruse. Dividing the workload and archival list, the four of us worked over several months to collect data. We established deadlines and plowed through documents, taking notes, keeping research journals, and making copies of significant documents. Throughout the process, Brian, in particular, asked for more structure, including clear timelines, deadlines, and instructions: "In prison, I had a lot of structure, I lived with strict structure. I need that now." We later developed this observation in our chapter.

A second stage in the navigation process was from a person-based inquiry model. We planned to interview friends and family who were formerly incarcerated, as well as conduct interviews at a Fortune Society GED program serving the formerly incarcerated. We collaboratively drafted questions and conducted 21 semistructured face-to-face interviews. The navigation stage took approximately six months; we then advanced to the analysis or scaling stage.

Scaling

Scaling involves the management of collected data (analysis) and researchers' time and participation level (Chevalier & Buckles, 2013). The first level of scaling involved deciding what data to use in our writing and meeting to analyze the data, looking for themes—a type of grounded-theory approach (Corbin & Strauss, 2008). The data, particularly from the archives, was exhaustive and sometimes did not seem to apply to our topic. We struggled with the right scale of data, aiming for a balance between text-heavy data from the archives and personal experiences of the interviewees.

We initially used a large poster board to write down all the pertinent concepts and issues around former incarceration and reengagement. After several hours of plotting, we clustered these concepts and issues into themes: policies, obstacles, GED, classroom atmosphere, advising, counseling, financial impacts, community support, curriculum, and reentry. Arriving at these

themes through collaborative analysis—coding, dialogue, and argument—
was a messy business and felt chaotic at times; however, all stakeholders
stuck with the process.

Another part of scaling is the management of time and resources (Chevalier & Buckles, 2013), so we decided in the interest of time and control of the
data to divide the emerging themes among the three student writers. Brian,
Joserichsen, and Timothy decided which themes they were most comfortable
writing about. We discussed getting thoughts down and not worrying too
much about editing, setting a three-week deadline for first drafts. Brian wrote
his drafts on his cell phone. For Brian, technology was new because in prison
he had little access. This made returning to a technological world overwhelming; we decided to include this in our chapter as well. As coach, editor,
and book editor liaison, I did not write.

Sense-Making

Sense-making is an interdisciplinary concept from human-computer interaction, organizational management, and adult learning, defined as the understanding of complex systems (Schwandt, 2005). Applied to this project,
sense-making meant using collaborative writing as a tool to understand and
interpret the data. During the three-week initial writing stage, we communicated by email, texting, and periodic phone calls, then met to read the initial
three drafts. Using hard copies, we read all papers orally and began the long
process of integrating the themes and three distinct writing styles. Timothy
later said that this stage was intimidating because you had to share and get
feedback on your writing, but these writing shares were invaluable in the
revision and sense-making process. The first drafts were very rough, so, after
discussion, the students extensively revised.

After a couple of meetings, we decided Brian would write the opening
section, a historical and social background, on past and present policies that
impact the formerly incarcerated in the classroom. Joserichsen would write
the second section on reentry into society, GED and early college, including
obstacles and success factors. Timothy would write section three about classrooms and teacher approach. After arduous writing, revising, and editing,
these sections later became major portions of our book chapter, balancing
people-based data and *evidence-based data*.

During the writing, we shared drafts with a few interviewees. In one
memorable member-checking session, a formerly incarcerated student read
through the manuscript line by line, meticulously giving feedback on the
content and writing style. As a group, we continued critiquing, suggesting
additions and deletions, and correcting spelling and grammar. On several
occasions, I edited the document, adding transitions for readability, but always tried to keep the writers' voices. Through writing, we thought through

the topic, communicated feelings, prepared for action, and made sense of a painful phenomenon.

We completed our chapter for submission to the book editors on time. Once the editors responded with feedback, we addressed each comment by assigning each of us portions of the manuscript to revise. Near the end of the writing process, the editors asked for one last major revision—to cut the chapter down significantly by 1,500 words. This was major cutting. Bravely, Brian, taking the lead, worked over an entire afternoon with Joserichsen and Timothy to delete words and cut sections of the chapter. I stepped back from this process as the young men seemed well able to tackle the task. I was afraid that the essence of the chapter would be destroyed, but that was not so. The final-cut version held together well and withstood the trimming.

About this time, the students had an opportunity to have lunch with the book's editors. Over lunch, introductions and conversation ensued, author copyright transfer agreements were prepared, and communication around the students' future plans was discussed. This was an opportunity to engage in the "culture" of academia and understand the editors' roles in the creation of the book and our chapter.

LESSONS LEARNED AND UNFORESEEN OBSTACLES

Consistent with adult-learning practice, we intentionally engaged in critical reflection around what we had learned and the obstacles that informed that learning (Mezirow, 1998). Sometimes over a meal, Brian, Joserichsen, Timothy, and I spent time discussing our experiences. Brian stated that he learned that writing is a process—long and demanding dedication. He appreciated the self-investigation and learned from his cowriters the diversity of the black experience while understanding that he holds a certain positionality as having been formerly incarcerated. Brian expressed feeling unworthy to be a writer, to publish, and learned that he would have to work through these insecurities. In Brian's words:

> In a way it [participation in the project] was audacity! The audacity of a dropout (push out) and two "community college students" students to collaborate and meet the standards set. That audacious belief and fearless presumption (fueled by an encouraging and affirming team) powered the project to new heights.

Timothy said he learned patience—"a lot of patience." Writing takes time, hard work, and adaptability. Like Brian, Timothy expressed insecurity as a writer and battled to overcome those feelings.

Joserichsen was amazed at "the multiple personalities putting their ideas together in collaboration and how we were able to actually write a chapter together—and speak as a single voice." As part of member checking and reflection, Joserichsen perused this article before I submitted it for review. Here is his feedback on both this article and the project:

> I loved it. I grasped the entire process from beginning to end, in full detail. It [this article] also grasped the feeling of it [the project]. It was cool. I practically re-walked the whole journey. It was surreal, viewing myself from a different angle. It felt good being a part of something.

And when asked if he preferred that I use his real name instead of a pseudonym [Mason] to identify him in the article, he emphatically declared, "And hell, yea, I wanna use my full name, Joserichsen Mondesir. I don't know who the hell this Mason guy is lol."

I learned that I have had an empathy deficit when it comes to *sensemaking* and the phenomenon of incarceration and reengagement. I relearned that the affective and cognitive cannot be separated when embracing issues of complexity, marginality, and social justice and that the mental and emotional work is frequently painful. Beyond that, I fully embraced and enjoyed, once again, the satisfaction of collaboration.

There were unforeseen obstacles as well. Timothy disappeared for a month and a half during the writing process. He did not show up for several meetings, did not answer emails, and generally couldn't be found. Finally, he responded and said that he had experienced an unfortunate incident and had briefly been in the hospital. We had become a community of writers and were both concerned and relieved when Timothy re-emerged back into our group.

Although we were a community, Brian, Timothy, and Joserichsen later admitted that there was competition among them. This competition can be viewed as both an obstacle and as a catalyst. Brian voiced it this way:

> There was a competitive nature of the assignment, unspoken competition, but present. None of us every mentioned it, but we knew it was there. We wanted to be the best, or at least our personal best! We all wanted to be better, because we knew we could. More important, we were being held to a high standard.

The writing process was long and tedious. Toward the end, before the final cutting, Joserichsen became discouraged, saying, "I am not doing anymore revising—enough is enough." This was at the same time that Timothy was absent from the group. So Brian forged ahead and, with my support, we moved the writing forward. These are common obstacles in most writing processes and surmountable through transparent communication and strong relationships. Both Joserichsen and Timothy rejoined the team and the work moved on to publication, dissemination, and celebration.

TAKING ACTION

Unfortunately, Brian recently said to me "You know, art really does mirror life." This was said as he was graduating from community college, transferring to a four-year institution, and attempting to secure his college transcript. To make a long and messy story short, he was living our chapter. He did not know the jargon of academia and was not privy to the social capital necessary in negotiating the financial aid and bursar's offices, causing grave difficulties and almost disrupting his college plans.

Another example was when filling out college applications, several asked whether or not the applicant had ever been convicted of a felony. If the formerly incarcerated has been released and paid their dues, why would this question be necessary? Obviously the applicant cannot lie, but it raises questions about the rationale for asking and whether or not the applicant should include the obstacles overcome after incarceration when submitting their personal narrative or when faculty write references.

When applying for campus employment, why should Brian be fingerprinted twice, or interviewed multiple times? Maybe this is justified and all applicants go through the same process, but all seems suspect in light of our collaborative inquiry. More action is needed to address these seeming injustices.

Action is the ultimate goal of any participatory learning project (Rahman, 2008). Writing is our first stage of action—being heard. Our chapter was published (Miller, Mondesir, Stater, & Schwartz, 2014). There were celebrations—book launches and public readings. Our goal is to engage others in meaningful discussion around our writing, encouraging administrators and instructors to use the chapter in the classrooms especially as they relate to current events surrounding black males in both Staten Island, New York, and Fergueson, Missouri.

We are already disseminating our research and writing through conference presentations. This past April, Brian, Timothy, and I presented in Philadelphia at the American Education Research Association (AERA). In an intimate setting, we were able to talk candidly about our research, writing, and our personal journeys. In addition, all of us are part of a college EXCEL conference which highlights faculty and student projects; our project will be included in a video collage of artistic and academic achievements. These kinds of presentations provide forums to engage our collaborative inquiry with audiences and provide further learning of valuable oral communication skills.

Finally, this project has inspired an additional research project—a phenomenological study that will further examine the phenomenon of returning to school after incarceration which will result in a documentary with again both student and faculty collaboration. Beyond the opportunity for Brian, Joserichsen, and Timothy to publish their writing on arguably the most crucial civil rights issue of our day, and writing is action; the anticipated follow-up documentary will engage more students and potentially reach even more audiences to further bring awareness and hoped-for change.

This chapter was previously published with the title "After Incarceration & Adult Learning: A Collaborative Inquiry & Writing Project" in the publication *Adult Learning-SAGE publishers*, Vol. 26, No. 2, May 2015.

REFERENCES

Alexander, M. (2010). *The new Jim Crow: Mass incarceration in the age of colorblindness.* New York: The New Press.

Bell, D. (1980). Brown v. Board of Education and the interest-convergence dilemma. *Harvard Law Review, 93(3)*, 518–34.

Brooks, A., & Watkins, K. (1994). A new era for action technologies: A look at the issues. In A. Brooks & K. Watkins (Eds.), *The emerging power of action inquiry technologies.* New Directions for Adult Education and Continuing Education. No. 63 (pp. 5–16). San Francisco, CA: Jossey-Bass.

Carlson, J. (2010). Avoiding traps in member checking, *The Qualitative Report, 15*(5), 1102–13.

Chevalier, J., & Buckles, D. (2013). *Handbook for participatory action research, planning and evaluation.* Ottawa, Canada: SAS2 Dialogue.

Closson, R. (2010). Critical race theory and adult education. *Adult Education Quarterly, 60*(3), 261–83.

Corbin, J., & Strauss, A. L. (2008). *Basics of qualitative research: Grounded theory procedures and techniques* (3rd ed.). San Francisco, CA: Sage.

Creswell, J. W. (2007). *Qualitative inquiry and research design: Choosing among five traditions* (2nd ed.). Thousand Oaks, CA: Sage.

Davis, L., Bozick, R., Steele, J., Saunders, J., & Miles, J. (2013). *Evaluating the effectiveness of correctional education: A Meta-analysis of programs that provide education to incarcerated adults.* Washington, DC: Bureau of Justice Assistance.

Denzin, N. K., & Lincoln, Y. S. (2008). *Collecting and interpreting qualitative materials.* Thousand Oaks, CA: Sage.

Dixson, A. (2007). *What is critical race theory in education?* [PowerPoint slides]. Retrieved from http://steinhardt.nyu.edu/metrocenter.olde/programs/TACD/Summer%20Institute/SummerInstitute2007/powerpoints/CriticalRaceTheoryandEducation.pdf.

hooks, b. (1994). *Teaching to transgress: Education as the practice of freedom.* New York: Routledge.

Horsman, J. (2000). *Moving forward: Approaches and activities to support women's learning.* Toronto, Ontario: Parkdale Project Read.

Kasl, E., & Yorks, L. (2010). "Whose inquiry is this anyway?" Money, power, reports and collaborative inquiry. *Adult Education Quarterly, 60*(4), 315–38.

Konrath, S., O'Brien, E., & Hsing, C. (2011). Changes in dispositional empathy in American college students over time: A meta-analysis. *Personality and Social Psychology Review, 15*(2), 180–88.

Ladson-Billings, G. (2005). The evolving role of critical race theory in educational Scholarship. *Race, Ethnicity and Education, 8*(1), 115–19.

Lincoln, Y. S., & Guba, E. G. (1985). *Naturalistic inquiry.* Newbury Park, CA: Sage.

Mesirow, J. (1998). On critical reflection. *Adult Education Quarterly, 48(3),*185–98.

Miller, B., Mondesir, J., Stater, T., & Schwartz, J. (2014). Returning to school after incarceration: Policy, prisoners and the classroom. In J. Schwartz, D. Rosser-Mims, B. Drayton, & T.

Guy (Eds.), *Swimming upstream: Black males in adult education.* New Directions in Adult and Continuing Education. San Francisco, CA: Jossey-Bass.

Milner, H. R. (2007). Race, culture, and researcher positionality: Working through dangers seen, unseen, and unforeseen. *Educational Researcher, 36*(7), 388–400.

National Research Council. (2014). *The Growth of Incarceration in the United States: Exploring Causes and Consequences.* Washington, DC: The National Academies Press.

NYS Department of Correctional Services. (2010). *Follow-up study of a sample of offenders who earned high school equivalency diplomas (GEDs) while incarcerated in DOCS.* Albany, New York: Harriman Office. http://www.doccs.ny.gov/Research/Reports/2010/GED_evaluation.pdf.

Pillow, W. (2003). Confession, catharsis, or cure? Rethinking the uses of reflexivity as methodological power in qualitative research. *Qualitative Studies in Education, 16*(2), 175–96.

Rahman, M. A. (2008). Some trends in the praxis of participatory action research. In P. Reason & H. Bradbury (Eds.), *The SAGE Handbook of Action Research* (pp. 49–62). London, England: Safe.

Rosenwasser, P. (2000) Tools for transformation: Cooperative inquiry as a process for healing from internalized oppression. In T. Sork, V. L. Chapman, & R. St. Clair (Eds.), *AERC 2000: An international Conference* (pp. 292-96). Vancouver: University of British Columbia.

Schwandt, D. (2005). When managers become philosophers: Integrating learning with sense-making. *The Academy of Management Journal, 4*(2), 176–92.

Schwartz, J. (2014). Classrooms of spatial justice: Counter-spaces and young men of color in a GED program. *Adult Education Quarterly, 64*(2), 110–27.

Solórzano, D., & Yosso, T. (2002). Critical race methodology: Counter-storytelling as an analytical framework for education research. *Qualitative Inquiry, 8*(1), 23–44.

Solórzano, D., Ceja, M., & Yosso, T. (2000). Critical race theory, racial microaggressions, and campus racial climate: The experiences of African American college students. *The Journal of Negro Education, 69*(1/2), 60–73.

Sue, D. W. (2010). *Microaggressions in everyday life: Race, gender, and sexual orientation.* Hobokon, NJ: Wiley.

Part II

Counterstories

Chapter Six

On the Other Side

The Reengagement of Formerly Incarcerated Students

Michael Baston and Brian Miller

As soon as you step off the bus, the smell hits you. You kind of know you are in another world, a different place; but the understanding that you are in a completely foreign country does not hit you until you taste the food, see the change in environment, hear the local dialect, and are briefed by the commanding officer who welcomes you to your commitment. You are told that the enemy is everywhere. Remain to yourself and your team. Keep your head up and your nose clean, and be prepared for combat at any time and maybe, just maybe, you will survive. You are told that for the duration of your commitment you will be in a war zone unlike anything you have seen or been prepared for. At any time, you can, and very likely, may be killed! After being debriefed you are escorted to the barracks by the sergeant who wishes you good luck in the years to come. He steps back, signals, and then the bars slowly close and you hear the infamous lock of your cell. You have walked into hell! Not in a foreign country, but right here on U.S. soil in a prison to begin your commitment as an inmate, an experience frequently hallmarked by trauma, sometimes leaving long-term emotional and mental residual effects after the incarceration.

Now it seems self-evident that having been socialized into such a hostile environment would require some attention after being released or *discharged.* It is the reentry portion of this ongoing story that this chapter seeks to understand and highlight; particularly the process of supports (or lack thereof) of those who are formerly incarcerated being accepted and welcomed into society. We examine higher education, and community college in particular, after incarceration.

RETURNING HOME

Across the nation, nearly 97% of all offenders incarcerated today are expected to be released and returned to the same communities from which they came. In 2010 alone, nearly 900,000 prisoners were released under community supervision back to their communities (Glaze, 2011). In New York State, there will be approximately 24,000 prison inmates who are to be released each and every year. The concept of reengagement is critical for the formerly incarcerated in an effort to prevent recidivism. "About two-thirds (67.8%) of released prisoners were rearrested for a new crime within 3 years, and three-quarters (76.7%) were rearrested within 5 years" (Bureau of Justice, 2014).

In light of these visible trends, federally funded programs and initiatives have been created to increase the employability and access to education for formerly incarcerated individuals. The Second Chance Act of 2007 is an example of one response to the unique challenges of postincarceration, which may include limited opportunities for long-term employment, human capital accumulation, career advancement and benefits. Although postsecondary education has seen a boost for former prisoners, there are still "dramatic education disparities by race among the formerly incarcerated population" (Pettit, 2012). Community colleges have been presented with a distinct opportunity to serve as an avenue for the reengagement, education, and reintegration of formerly incarcerated individuals. "For the formerly incarcerated, engagement in adult learning, whether high school equivalency (HSE) or college, decreases the likelihood that they will return to prison, increases opportunities for employment, and serves as a powerful reintegration tool in society" (Schwartz, 2015). This chapter takes a look at this phenomenon of community college as a reentry tool but first provides some definition of terms and historical context.

DEFINING TERMS

Prison reentry and recidivism are thrown around as common terms, but in fact are often misunderstood. To many steeped in the work of prison reentry and criminal justice these terms are familiar, but for the sake of clarity when this chapter uses the term reentry it is referencing policy and theory as reflected in the federal government's "Serious and Violent Offender Reentry Initiative" (SVORI) which was initiated in 2002 (National Institute of Justice) and the federal "Second Chance Act" (P.L. 110–199) enacted on April 9, 2008. The act expanded the existing offender reentry grant program at the Department of Justice and created a wide array of targeted grant-funded pilot programs. The term "prisoner reentry" or the less appropriate expression "offender reentry" will be used to describe individuals who are returning from a jail and/or prison term, but will be extended to include "at risk" populations that are on probation and parole, under direct correctional extended supervision. When the authors use the term reentry it is to be understood as "the processes and interventions that equip incarcerated individuals to return home and stay home."

This chapter further assumes that reentry is the experience of individuals who are returning to the community following a period of punitive action stemming from conviction of a crime. It assumes that the system of incarceration was not one solely of punishment but instead of rehabilitation. Ideally this causes the individual to reflect upon his or her actions, ultimately leading to a personal and individual transformation.

Reentry encompasses all activities, programming, and policy research that is used to understand, access, and prepare the formerly incarcerated to return to their communities with the intent of preparing the individual to become a productive member of society. These programs stratified into three distinct categories: first, the participatory programs that require an inmate to establish a plan of action intended to secure and ensure a viable existence outside the institution—"home plan." Then there are the programs that are community based; these programs generally partner with not-for-profit organizations whose mission is to aid an individual to execute the home plan as soon as they are released. Lastly, there is the collection of programs offering long-term support structures and supervision. It seems fair to argue that the best program would be one in which all three elements are included.

Finally, in this chapter the term recidivism refers to two separate criteria: "reoffending," meaning catching a new charge, or committing a new crime not associated with the initial offense, or a recommitment based on a parole or supervision violation not necessarily related to a new charge. Reentry support is designed to prevent both types of recidivism.

A BRIEF HISTORY AND CONTEXT

It seems pertinent to any discussion of reentry to revisit the earliest practices of rehabilitation and the systems designed to manage "crime." Among early penal measures were militias and slave catchers whose job was to ensure a racial system of control and the rule of law (Campbell, 2012). This is an important argument in that it sets the foundation for the establishment of an unjust system and thus the fruit gleaned are tainted by the root of racial disparity and unfairness from the system's earliest inception. As time progressed, the necessity of jails and prisons increased and, with it, a mentality of punitive rectification of justice which was intentionally anything but rehabilitative. In fact, its central purpose was to be punitive and punish the "offender" (Rothman, 1998a), the general idea being the individual would serve their time and their debt to society and eventually be forgiven for that debt. It is during this epoch in which the earliest prisons were created and designed with the belief of transformation of a prisoner's heart and minds (Rothman, 1998a; 1998b). This concept of transformative adult learning (Mesirow, 1978) is at the core of higher education as a tool of reentry and rehabilitation as contrasted to punishment. This chapter examines the phenomenon of higher education as a vehicle of rehabilitation and the prevention of recidivism by unpacking the experience of those who have fallen victim to the prison industrial complex. By way of a phenomenological study, reengagement into a higher education setting is examined and one potential community college program is highlighted, showing the potential formerly incarcerated students have to thrive and succeed after being rehabilitated.

STUDY DESIGN

Data Collection

Utilizing the lived experience of one of the co-authors of this chapter as well as six formerly incarcerated males currently enrolled in community college, the phenomenon of reengagement into a higher education setting and society was examined. The aim was to understand or unveil the potential restorative capacity of community colleges for the formerly incarcerated and to understand engagement as a prevention method to recidivism.

Six formerly incarcerated male students at LaGuardia Community College of the City University of New York college system voluntarily participated in a two-hour focus group and provided at-length and descriptive interviews detailing their post-incarceration higher education experiences. LaGuardia is a community college with a highly diverse student body profile providing academic and co-curricular services to a range of students from different races/ethnicities, countries of origin, ages, and socioeconomic backgrounds. LaGuardia serves a student population of nearly 50,000 and awards degrees from a host of academic programs. By challenging assumptions about who learns, who teaches, and who benefits from community colleges in America, LaGuardia has changed the thinking about two-year institutions and their place not only in the landscape of higher education, but their role in strengthening our nation's economy. The enhanced skills and abilities of community college students bolster the output of U.S. employers, leading to higher income and a more robust economy (American Association of Community Colleges, 2014). Purposive sampling was employed in this study to gather a group of formerly incarcerated students to participate. While it would be ideal to test the entire population by random selection, LaGuardia does not require that all formerly incarcerated persons self-identify postincarceration status. Therefore, it would be impossible to use the random sample technique. Access to students who self-identify as formerly incarcerated persons and their willingness to participate in the focus group necessitated the purposive sampling approach. Also known as selective or subjective sampling, this technique relies on the judgment of the researchers to select the participants of a study, as the researcher chooses what data they are eliciting and sets out to find people who can and are willing to provide the information due to their acquired knowledge or lived experience (Bernard, 2002; Lewis & Sheppard, 2006). While utilizing a campus service, they indicated that they were formerly incarcerated which enabled the researchers to have access to the participants. These students, ages 27, 33, 33, 45, 49, and 52, all served federal time in a correctional facility ranging from 3 to 20 years. It should be noted that the names of the study participants have been kept anonymous, but the students desired to have their identities be revealed to personalize their stories for the purpose of helping someone in a similar situation. Six critical questions were asked:

1. Think broadly about your experience in community college—your classes, outside-of-class time, the services you received, your faculty in your major, as well as the campus as a whole. Use one word or phrase to describe the impact on your life.
2. To what extent did your lived experiences and incarceration play a part in your decision to attend college?
3. Once you started college, what were barriers or challenges that you faced and where did you seek out help to overcome them?
4. What about you has changed that allows you to make good decisions that will lead to your finishing your program?
5. Do you feel prepared for the next step after you graduate?
6. What advice would you give to other formerly incarcerated students who are starting college to help them succeed and graduate?

In addition to the focus group, the lived experience of one of the co-authors of this chapter also informed the analysis of post incarceration and the discussion.

Data Analysis

The focus-group interviews of these formerly incarcerated students shed light on the experiences and processes institutions should take to successfully reengage them. Participants of the study were ascribed a pseudonym and their accounts were written down accordingly. Notes taken during the focus group were transcribed and coded by hand according to themes that surfaced through the participants' responses to the posed questions. The emergent codes were visible in the transcription of the participant interviews and responses were analyzed accordingly. Several key themes presented themselves, including: increased self-determination; need for structure, communication, and engagement; developed cognition; and a desire to help others change the direction of their lives and impact their communities. Through analysis of the data gathered from the focus group, it was concluded that crucial points of interaction within a *Guided Pathway*, between the formerly incarcerated and those in higher education, must be established in order for successful reengagement to occur.

ONE POTENTIAL MODEL

There is in fact no "magic bullet" that will fully fix the problem of recidivism (Lipsey & Cullen, 2007), to that end, there are problems that can be identified in all areas of the movement; some working better than others and some having effects long term and some, short term. The question that must be asked and addressed is what methodology is being used and, equally as important, is to reject the assumption that said methodology will automatically do well for the intended population; there should be a serious reflection and appreciation for the very real harm that could come from the initiatives. As a wise man once said, "all programs are not created equal" (Rosenfeld, Petersilia, & Visher, 2008). Having made this disclaimer, we move to one potential community college model in the light of our study.

Many community colleges and four-year institutions are discovering that student outcomes and degree completion are heavily impacted by lack of structure. "Under the prevailing model common to community colleges, students are left to navigate a complex and often confusing array of programs and courses and support services mostly on their own. Instead of letting students figure out their own paths through college, a growing number of colleges and universities are creating *guided pathways* for students" (Jenkins & Cho, 2013). Under this model the institution presents courses in the context of highly structured, educationally coherent program maps that align with the student's career and future education goals (Baily, Jaggars, & Jenkins, 2015). Imbedded in the model are comprehensive student supports including proactive advisement and monitoring student progress to support college completion. Using the *Loss and Momentum Framework of Completion by Design*, which looks to support student progression at the four critical junctures of the student experience: *connection, entry, progression, and completion*, LaGuardia has been seeking to develop its own *guided pathways* approach for students. *Connection* is the effort to recruit students into programs of study and covers the period from interest to application. *Entry* represents the student's steps between enrolling into the school until their completion of gatekeeper courses, which are generally during the first year of study. Once students enter a program, *progression* is the time students are taking courses until 75% of the requirements are completed. *Completion* is the period of the student's experience where they have finished their desired credential and are advancing to their next stated goal (Completion by Design, 2017).

CONNECTION

Results from this study suggest that the model for reengaging formerly incarcerated students may be moderately different in the connection phase to raise awareness of the opportunities afforded by the community college. As noted by the participants, knowledge of and access to the benefits and opportunities of a community college education are not always readily available or articulated as a viable path prior to release. For anyone in a predicament where they find themselves with a lack of access to education, being provided with the information or even simply the idea to attend a higher education institution can be the difference between making good life choices and continuing down the wrong path. This is especially true for those who are currently or were formerly incarcerated.

ENTRY

Given the unique challenges this population potentially faces and with special attention to increased structure, appropriately placed communication, targeted engagement, and the recognition of the frequent desire of the formerly incarcerated to give back—the themes that emerged from this chapter's study are also important for consideration in the entry and progression phases. Once the idea of college attendance has been implanted into the mind of someone who is formerly incarcerated, the next step to ensuring a successful reengagement is their actual entry or acceptance to a degree-granting program at a higher education institution. The point of this phase of interaction with this population of students is to ensure entry into an institution and getting them to pass their first gatekeeper courses in a fashion that is as seamless as possible. From the formerly incarcerated participants it is evident that a sense of consistency and regularity in the schedules of students helps ease their transition from detainment and reduces their risk of recidivism after being reintegrated into higher education.

PROGRESSION

A large part of the *Guided Pathways'* academic planning model is following students throughout their time at LaGuardia Community College and engaging with them through proactive advising. This allows students to progress from entry into their degree program, to completion of their program requirements. "Prisoner reentry is fundamentally rooted in the need to access information and social connections that enable successful reintegration" (Lynch, 2006). Being provided with the proper channels of support, formerly incarcerated students can be successful.

COMPLETION

The ultimate goal of a community college should be degree completion and the facilitation of growth and development within their students (Bushway, Stoll, & Weiman, 2007). LaGuardia Community College encourages and challenges its formerly incarcerated students to pursue further education as well as labor market advancement opportunities. When asked if they felt they were prepared for the next step of their lives, the focus group participants said:

> I feel like because of community college I'm prepared for anything that comes my way.
>
> I'm getting there. I'm getting ready to make decisions on a four-year school and I never thought that would happen.
>
> I feel like I'm prepared. I'm making moves to better myself. I go to public speaking sessions. I'm attending church. I'm prepared. Now I'm just looking to get paid!

Ultimately by implementing a *guided pathways'* model that seeks to interact and impact students at critical points in their reengagement process and providing the appropriate resources, guidance and advising connections, and academic/social support, formerly incarcerated students are capable of taking charge of their destiny and making a positive change in the lives of others.

The *guided pathways'* model is a great way to ensure that community colleges and other higher education institutions are effectively reengaging formerly incarcerated students. By providing incarcerated individuals with information about higher education during their detainment, encouraging them to pursue a degree after their release, progressing through their core classes and ultimately completing their programs and graduating, this pathways' model can be a tool for any institution seeking to assist a very unique population. Within *guided pathways* there exists elements that aid the overall development of the student. Clarifying aspirations and enhancing commitment, developing college know-how, creating social relationships, and making college life feasible are all methods for reducing the potential of recidivism with these students. At every point in the guided pathway, there is an opportunity for educators to challenge and support formerly incarcerated students through each of these elements. When formerly incarcerated students complete they should not feel the way they did when they left prison; fearful, controlled, and captive. They should feel liberated, hopeful, and alive.

FINDINGS

Overall, the findings indicate evidence of transformative adult learning (Brookfield, 2000). Focus-group participants spoke about the many ways that they had changed or were transformed as individuals and the benefits they have reaped from their experiences reengaging with an academic institution. They described their college experience as "a foundation for improvement," "a jumpstart," and "a boost of confidence." Participants communicated that when they are effectively reengaged they acquire a surplus of motivation and drive to continue succeeding, a developed sense of cognition and newfound self-awareness, and lastly a sincere desire to give back to their community, after seeing themselves in a better place and wanting the same for others like them.

Functioning in an academic environment on a regular basis, one is expected to experience a certain degree of cognitive growth and development, but this was the case even more so for the formerly incarcerated. These students exhibited a highly sophisticated level of cognition and awareness of self that can be attributed to their reentry into the higher education system. They were able to reflect on the questions they were asked, formulate thoughts and opinions, and provide insight on the experiences they have had from their perspectives as formerly incarcerated students. Participants spoke to the lessons they have learned about themselves and about the new way in which they see the world. "Twenty years later I'm back in school and I'm being shown what I missed out on academically and in life when I was growing up." Responses indicate a looking back on their lives, the major mistakes, and reflecting on why they chose the route they did. Participants indicated how they made improvements and how they don't want to regress into old patterns. "I learned about the things that made me want to make bad decisions. After being exposed to consequences and then education, the more I learned the less I realized I knew." In addition to this transformative learning about the self, the following four themes emerged in the findings.

NEED FOR STRUCTURE

The participants of the study share their experiences with navigating college life and how LaGuardia has made this process much more feasible for them personally.

> LaGuardia was not my first choice after being incarcerated. It was the only school I was accepted to. I attended a four-year institution before this. My GPA was a 1.1 and I just could not get accepted to any other school after dropping out and being arrested. LaGuardia never really crossed my mind but it was the only place I could get into. Everything about the school made me want to stay and graduate from here once I started attending classes.
>
> Set a schedule that works for you. Don't overdo it. Time management is key and very important in knowing what you want. Stay with it, it's definitely worth it!
>
> If you can withstand the pressure of doing time behind bars, you can withstand the pressure of doing time behind some books!

COMMUNICATION

One student mentions, had this student not seen the opportunity to attend LaGuardia Community College presented in front of him, he may not have made the strides that he is currently experiencing in his life. Another student explains his first point of connection with LaGuardia Community College by plainly stating that his initial point of interaction with information and testimonies from individuals from similar backgrounds and experiences is pivotal to reintegrating formerly incarcerated individuals into a higher education setting. Communication is key in setting expectations, goals, and ultimately a vision for these students.

> I saw flyers and other promotional materials while I was inside and at that point I made the decision to go to a college nearby me once I was released.
>
> I was moved to Queensboro Correctional and I physically saw the college building every day from my jail cell. I said to myself, "that's where I want to go to school." I also came across someone else who had did time who studied at LaGCC and they were making it. It gave me hope to see myself doing the same.

Community colleges and four-year institutions must dedicate themselves to sending admissions information packets to incarcerated populations for this very reason. "A majority (66%) of colleges collect criminal justice information, although not all of them consider it in their admissions process. Private school and four-year schools are more likely to collect and use such information than their public and two-year counterparts" (Center for Community Alternatives, 2011). Poor academic records combined with a criminal record can definitely serve as a barrier to accessing an education postincarceration but that should not deter students from pursuing a better life for themselves.

ENGAGEMENT

"Dropping classes because of work was tough for me but I had to cuz they were breaking me down. Finding classes that fit a working man's schedule is frustrating because these academic class offerings are very strict." For formerly incarcerated students, it is critically important to stay well connected so that they do not fall through the cracks or become discouraged by the unique challenges they are facing. One student speaks about their experience in the Accelerated Study in Associate Programs (ASAP) initiative at LaGCC, designed to help motivated community college students earn their degrees as quickly as possible by providing academic, social, and financial support, through enrollment in LaGuardia's academic programs, co-curricular initiatives, and access to advising from financial aid officers. "My college initiative advisor helped me get into the academic programs and that helped because it's a grip paying for all the stuff we need here like books and metro cards." Another student indicates how financial difficulty was a major struggle for him when he explains, "Financial situations are tough. Working minimum wage jobs until midnight is a challenge, but I'm learning how to navigate it." When working with students with a criminal background, providing resources to work-study opportunities, financial aid information, and other ways to lighten their financial expenses is a great way to facilitate the reengagement process. Formerly incarcerated students need consistent, readily available support structures. Providing them with the appropriate resources can make a huge difference in the degree to which they are reengaged academically and reintegrated into society.

> I feel prepared going to my next job because I have a good network out there.
> We know what to do. Participate. Go to class. Get involved. Take advantage of resources. Start a relationship with your teachers. Relationships matter. Create them.
> Seek out a mentor. They can be either a formerly incarcerated person or not, as long as they know the proper resources you can go to for help. Don't be afraid to ask questions. There are plenty of opportunities to give back later on.

GIVING BACK

This initial point of interaction, within the *guided pathway*, in the form of information and testimonies from individuals from similar backgrounds and experiences is pivotal to reintegrating formerly incarcerated individuals into a higher education setting. "When something happens to you that you didn't cause yourself and then you engage in self-destructive behaviors because of it, it just gives me the realization that there are a lot of ways I can be a positive change for others going through similar situations as me." Remarkably, a fourth theme that presented itself in the analysis of the focus-group notes is the desire to help others change the direction their life is going and to make an impact in their surrounding communities. Many of the students talked about their educational experiences bringing everything full circle for them and realizing that they have made mistakes. They don't wish to see anyone else go through what they have. "I wasn't born with a silver spoon in my mouth. I really just don't want them to follow the same path I did. If you see somebody walking towards a cliff, wouldn't you want to lead them away? I don't want anyone around me to have untapped potential." The reengagement process for students with criminal records is cyclical in itself. "I came across other formerly incarcerated individuals studying in college who were making it and it gave me a vision to see myself doing the same."

With so much growth, knowledge, and progress that is to be experienced by students who manage to be successfully reintegrated and accepted into a community college, the formerly incarcerated students of LaGuardia were given the opportunity to share words of wisdom with students like themselves. They believe that these insights will help them graduate and succeed as well.

> Give yourself a chance and stay open-minded. It can happen for them also!
>
> You are the creator of your own destiny. You can create whatever you want. You can go the right way or the wrong way. Don't believe that a criminal record or a previous criminal background is going to stop you from doing what you want to do. You can do anything!
>
> I knew that the school could help me get to where I wanted to be and has been a great place to even help me eventually start my own non-profit organization for the homeless.

ON THE OTHER SIDE

> I couldn't wait to get out of there, I could not stop thinking about my freedom, doing what I wanted, when I wanted, how I wanted, not having to smell the drill sergeant's breath in the morning, not having to make up this damn bed every morning, and most important no more damn letters, I get to see my real family, and childhood friends as much as I want when I want.

Soldiers, like inmates, are institutionalized into a new world, a new language, a new environment of expected violence, carnage, and demanding structure. The demand for rigidity is absolute, requiring complete acquiescence to the prevailing rule of law. Ex-military after returning to their communities have the benefit and the expectation of "three hots and a cot" and are allotted resources like free education and stipends to offset expenses. Alas, for the returning inmate, not so much. This chapter has looked at the resource of college as reentry and proposed that, not totally like returning from military combat, the formerly incarcerated have expressed certain unique needs: structure, connection, engagement, and giving back. In addition, one community college model was described.

College is a potentially powerful tool for reentry and reengagement, and community college in particular is often well situated to embrace those returning citizens. The themes that emerged through the focus group evidence how LaGuardia Community College has been able to develop its formerly incarcerated students. The students developed a greater sense of motivation and drive, which ultimately lead them to develop their aspirations, and definitely enhanced their commitment to their academic journeys and lives as a whole. Students have learned how to navigate the community college system, applying for work-study positions, scheduling classes around their work schedule. This acquisition of college know-how further assists the process of reengagement. Students were able to foster healthy social relationships with other students, faculty, and administrators through their access to programs like ASAP and this ultimately made their college life experience more feasible by giving them additional resources to succeed. Furthermore, it is a substantial way of showing other individuals who have been incarcerated because of criminal behavior how taking advantage of opportunities not only affects you but every generation after you. Access to higher education offers an excellent opportunity for that to happen in a positive way and no one should be excluded.

In the words of one citizen and study participant:

> I finally get to make my own choices! I am free, my first choice? To return to school and get a degree! All this time out here has messed me up, it's time to look to the future and embrace my discharge, it will be hard to get on my feet, but I will do what I have to!

REFERENCES

American Association of Community Colleges. (2014). *Where value meets values: The economic impact of community colleges analysis of the economic impact and return on investment of education.* Washington, DC: Economic Modeling Specialist International.

Baily, T., Jaggars, S. S., & Jenkins, D. (2015). *What we know about guided pathways.* New York: Columbia University, Teachers College, Community College Research Center.

Bernard, H. R. (2002). *Research methods in anthropology: Quantitative and qualitative approaches,* 3rd edition. Walnut Creek, CA: Alta Mira Press.

Brookfield, S. D. (2000). Transformative learning as ideology critique. In J. Mezirow & Associates (eds.), *Learning as transformation: Critical perspectives on a theory in progress* (pp. 125–50). San Francisco, CA: Jossey-Bass.

Bureau of Justice. (2014). Recidivism of prisoners released in 30 states in 2005: Patterns from 2005 to 2010. Bureau of Justice Statistics Publication No. NCJ 244205, http://www.bjs.gov/index.cfm?ty=pbdetail&iid=4986.

Bushway, S., Stoll, M. A., & Weiman, D. F. (2007b). Introduction. In S. D. Bushway, M. A. Stoll, & D. F. Weiman (Eds.), *Barriers to reentry? The labor market for released prisoners in post-industrial America* (pp. 1–25). New York: Russell Sage.

Campbell, S. W. (2012). *The Slave Catchers: Enforcement of the Fugitive Slave Law, 1850–1860.* Chapel Hill: University of North Carolina Press Books.

Center for Community Alternatives. (2011). *The use of criminal history records in college admissions reconsidered.* New York: Author.

Completion by Design. (2017). http://completionbydesign.org/.

Glaze, L. E. (2011). *Correctional populations in the United States, 2010.* Washington, DC: Bureau of Justice Statistics.

Jenkins, D., and Cho, S.-W. (2013). Get With the Program … and Finish It: Building Guided Pathways to Accelerate Student Completion. *New Directions for Community Colleges,* 2013: 27–35. doi: 10.1002/cc.20078.

Lewis, J., & Sheppard S. (2006). "Culture and communication: Can landscape visualization improve forest management consultation with indigenous communities?" *Landscape and Urban Planning* 77: 291–313.

Lipsey, M. W., & Cullen, F. T. (2007). The effectiveness of correctional rehabilitation: A review of systematic reviews. *Annu. Rev. Law Soc. Sci.,* 3, 297–320.

Lynch, J. P. (2006). Prisoner reentry: Beyond program evaluation. *Criminology & Public Policy,* 5(2), 12.

Mezirow, J. (1978). Perspective transformation. *Adult Education Quarterly,* 28:2, 100–110.

N.Y. State Div. of the Budget. (2014). *Investing in What Works: "Pay for Success" in New York State.* New York.

Pettit, B. (2012). *Invisible men: Mass incarceration and the myth of Black progress.* New York: Russel Sage Foundation.

Rosenfeld, R., Petersilia, J., & Visher, C. (2008). The first days after release can make a difference. *Corrections Today,* 86–87.

Rothman, D. J. (1998a). "The invention of the penitentiary." In T. J. Flanagan, J. W. Marquart, & K. G. Adams (Eds.), *Incarcerating criminals: Prisons and jails in social and organizational context* (pp. 15–23). London, UK: Oxford University Press.

Rothman, D. J. (1998b). "Perfecting the prison: United States, 1789–1865." In N. Morris & D. J. Rothman (Eds.), *The Oxford history of the prison: The practice of punishment in western society* (pp. 100–116). New York: Oxford University Press.

Schwartz, J. (2015). After incarceration and adult learning: A collaborative inquiry and writing project. *Adult Learning,* 26(2), 51–58.

U.S. Department of Justice Office of Justice Programs. (2014). *Prisoners in 2014: Bureau of Justice Statistics.* Washington, DC: Ann Carson, E.

U.S. Department of Justice, Federal Bureau of Prisons. (2015). *The Reentry of Formerly Incarcerated Persons: Key Accomplishments, Challenges, and Future Directions.* Carter, Madeline.

U.S. Department of Justice, Office of Justice Programs. *Learn About Reentry.*

Chapter Seven

Mentoring

Compassion Without Condescension

Tiheba Bain and Joshua Halberstam

Rabbi Khanina remarked, "I have learned much from my teachers, more from my colleagues, and the most from my students."—Talmud Ta'anit 7a

The mentor/mentee relationship poses many of the trickiest challenges of the best of relationships. Expectations are misconstrued, disappointments inevitable. Commitments, overt and unvoiced, are often ignored. However, when the relationship flourishes, the satisfactions are truly wonderful. This is so especially in the realm of intellectual exchange where the mutual learning always deepens the participants' lives.

There is an easy way to tell when mentoring goes well: look for an ongoing, fluid shift between who is doing the instruction and who is doing the learning. The connection between us (Joshua Halberstam and Tiheba Bain) is—and hopefully will continue to be—one of those instances of reciprocal learning.

Two features of our connection that one might have expected to undermine its success actually underscored its vitality: the significant difference in our personal backgrounds (including race and gender) and the insistence that in our philosophical discussions, the appeal to rigor and reasoning always remain independent of our personal feelings. Both of these features—making explicit one's different perspectives, but also adhering to a shared commitment to learning that transcends those differences—are essential to the effectiveness of mentoring, especially so with regard to mentoring post-prison college students.

This is how we met those challenges.

JOSHUA HALBERSTAM

Bronx Community College had instituted a program whereby students who had excelled in designated courses would serve as mentors to students taking the same course. Tiheba was assigned to tutor students in my class *Fundamentals of Interpersonal Communication*, a course she had taken the previous semester and aced. She proved ideal for this role, providing the requisite balance between enforcing high standards and a compassionate understanding of the students' situations; her own ownership of these traits was clearly manifest. Not surprisingly, Tiheba became a highly valued mentor to the group of students she tutored.

During that semester, Tiheba was also a student in my philosophy class, so we had numerous occasions to talk—talk and listen. I was aware of the real asymmetries during these exchanges. This was my office and I sat behind my professorial desk. I determined the curriculum, the course requirements, and I did the grading. Nevertheless, when the conversation turned to our life stories, what we had learned from our lived experiences, this asymmetry largely dissipated. I clearly had a great deal to learn from Tiheba about what it means to "pull yourself together," and what determination really looks like.

TIHEBA BAIN

On the cold and dreary day of September 27, 2011, I was released from Danbury Federal Prison after 10 years of incarceration. What was supposed to be one of the happiest days of my reformed life was actually rather scary. Leaving behind the people I grew to love and respect as family left a bitter taste in my mouth and an emptiness in my heart. As I said my goodbyes and ate my last meal behind the walls of incarceration a sudden grip of fear of the unknown latched onto me. A part of me wanted to stay, the other part wanted to be with my sons and my family.

They called my name over the intercom system to report to Admissions and Discharge (A&D). An officer escorted me to the gate. Discharge was a long process because they had a fog count. Free at last after sitting in a cold holding cell for approximately two and a half hours, an inmate driver drove me to the bus station. The very first indication of how society would view me came from the Greyhound bus attendant. Unfriendly and unwelcoming, he dealt me a look of disgust. I prayed that he was not the rest of the world but if so, Lord teach me to cope, deal, and adjust to what was in store.

Life may throw you curve balls, but that is what makes winning in the game of life so much more interesting. I always understood that higher education was going to be the key I'd need to unleash my full potential and become the bright and shining star I sought to be. Raised by my grandmother along with my sister and my brother, despite our poor existence, we experienced some good things in life, frequently went to Madison Square Garden to see horse shows, dog shows, and the circus. I was lucky enough to enjoy horseback riding, hayrides, swimming camp, and other activities that most inner city kids were not as fortunate to experience. I was a curious kid, interested in knowledge—my siblings called me "big head." I did well in school, an "A" student, and saw myself as an aspiring lawyer. I was even good enough in junior high school to be able to skip from the seventh grade to the ninth (though my grandmother vetoed the offer). Still, I always had a fear of failing, and unsure of myself, I dropped out of school in the twelfth grade and went on to make some truly poor decisions that resulted in my 10 year prison sentence. I'd grown older and more curious, but about the wrong things. My life took a turn down the road of fast money, darkness, and uncharted adventures, which led to many run-ins with the law. During that time of madness, I still managed to get married and have two beautiful boys and went back to school. I took an intensive paralegal course under the auspices of the Department of Labor while studying business at Three Rivers Community College. I thought I was still on my way to accomplishing my long-lost dream even though I was still using controlled substances; I was living in a false reality. I ended up going to prison for 10 years and with no accumulated college credits from either school due to my untimely and dishonorable departure. The drugs, anger, and resentment that had plagued my life derailed me from my educational goals.

But my desire for education never abated. Most of my time spent in prison was dedicated to self-rehabilitation and I took full advantage of every opportunity afforded to me to better myself. I made sure to continue my education while incarcerated. I received my paralegal certificate through the Blackstone Career Institute. I studied psychology via correspondence with Ashworth Community College, finishing with a 3.5 GPA. I worked in the education department teaching Microsoft Word, Excel, and PowerPoint. I became strong in my faith and continued to seek educational outlets to help me enhance my knowledge. The last academic endeavor I conquered while incarcerated was a yearlong Business Management Certificate Program with Naugatuck Valley Community College. I felt alive and renewed from within and did not want to waste all that I had accomplished by not continuing my education. So, returning to society in September of 2011, I learned of the college initiative program and happily enrolled in Bronx Community College (BCC).

During my first semester at BCC, I met some wonderful people, professors and students alike. I took a communications course and received an "A." After my first semester, I realized I was in the right place. I must have made an impression on my professor because soon after I was invited to do a pilot program, *Supplemental Instruction Leader*, another fancy name for a tutor. Yet it was an honor and privilege to be chosen for the newly implemented pilot program.

After attending the training and qualifying for the communications course in the program, I became the Supplemental Instruction Leader for Professor Halberstam's class. And because I was taking his philosophy class at the same time, we had two explicit reasons to engage in many conversations—and I had reasons to bug him all the time. I told him my story. I told him about my past criminal lifestyle that had brought me to a federal prison facility where I knew it was now or never. Professor Halberstam never criticized or judged; he listened and gave me advice on what to do moving forward. He also allowed me to see into his world by sharing his background of studying and the strictness of his Jewish upbringing. Yes, he did not endure the struggles that I overcame. Yes, he was privileged in ways that I was not, but yes, too, it was clear that he, as well, had struggled to become his own person. He proposed I adopt a different lens on life, not one as a formerly incarcerated woman but a person who overcame life challenges. He helped me to see myself as a victor and not a victim. The wisdom that came from him and my other professors at that time solidified my trajectory of success.

JOSHUA HALBERSTAM

Here is a memory. I'm about six years of age, and I learn that Europeans, unlike Americans, cross the number seven. I learn this by reading the numbers branded on my uncles and aunts arms in the concentration camps. These were the uncles and aunts who were slaves in those camps but were the lucky ones who survived—unlike the others, unlike my many other uncles and aunts and cousins who were murdered in those horrific years. My parents escaped the direct horrors, having arrived to the United States before the war. I grew up in a world of reeling, traumatized adults trying to figure out how to make their way in their new world. Understanding communal suffering was never some distant theory for me. I get it, from the inside, where it matters.

I also get that in this country, being who I am—what I look like—does confer distinct benefits. To be sure, my so-called "privileged" status surely made my path easier than Tiheba's. Indeed, on some accounts, I possess the upper reaches of such privilege: a PhD white, middle-class male. The implied advantages are real: these include the residual benefits conferred on me but not African Americans by dint of America's awful history of racism. Although I do not share *the guilt of that history*—my impoverished ancestors in Eastern Europe were hardly slave owners—as a citizen of this country, I share in *the responsibilities of that history*.

Part of that responsibility is responding to the staggering number of persons incarcerated in our prisons, and the deeply troubling proportion of these persons who are Afro-American and Latino. The reasons for this are complicated; tracing this confluence of factors is well beyond my expertise. However, of immediate concern, whatever are the reasons so many find their way into prison, we must make sure they do not return there. Tiheba's remarkable, ongoing journey provides some useful clues of what it takes to thrive outside the prison system.

Tiheba had been to prison for 10 years. Ten years! Returning to life on the outside would clearly be a challenge. She needed to earn a living. In addition, she had sons with whom she needed to refurnish a frayed mother's relationship. She had a real life to construct and reconstruct. Schooling was the constant of it initially and it is also presents the best long-term solution.

From the outset, there was this striking aspect in our talks. Never, ever, did Tiheba ask that her past tribulations, the prejudices she faced as a black woman in addition to her difficult years in prison, mitigate what she needed to accomplish. While she was open about the hardships she faced in her current situation, a subject we sometimes considered in some depth, she never allowed those personal impediments to deduct from what she knew she was capable of achieving.

I think this compartmentalization needs to be made explicit. Post-incarcerated students are emerging from an extraordinarily rough past and many, if not most, are still in the same difficult environment that allowed them to get into trouble in the first place. But the world isn't going to care. The job market is going to focus on the skills that are on offer now and going forward. Mentors who work with these students need to make sure this reality is understood. Interestingly, I think most of these students, as is the case with Tiheba, are, in fact, eager to deal with the challenges of the here and now, and move on from the handicaps of their past. Easier said than done, to be sure. But the past can't become the sole determinant of the future.

TIHEBA BAIN

Everyone is impacted by the traumatic experience of the criminal injustice system, either directly or indirectly. The realities of post incarceration are stark. Housing, employment, and criticism from the ones closest to me have been the most difficult challenges I faced. I came home after those 10 years in prison with no more than the clothes on my back and 100 dollars in my pocket. I lived five months in the halfway house and one year and three months with my aunt. I saved enough money for the first month's rent and a security deposit to live in New York, but I needed to earn three times the amount of the rent to be considered eligible for the cost of living in New

York City. The tedious task of finding housing in New York tri-state area suitable for my income was exhausting. I opted to move to Bridgeport, Connecticut, which also required, among other hassles, permission from one probation officer who, in turn, assigned me to still another probation officer and another set of rules. Welcome to living in one state and the long commutes to work in another state. Complications upon complications!

But through it all, I was determined to continue my education and thereby access different employment opportunities. After completing the college initiative program, I enrolled at the Osborne Association and completed their Green Career Program. It took some doing, but I started working as a maintenance worker in the HRA building in the Bronx under a one-year contract. Other jobs were only part time or per diem. My criminal record and the nature of my crime were boulder-sized roadblocks that kept me from obtaining full-time employment for some time. But I knew if I completed my higher education goals I'd be able to overcome those expected roadblocks.

JOSHUA HALBERSTAM

Formerly incarcerated people who seek a college education are a select group of determined men and women. The numbers aren't reassuring. Incarcerated people in America are far less educated than their non-incarcerated peers. According to the recent U.S. Census Bureau (2009), nearly 40 percent of incarcerated individuals over 18 years old have not graduated from high school, compared with just over 14 percent of the general population; nearly 20 percent have as their highest educational attainment either a GED test credential or other high school equivalency, compared with only 4 percent of the non-incarcerated adult population; and only 23 percent of incarcerated people have any postsecondary education, compared with more than half of the general population. And the situation is worse for incarcerated people of color: 27 percent of whites, 44 percent of blacks, and 53 percent of Hispanics lack a high school education (U.S. Department of Justice: Bureau of Justice Statistics, 2004).

So, those post-prison post–high school students now in college are truly extraordinary and it's "criminal" not to provide them with the opportunity to get this education they seek. It's also incredibly shortsighted. The research on this is dispositive (Wheeldon, 2011): post-secondary education, both in and outside correctional settings, is one of the most effective ways to reduce recidivism and ease the post-release path to employment and reintegration into the larger community.

It's worth emphasizing that reentry is especially tough for post-prison women, and even tougher for women who are also mothers of adolescent children who suffer because of their mothers' imprisonment. Indeed, the difficulties these adolescent children experience are highly correlated with the educational levels of their incarcerated mothers: the less education, the greater the levels of delinquencies of their children (Trice and Brewster, 2004).

We need to recognize, too, that when teaching adults, and especially, formerly incarcerated adults, alternative standard teaching methods are sometimes called for. Much of that teaching takes place outside the formal classing, in particular when one serves as a mentor. These students are often weighed down by heavy emotional luggage and insecurity and need ongoing reinforcement. This might translate into more collaborative pedagogical approaches; incorporating the input of these students into the learning process can go a long way (Schwartz, 2015).

But we also need to make sure these considerations are not a call to reduce standards. Post-incarcerated students, and, again, especially post-incarcerated people of color, have been patronized enough in their lives. They aren't looking for excuses . . . and they value merit. That means that even with their best effort they will sometimes not ace every class. So be it. Mentors should be wary of confusing compassion with condescension.

I teach communications and philosophy. The first of these subjects cautions students to be aware of subtle differences in the different ways we communicate not only as individuals but also within and across our respective cultures and subcultures. Philosophy, on the other hand, at least philosophy as I see its most noble aim, recognizes these historical and cultural differences but seeks to understand our shared human condition and desire to understand the world we all live in irrespective of those differences.

I warn my students on the first day of my philosophy class that I fully intend to be "offensive." They should expect that their basic assumptions about how the world works and how it should be organized to be directly challenged—or offended, if you will. Do you believe in free will? Get ready for the argument from determinism. Think it's all determined? Here's the argument for free will. So, too, with your assumptions about democracy, socialism, capitalism, beauty, death, and other basic convictions. As college students, expect to be challenged. There are no safe spaces when it comes to intellectual honesty.

This insistence on rigor and reason was especially manifest when the discussions with Tiheba in and out of class turned to religion. Tiheba solidified her religious roots while in prison and emerged a devout Christian. That religious commitment was integral to her newfound resolve and needed to be respected. However, her religious sensitivities—along with the anti-religious sentiments of other students—were on hold when we examined the validity of the cosmological arguments, appeals to miracles, existential theology,and all the other topics in our study of theological arguments. And that, I contend, is as it should be. There is no black or white way to do calculus; there is no male or female astronomy.

And here I part company from those critical race theorists who deem standards of merit as yet another way the powerful reinforce the social subordination of other groups, for example, John Calmore, "Cultural bias, sets standards for performance in terms of the tendencies, skills, or attributes of white America, and it is against these standards that all other groups are measured"; Richard Delgado, "[M]erit is that which I . . . use to judge you, the Other. The criteria I use sound suspiciously like a description of me and the place where I stand," and similarly Duncan Kennedy, passim. When proponents of this view are asked why they have no problem with applying merit to scoring points in a basketball game or winning chess matches and so forth, the usual answer is that these domains aren't vital to those of genuine power. This response tends to be stipulative and non-falsifiable, nor able to explain adequately (without circularity) the economic success of other non-white groups. But this is not the occasion for the deployment of arguments against this aspect of critical race theory. It is an occasion to underscore the immediate aim of mentoring to this population of post-incarcerated minorities, and that is to help them succeed in the world as it is, however deep the structural legacies of racism might be. The motivation to make it a bit easier for these mentees by reducing standards of performance is understandable, but, finally, unwarranted and counterproductive. It is also condescending. These are highly motivated individuals who deserve to be held to, at least, the prevailing standards of excellence.

TIHEBA BAIN

We live in a white patriarchal society, so being black, a woman, and a former inmate placed me under the totem pole. I should note that my blackness and my womanhood perpetuated the cycle of verbal abuse from opposing cliques inside prison as it did outside those walls. The nature of my crime, violence against a minor (though, at the time, I didn't know the victim was a minor), makes it difficult enough to "prove" myself now. Being a black woman certainly makes it even more difficult. The disparities between black women and others regarding employment and housing are readily apparent. For a man, it is much easier to get a room, find work, and start rebuilding his life. Not so for a woman, especially women like me who are also responsible for our families and need to find not just a room but housing for children. So too with jobs. Housing agents and employers are more apt to take a chance on a male and a non-black than with a black woman.

I think mentors need to have that extra compassion and recognition for students with similar experiences to mine and try to understand why sometimes they may be late to a meeting or late with an assignment, as long as they're making the effort to complete that assignment and to show up when expected. We should be able to weed out the nonsense excuses from those that occur because of actual, real-life difficulties.

JOSHUA HALBERSTAM

I imagine white mentors might feel some "discomfort" about how to deal with their African-American students. These mentors do need to see that racial divide but also see beyond it. For one thing, we should similarly be aware that all sorts of traits make a significant difference in our lives, even if those attributes aren't now designated as "privileged." Being talented is a privilege, as is being smart, tall, thin, good-looking, a sibling, healthy, born in a first-world country, and a hundred other largely "given" traits that have an enormous effect on one's life trajectory. Certainly, these other advantages might have innate status, whereas the advantages of class, gender, and racial privileges are not hardwired in the same way and therefore, more inexcusable. To be sure, determining the acceptable role of luck in the distribution of social goods is a complicated issue in moral theory. Nonetheless, a comprehensive analysis of successful mentoring to recently released prisoners, minorities or otherwise, should be wary of limiting its scope to specific kinds of privileges. A mentor doesn't make policy but deals one-on-one with an individual person. And while these personal interactions need to be sensitive to the respective group's history, they need to focus on the personal interaction that characterizes an effective mentor-mentee relationship.

TIHEBA BAIN

One profound lesson I learned from my mentor is never take a professor's word for the truth of an idea; research and dig to find the truth for yourself. When a person teaches a course like philosophy, it is easy to persuade the class to think along the lines which the professor favors. So, I really appreciate that this was not the case with my mentor, Professor Halberstam. While respecting my views, he challenged me to justify those views with clear arguments. And this is a useful lesson for all teachers and students, mentors and mentees, in all subjects.

My suggestion to anyone searching for a mentor is to let the mentoring begin without deciding that particular person will be your mentor. When you ask questions, and find yourself returning to bend his or her ear to seek their guidance on other issues outside of the subject matter of academics, about life in general, that is when you will realize that a mentoring relationship has been developed. An assigned mentor may not be compatible to your needs and goals. You must make sure that you two are a good fit. And it shouldn't matter whether that mentor is male or female . . . it's this fit between you that matters.

It's the same when it comes to race.

Professor Halberstam is white and I am black, but to be honest that was the least concern or interest of mine. The pervasive American racial divide didn't figure at all in our mentor-mentee relationship. I love and accept everyone for who they are, as I want to be loved and accepted for who I am. The dynamic between Professor Halberstam and me was not one of racial inequality, or the discomforts this might bring, but one where each of us was open to exploring the other's world on an equal playing field of interest. I am grateful for his insights.

I have a few more months until my supervised release of five years is completed. By next year this time, I expect to be free from a lot of things that have caused me to be in a state of bondage, and will be able to start fresh with no chains, obstacles, no more of trying to live up to other people's expectations, worrying about reaching their goals for my life, not my own goals for my life.

I am proud to be a liberated and educated black woman. My education has been key to providing me with this hope for the future. I've been fortunate too in having helpful mentoring. And I look forward to maintaining our mentor–mentee relationship—and friendship—with Professor Halberstam as I move on with my life.

REFERENCES

Calmore, J. (1992). *Critical Race Theory, Archie Shepp, and FireMusic: Securing an Authentic Intellectual Life in a Multicultural World*, 65 S. CAL. L. REV. 2129, 2160–61

Delgado, R. (1991). Brewer's Plea: Critical Thoughts on Common Cause, *44 Vand. L. Rev. 1, 8–9) supra note 40, at 9*.

Kennedy, D. (1990). *A Cultural Pluralist Case for Affirmative Action in Legal Academia*, Duke LRV.

Schwartz, J. (2015). After incarceration and adult learning: A collaborative inquiry and writing project. *Adult Learning, 26*(2): 51–58.

Trice, A. D., & Brewster, J. (2004). The effects of maternal incarceration on adolescent children. *Journal of Police and Criminal Psychology, 19*(1): 27–35.

U. S. Department of Justice: Bureau of Justice Statistics. (2004). Prisoners in 2003. NCJ 205335. Washington, DC.

Wheeldon, J. (2011). "Visualizing the Future of Research on Post Secondary Correctional Education: Designs, Data, and Deliverables." *Journal of Correctional Education, 62*(2): 94–115.

Chapter Eight

Short-Term to Long-Term Incarceration and Educational Reengagement

A Comparative Case Study

Dwayne Simpson, Davon T. Harris, and
John R. Chaney

No responsible critical race perspective would be complete without analyzing the development and teaching of value systems within the family unit and community that are then internalized by our youth (Carter, 2003). Our contributing authors have provided poignant and often disturbing counterstories that highlight many challenges experienced by those growing up poor and black in urban America, often resulting in the incarceration of our best and brightest. Each author offers a unique opportunity for the reader to safely walk down the fascinating and treacherous paths their respective lives have taken, including boyhood, crime, and incarceration, and finally reclaiming their lives through education. Both present stories with distinctive life experiences as common themes begin to emerge, including the ongoing state of the economic and psychological health of their respective communities. We also see patterns of microaggression, stigma, and collateral consequence episodes typically associated with men of their demographic profiles and life experiences (Wheelock, 2005). Parenting, self-esteem and self-efficacy development, with feelings of being "on the outside" are frequent topics explored in each narrative. Each author also offers experiential discourses on the limits of educational success in eradicating the pervasive sting of marginalization experienced by formerly incarcerated citizens. Neither offering illustrates definitive conclusions regarding the complex issues addressed; nevertheless, the reader will likely be compelled to explore the validity of any argument negating that subliminal racially driven policies continue to impact the outcomes of returning citizens, even for those who choose post-release education as a pathway to social acceptance and successful reintegration.

DWAYNE'S STORY: THE EARLY YEARS

Dwayne, now a successful middle-aged human services professional, MSW recipient, and proud father, shares his life journey, including a courageous and ultimately successful effort to end a vicious cycle of "doing life on the installment plan." Part one explores the impact of his family life, how he began to embrace a criminal lifestyle, and his descent into addiction and eventual incarceration.

I grew up the oldest of three children to young parents in a housing project in Brooklyn, New York. I had a sister with my little brother not being born until I was about 10 years old. My parents tried to do the best they could for their children, but my dad discontinued Christmas when I was also about 10 years old. That was the first experience of my dislike for him. I heard kids on the floors above me, heard kids in the halls with their toys, then went outside and saw kids with their new bicycles. It really made me feel inadequate. My father later became very abusive to the family. He beat my mother, me, and my sister. I thought this man didn't love us.

My father was someone I looked up to, and I felt that I needed to make him proud of me so the family wouldn't suffer so much. I started to fight over frivolous stuff because I thought my wins would make him proud of me. Lacking the attention of my father, I began to really act out and he began to beat me even harder, and he took my behavior out on my mom and sister as well.

I used to get whipped with extension cords that tore slices of skin from my legs, back, and arms. My clothing used to stick to my wounds. The beatings somehow in my mind made me believe that this was the way he cared for me. Hey, that was the only attention I was getting from a male I was identifying with, and I became good at acting out.

I had excellent grades, but my behavior was unacceptable. My father made a lot of broken promises to me. Never bought me a baseball glove, never hung out with me or did what fathers do with their sons. My issues with women began to manifest themselves. I just saw them as a piece of meat. I had no compassion, and I didn't love. I can remember joking as a young kid by telling my peers that I was having sex since I was nine years old. I guess that was a way of suppressing the realization that during this time I had been repeatedly raped by female babysitters.

My little brother then came along and for some reason I felt I needed to protect him. My hatred and pain grew deeper and deeper and there was lot of weight on my shoulders. I was able to get a little part-time job in a variety store in the neighborhood. I used to steal cigarettes, Parker pens, 110 Kodak film, and I used to sell them to my teachers. Not one teacher ever asked me where I got the stuff I was selling; they simply placed their orders with me.

I eventually got caught and lost my job. I didn't know what to do. I couldn't give my sister any money for the ice cream truck or couldn't buy and wear the sneakers and jeans that my peers in the neighborhood were wearing. This is when I began focusing on the older teenagers in my neighborhood and asked them how they earned money. Some of them said by selling loose joints on 42nd Street. Now all I had to do was think how I could manipulate school so I could hang out on 42nd Street and sell joints during school hours.

I knew I had to pass all my exams and impress all my teachers with the retention of the information taught. Man, I was good, I mean straight A student good! I even used to help other students cheat, all so that every couple of days I could be missing from school without any questions asked, then I could sell loose joints to make some cash.

The karate movies on 42nd Street were a great place to start. Nobody bothered you really back then in the movie theaters. You were allowed to smoke and pretty much do anything, and nothing was ever said. I then began to sneak into the X-rated movie theaters and boy, the experiences I had in there! Besides witnessing men give each other blow jobs in the theater, I began to actually see people have sex on screen; meanwhile the money flowed in nice in these rated-X movie theaters and my grades started dropping. I then began to get pressure from my teachers and parents, and I had to step back for a minute. I didn't want to blow my operation.

I then received a 98 on the civil service exam and was called to work for the transit authority at 18 years old. I felt like I was on top of the world. I began to frequent the clubs and was introduced to cocaine. The women there loved cocaine so hey, it was my responsibility to make sure I had enough of it whenever I went clubbing. My new pastime eventually got me into major money trouble with American Express and Visa. Thinking about what I could do to get out of this, I came across some information saying that if I joined the military the transit authority would have to keep my position until I returned. Nineteen years old at the time, I figured I could pay all my credit card bills and also become a soldier just like my dad.

While this was going on I still hadn't gotten any acknowledgment from my father, a Vietnam veteran who had served two tours of duty. I thought that he would be proud of me, once again trying to find something I could do to make my dad hug me and tell me that he loved me. Well, that didn't work. Coming home from the military, I got my job back with the transit authority, began to party hard and use drugs heavily. They sent me to a treatment program with a bunch of heroin addicts.

Here I am, probably about 20 to 21 years old, in total denial. My counselor could have taken my job plenty of times because the seven months that I was in the program I had never given him a negative urine. He gave me several breaks but in time, because of testing positive for marijuana and cocaine, I was stripped of my transit authority train pass. I had to empty out my locker and must have cried for days. Getting that job was the only thing that made me feel good about myself, that and the things I did to make sure my sister and brother were ok. My self-esteem dropped dramatically, and I became aware of crack cocaine. It was in the late eighties. I began to sell hard drugs. I also began to smoke base, rationalizing that it was better than crack. After a while, smoking base became expensive. The introduction to crack, and how inexpensive it was, helped me to make the decision to begin using it. One of my addicted criminal friends suggested that I take a couple of hits of heroin to take away the hyper feeling crack cocaine gave me.

I began sniffing heroin from age 22 to about 30 years old, becoming very dependent. I robbed, stole, and did anything to have the drug because without it, the pain of withdrawal made me very desperate. My behavior began to land me in places that I really didn't want to be: treatment programs, drug houses, and finally jail.

I served my first sentence on Rikers Island, then another in New Jersey, and yet another in Virginia. Jail broke me down, and I couldn't stand being called an inmate. I couldn't stand being locked in. The very next time I found myself in Rikers Island awaiting sentencing, one judge wanted to sentence me to state prison time. For reasons that I didn't understand at the time, I was miraculously given an opportunity to serve a sentence of intensive probation.

DAVON'S STORY: THE EARLY YEARS AND INCARCERATION

Davon, a former Sing Sing resident and now a talented young college student, accomplished writer, and aspiring attorney, offers strong viewpoints commonly expressed by gifted young black males dissatisfied with the inequities of the current system. Recollections of his upbringing focus upon his selection of role models and lifestyles sometimes emulated and admired by segments of socioeconomically distressed urban communities, as well as his experiences while in prison.

I grew up in a single-parent household in the ghettos of New York City. I and the children in my neighborhood wanted to become professionals of some type. While our parents may have encouraged us with aspirations of success, their eyes told us that our chances for success were very limited. I recall speaking to a neighborhood elder about wanting to get back into school when I was about 19. The elder looked at me and said: "Oh, that's nice." *Later when she heard I was selling crack cocaine, she took time to have an extended conversation with me, her last words being, "Be the best at it." I knew there that these broken spirits living check to check, hopeless people relying on social welfare to survive, didn't believe they were ever going to be successful. I knew then that they thought crime was the only true road to success for people like us unless you were an entertainer or some sort of athlete. I discovered this in the conversations of the old timers speaking about how much money their favorite artist had, and observing the eyes of the young women when the drug dealers road past them in their pretty cars. I was a bad athlete and even a worse rapper, so I knew the only option for me was crime.*

From the age of 17 I sold all kinds of drugs and even engaged in armed robbery when there was no money to be made on the corner. I can recall a job that I held when I was 20 years old loading trucks, and my boss told me "If you work a little harder we'll keep you on at a guaranteed 20 hours at $12/hour." I went home and put on my TV and watched MTV cribs. I left that job after two months. I saw these extravagant lifestyles and when I walked the streets in my shabby clothing people looked at me as if I done something wrong. Even in the ghetto, there is a desire to be elite and those who cannot reach to such a standard are labeled as losers, dirty, and cornballs. I could not tolerate being any of those things. So, I took my checks and went right back to selling crack. After about two good years I found myself in jail.

While there I looked into the eyes of the young men in jail and saw desire. I looked into the eyes of the older ones who had failed at their attempts to acquire their desires and saw resentment. Young men filled with hope and old men with little belief that their hopes would become a reality. I served one year and was released. Nine months later I was back on a four-year prison sentence.

While there, offers then came for me to join gangs, become a Muslim, and even to arm me with prison shanks. I declined them all. I must admit my respect was constantly challenged but never assaulted. Many of the men around me could not understand why I was so proud, so cocky, so determined. I knew that I would never be able to live with the life that was being offered to me, therefore it was "do or die." Many of us were culturally different; I came from a culture of hustlers, while many mostly came from a culture of gang bangers. I felt sorry for some of these young men, they were not cowards, but definitely not killers. I know hustle, I know money, but I learned the cost of acquiring such things in prison. The guards who would look at me and call me boy, and the junkies who had very little to live for and now in prison becoming violent alpha males, for they had no life to live for. All these lessons amounted to wisdom; priceless wisdom. I finally left prison in the year of 2014 determined never to go back.

DWAYNE'S STORY: THE IMPACT OF
POST-RELEASE EDUCATION

Upon my release, I had to spend time living in a men's shelter, eventually managing to secure employment as an outreach worker and get myself an apartment. I realized that I didn't know anybody anymore and was lonely. Someone suggested I should go back to school.

I decided to return to school to earn my bachelor's degree. In college, I became friends with other males. Education helped me understand that sometimes family systems play a role in a child's ability to make healthy decisions. Through education I began to heal emotionally. I went back to school, got my degree, and met some really great people. We accomplished four years of undergraduate school together. I found myself learning but I was also learning how to socialize and occupy my idle time a lot more constructively. We visited libraries, learned how to research, and I found it all very interesting, very exciting!

I decided to also pursue my Credentialed Alcoholism and Substance Abuse Counselor (CASAC) certification because it would enable me to counsel other substance abusers. I would help them make connections with their childhood experiences so they could make better choices as young adults.

It took me two years to finally enter a master's program. I had excellent professors in graduate school and while earning my degree in social work I made strong connections between my life experiences and the choices I made as a young adult. I became a better person.

I went on to become a substance abuse therapist for the forensic population (criminal justice). After two years at a treatment center, I became a program coordinator for a project providing services for federal probationers, later receiving a promotion supervising staff working with state parolees. My duties now included teaching new staff how to provide substance abuse treatment, make referrals for vocational services, teach parenting skills, and provide other ancillary services to the criminal justice population.

All the above was a spiritual awaking for me. During this process my father began to talk to me about his experiences as a child and his experiences in Vietnam. These dialogues also helped me heal and validated my self-worth. African American families often have secrets that they don't share with their children. They simply don't understand that those secrets, however gross and painful they might be, if put on the table for resolution, could give their children an opportunity to live a healthier life. Perhaps when these parents were being reared by their own parents they also experienced suffering. I suspect they likely thought they were doing the right thing by continuing this cycle.

I then took an exam to become a Substance Abuse Treatment/Offender Rehabilitation Coordinator for the NYS Department of Corrections. I passed the exam and was called in for an interview that went extremely well. My employment package was then forwarded to Albany, where it was rejected. This really hurt me. I began to think that after 18 years of reeducating myself and the hard work I put in at community-based organizations that some still think that people cannot change. Then again, maybe they simply don't want to give people a second chance.

But I remained on the Civil Service list for passing the exam and was called a few months later for an interview for another NYS prison. Surprisingly I was approved. I rejoiced because after all the years of working with people on state parole/federal probation, now I had an opportunity to work inside the prison and provide substance abuse treatment and guidance services to motivate them in living a pro social lifestyle as well as prepare my clients for success once they transition back into their communities.

Now I'm a father myself. My first and only child, a girl, was born when I was 40 years old. She is now 10 years old in private school She is learning different cultures, attending swimming classes, acting, gymnastics, dancing, among others. Her mother and I earn enough for our child to attend private school. I had strong concerns with allowing my child to attend public schools in New York City.

What we see today in public schools, in my opinion, in some degree reflects on how children are being reared by their families. It reflects the hurt and pain I experienced as a child. I did not want my child to be victimized or influenced by another child's pain. I want my daughter to navigate all stages of childhood development with very limited stressors, especially stressors within the family unit. I want her to be an educated strong black woman with the ability to make healthy decisions in her life.

DAVON'S STORY: THE IMPACT OF POST-RELEASE EDUCATION

During those four years of incarceration my hopes became resentments. I went in for a crime that was no more than criminal mischief and was given four years in prison for attempted arson. I started to get the picture; it will always be something that I did wrong even when I was right. I engaged in many conversations there and acquired some very interesting learning experiences. I still believed that once I became completely free, this time, I would not be caught; for now, I truly understand slick old Uncle Sam. I was 27 years old when I was set to be released and well into an adulthood when I realized the restrictions on me because of my color of skin. It became evident that my peers knew their adulthood had restrictions too as they called grown men in their thirties "my boy" and their closest peers "son."

My parole officer was very hesitant about allowing me to go to college, and at that point I decided I was going to walk in and tell her to send me back to jail if I could not educate myself. I reached out to the Urban Justice Department and met an amazing brother by the name of Johnny Perez. This brother connected me to College Initiative and advocated to the parole board for me to begin college.

I finished my first semester at community college with a 3.8 GPA. I felt my confidence grow knowing I could perform in the legitimate world. At times, though, I had to grow comfortable with sly remarks being made whenever I spoke in class. Prior to entering school, I had served four years in prison where I encountered lots of disrespect and assaults on my manhood. I remember going into my second semester when I was living in a homeless shelter, and I went to the library or to recreational center and there were young men smoking K2 while I was reading my homework. Someone blasted music while I was trying my hardest to understand algebra. I saw the look on these men's faces—hopelessness. Whenever I walked through the metal detector with my book bag, the guards asked, "Do you live here?" I simply replied, "Parole mandated me here." Once in a while I got a cheer of support from someone telling me I was going to make it and not to make the decisions they made. I appreciated every lesson taught, but I had and still have no other option, but to make it.

I was victim of many illegal actions prior and during prison. I endured four years in prison in a psychotic state of mind. At times the stress was so intense I wondered how suicide felt, but simply did not want to die in prison and be buried in potter's field. I dealt with an induced psychosis due to my conditions. I remember looking at my judge and telling him my story; he never denied it or ordered psychiatric attention. He simply cut his eyes at me as if to say "you're a nigger" and when I reacted, he cut those eyes again and actually asked me, "Do you want me to hang you?"

While in the shelter I wanted so badly to tell those brothers "What are you doing with your lives? This country makes a living off of destroying black lives so please don't make it easy for them to destroy us!" I wanted to tell them even though your life may be down, your actions are causing someone to lose their favorite uncle, father, or son. Eventually, I got housing, employment, and moved out of that shelter and was ending my second semester in college. For the first time in five years I slept in a free environment and could study all night without being told "lights out" or "bedtime." I was not content, though. I would sit on my couch thinking, "This is my existence?" I reached for my neck thinking about my prior $5,000 chain, I looked out my window and thought of all the cars I once owned. But by my third semester, I decided never to commit a crime again for luxury; living under constantly threatened existence was not worth it. Plus, I could see children who would not have food in their refrigerator because of chains and cars. This was when I knew the legit life would be the only life for me.

My readjustment to society taught me that sanity can be just as scary as insanity when you are not accustomed to it. For a very long time, I rejected society's logic and stayed in my shell. Even now after 30 months free, I no longer see this world in the same way I previously did. I watch the young men and women lose themselves in their phones while they pose for selfies and the only thing that comes to my mind is wondering why are they so happy. When people stare at me or bump me, I think do they really know what that can cost them. Then strangely, I develop a sense of a parental obligation to share my story with those on the verge of destruction and to stroke the ego of those questioning destruction. I have stopped and talked with several brothers and explained to them the price their actions may cost them.

College has been a non-stop learning experience and the lessons I've been taught allow me to understand so much that was once foreign to me. My favorite class was Honors Philosophy. I feel as if I was born to study philosophy. Imagine! The intellectual audacity to challenge what is normal, what is standard, and even what is divine. From Sartre to Socrates to Garvey I fall in love with their words every time I hear them. I believe that philosophers and politicians are the only preventers of chaos, war, and oppression. College has become my research lab where I study varying cultures and people desiring a better existence. I have worked as a research assistant; this became doable when I finally got housing, all while currently finishing five years of parole. This sane lifestyle has taught me responsibility, but the greatest gift has been the comfort I feel within. No sleepless nights worrying if I will be jailed or killed.

I am now scheduled to begin my last semester to complete my associates degree, currently working full time in a paid internship with MetLife. I look at myself now and can see myself making steps toward success. This has been a totally unpredicted path toward success, but due to wisdom acquired from lessons learned and circumstance, this is the path I walk. I find myself at times listening to my favorite songs and walking with aggression as I I stroll through my old neighborhood. My life has brought me much misfortune— misfortune which I once mistook as mistakes. From Sing Sing to college, from an inmate to a student, one thing does not change: the color of my skin. America may have taken great leaps toward change, but it is still evident in the acquittals of murdering police, I am sacrificial. My life can be sacrificed at any given time in the name of traditional values. I can easily go from a reformed ex-con to a hostile black man who puts a cop in fear for his life and is shot dead. This is reality. As a child, you simply believe that all of those people killed or wrongfully incarcerated did something wrong. As an adult I know that we can be killed even if what we were doing was right. My aggressive posture while singing along to my music should not be mistaken as the attributes of a thug, but instead emotional reactions to threats to my exis-

tence at any given moment. While I still exist, and strive for a more secure existence, I hope to learn as much as I can.

Knowledge is truly power, and only through education does one learn to understand what was once unknown. Reality is constantly in motion and no one thing remains the same. Men grow old, rivers become lakes, and volcanos become mountains. Only through education will we understand the processes time creates and learn to readjust with society. Life is a constant learning experience and we are all students. College has provided structured learning and is guiding me on how to understand what I learn. So, from the prison yard to the college cafeteria, I stand a man who has undergone a process of change and as time continues I will undergo further change. These are my lessons learned, my wisdom to those trying to understand the things I have undergone. These lessons have cost me chunks of my life and degradation that were unfathomable but I would not trade in my existence for another. Like the soldier who endures hardships on the battlefield and sees a man of honor when he comes home and looks in the mirror, I am the sacrificial existence who has endured extreme hardship to see a man prepared for anything when I look in the mirror. I was recently admitted into NYU and hope to enter law school after that. Life will continue to teach me, and I will pass my lessons on to those looking to learn.

REFERENCES

Carter, P. L. (2003). Black cultural capital, status positioning, and schooling conflicts for low income African American youth. *Harvard University Social Problems, 50*: 1; 136–55.

Wheelock, D. (2005). Collateral consequences and racial inequality felon status restrictions as a system of disadvantage. *University of Minnesota Journal of Contemporary Criminal Justice*, vol. 21, no. 1.

Chapter Nine

A New Normal

*Young Men of Color: Trauma and
Engagement in Learning*

Carlyle Van Thompson and Paul J. Schwartz

Black males killing black males, white males killing black males, and white police officers killing black males: these are the tragic circumstances that we face in this so-called post-racial society where we have twice elected a black male President. Barak Hussein Obama, his charismatic wife Michelle, and their two daughters have changed the iconography of blackness in profound ways. Despite this positive imagery, almost every day across America we are confronted with tragic news concerning the shootings and deaths of young black males. The prevalence of racial violence vibrantly underscores the institutionalization of white male supremacist culture.

Regardless of skin color or class, young black males are too often viewed as inherently aggressive, dangerous, and criminal. There is little evidence that change will come any time soon. The snarling winds of white supremacist culture create a perpetual winter in the lives of many black people, leaving black communities in a nihilistic state of hopelessness. As in the past, when wealthy white male landowners exploited free black labor, black males still represent a disposable commodity and a pervasive threat to white America's notions of security.

The tragic shooting of Jonathan Ferrell, a former Florida A&M football player who recently moved to the Charlotte, North Carolina, area, provides dramatic evidence of white America's notion of safety and security. After he had a horrible car crash, the 24-year-old escaped through the back window and walked, injured, to knock on the nearest door for help. Soon, Ferrell would be dead. The white neighbor he asked for assistance called 911, reporting Ferrell was attempting to break down her door (McLaughlin, 2014). One of the responding white male police officers shot the unarmed Ferrell 10 times. We wonder what explanation the police department will give to Farrell's fiancée, his family, and his community. This chapter aims to help educators understand the profound impact of trauma on our young men. It will identify approaches that will help educators aid learners in confronting effects of past trauma.

THEORETICAL FRAMEWORK

Two texts supply a framework for our discussion. Judith Herman's (1992) *Trauma and Recovery* describes the stages of trauma recovery. Herman divides the process of healing from trauma into three stages: Establishing a Safe Environment, Remembrance and Mourning, and Reconnection. The task of Herman's first stage, Establishing a Safe Environment, involves naming the problem, restoring control, and establishing a safe environment (p. 159). The task of the second stage, Remembrance and Mourning, involves retelling the trauma story and reconstructing the traumatic memory so that it can be "integrated into the survivor's life story" (p. 175). Reconnection, the final stage, involves the task of creating a future (p. 196). Complementing Herman's stages of trauma recovery, selections from Frederick Douglass' (1845) autobiography, *Narrative of the life of Frederick Douglass, an American slave*, provides historical context.

The chapter remains true to the tenets of critical race theory that emphasize the importance of the voices of people of color (Delgado & Stephanic, 2001) and the centrality of experiential knowledge through counterstorytelling (Solórzano, 1998). It will present the findings from a phenomenological study that posed the research question, "How does trauma experienced by young men of color affect their learning engagement and their access of counseling and support services?"

Readers will hear directly from our research participants, 20 young men, ages 18–27. The following data collection techniques were employed for the ethnographic study: a questionnaire soliciting the young men's experiences with trauma; in-depth semistructured interviews with open-ended questioning; and focus groups and member-checking activities where participants came together and gave feedback. The names used in the study are pseudonyms.

FINDINGS

The findings indicate that many young black and Hispanic men are coming to the educational setting with post-traumatic stress (PTS) that they perceive as a normal part of life. Data suggest that for the young men, trauma is an ongoing, sometimes daily series of experiences. We use the term "new normal" to describe the cumulative traumatic experiences, in and out of school, that the young men described as normal in their lives. All the participants resonated with the concept of *trauma*; understood trauma as "a given" in their lives; and accepted the inevitability of it. The shared wounds caused by past trauma for many young black and Hispanic men may be better understood in a larger historical context and framework that further complicates both the injury and the healing necessary for optimal engagement in learning.

ESTABLISHING A SAFE ENVIRONMENT

The problem of Establishing a Safe Environment has been critical for black males in American society from the chaotic times of enslavement to the present. As Herman (1992) states,

> Trauma robs the victim of a sense of power and control; the guiding principle of recovery is to restore power and control to the survivor. The first task of recovery is to establish the survivor's safety. This task takes precedence over all others, for no other therapeutic work can possibly succeed if safety has not been adequately secured. (p. 159)

Whether enslaved or free, black males lived in a society where violence was always present and unpredictable. Laws during the period of enslavement and the Jim Crow laws and Black Codes that came afterward were designed for the enduring socioeconomic disenfranchisement of black people.

Frederick Douglass is one of the most important black voices with regard to the issues of black male subjectivity and democracy within the paradoxical context of America's white supremacist culture. In terms of safety, Douglass' (1845) narrative provides examples where black male slaves were maimed or killed. Today, reports of young black males being killed in cities like Chicago and New York create ongoing trauma for young black males and their families. The pervasiveness of trauma among the young men in the study and documentary was evident as they spoke about horrific experiences as if they were talking about eating dinner or going to the store. Their words and conversational tone connoted resignation that this is how their life is: Nigel said, "Losing people—the reason why it's normal to me is that it happens a lot." Donovan said, "A guy I grew up with, he got shot, whatever . . . it was the second death in a year . . . I lost my best friend, and my cousin was killed." The young men related to each other's life histories that included gang violence, threats with weapons, and violent deaths.

Teachers and staff in educational settings, however, might not understand trauma as a habitual, inevitable, expected part of life for learners. Pedro

Noguera (2003) captures the disparity in school experiences that often exists between students and their teachers. When discussing the climate of violence that is typical in an economically depressed inner-city middle school where he was working, he stated, "I became increasingly aware of the fact that many adults at this school had no idea of how kids experience violence in their everyday lives" (p. 112).

The fear of constantly witnessing and experiencing violence is no doubt a major reason why students disengage from learning and drop out of school (Schwartz, Schwartz, & Osborne, 2012). Although the documentary participants are overcomers—each one either graduated high school or obtained his General Equivalency Diploma (GED)—the impact of traumatic experiences on their emotional health and sense of safety and stability was evident.

Now, as in the past, legal dictates in America are often designed to provide socioeconomic benefit to the dominant white male society. Paradoxically, legal issues such as racial profiling have created another slave-like reality manifest in the prison-industrial complex (Wood, 2003), where black males (many in the prime of their lives) are facing life in prison for drug-related criminal activity. There is a clear connection between black bodies and white wealth and leisure, just as when Douglass lived.

Detention centers and prisons full of black and Latino males provide tremendous economic benefit to rural white communities in terms of jobs and services; this cheap and slave-like labor force is also beneficial to major corporations that use prisoners for numerous tasks. The Corrections Corporation of America (CCA), the nation's largest owner of private prisons, has seen its revenue climb by more than 500 percent in the last two decades (Kroll, 2013). And CCA wants to get much, much bigger: Last year, the company made an offer to 48 governors to buy and operate their state-funded prisons. But what made CCA's pitch to those governors shocking was that it included an occupancy requirement, a clause demanding that the state keep those newly privatized prisons at least 90% full at all times, regardless of whether crime was rising or falling (p. 3). With a deal like this in place, state and city law enforcement policies would be designed to support the incarceration of the most vulnerable populations. Not surprisingly, private prison companies such as CCA and the Management and Training Corporation have supported and helped write "three-strike" and "truth-in-sentencing" laws that drive up prison populations (p. 4). Between 1954 and 2004, incarceration of African Americans increased by 829% (98,000 to 910,000) (Mauer, 2006, p. 134). One New York study showed that minorities were more likely than whites to receive jail time for misdemeanors and property crimes resulting in an additional 4,000 sentences a year (p. 145). The impact of penal policy on our young men can be seen in the educational system.

EDUCATIONAL TRAUMA

For the purposes of this chapter, educational trauma is defined as trauma that, according to participants, was experienced in middle school or high school, before and after school sessions, with the perpetrators being peers or teachers. Experiences of trauma included, but were not limited to, verbal abuse in the form of ongoing name-calling; bullying; condescending and demeaning language by teachers and school officials; out-of-control classrooms; and criminalization of school settings (substandard to institutional, prison-like facilities, armed security guards).

Educational abuse was noted in statements made to participants by their teachers that revealed low expectations of student's ability and potential. These messages were seared into the young men's consciousness. Terrance stated: "Teachers said to us, 'I don't care if you don't learn, I still get paid.' Teachers don't care. No motivation. Teachers basically told us the answers . . . made me feel stupid, a little lower." Feelings of inferiority, incompetence, even hopelessness can become internalized when perpetuated by supposed educators making demeaning remarks.

Study participants reported these events with clarity and detail, almost as if they had happened yesterday. The impact of early school experiences had traveled with the young men to other learning environments and was manifested in trauma responses. The young men were less trustful, less assertive, and wary of educational settings. They described how they often "scoped" classrooms as they entered to make sure they were safe. They chose to sit in the back of the room to make sure that everything was okay before they engaged with the teacher and other students. "When you come into a new environment, you don't feel safe at all. You know if you don't say the right thing it's gonna stick with you throughout the semester, year, whatever," Rudy explained. He recalled being teased and taunted with demeaning racist "jokes" by white classmates in elementary school. Lowering his head, he reflected, "Some were funny, but they stick" (gesturing with his fist toward his heart as if the cutting remarks had settled deep within his being).

The need to establish safe classrooms is foundational. During the interviews, focus group and member-checking activities, participants claimed ownership, stating they felt part of the process. A therapeutic climate was created. This was not therapy, but the provision of "safe spaces" where healing could occur. These were spaces where the young men felt empowered, emotionally safe, and grateful to be given a voice, and to have their voices heard and valued. Sharing in a safe environment with mutual support led to a normalizing of their experiences. This helped participants to understand and name past experiences as trauma, thus helping restore control. The creation of a safe space that gives voice to marginalized experiences aligns with emancipatory transformative learning that espouses inclusion, empowerment, self-expression, and critical thinking (Johnson-Bailey & Alfred, 2006).

REMEMBRANCE AND MOURNING

After the educator or helper has established a safe environment and a personal relationship with the young male student, as a trauma survivor the student needs a new language to rename experiences that have been nameless, voiceless. According to Herman (1992), "Remembering and telling the truth about terrible events are prerequisites both for the restoration of the social order and for the healing of individual victims" (p. 1).

In *Narrative of the life of Frederick Douglass, an American slave*, Douglass (1845) also allows us to connect to the issues of remembrance and mourning. It is important to remember that Douglass was a free man when he wrote his narrative, and the memories of his horrific days flooded into his mind. At one point, Douglass commented that the pen that he was writing with could be placed in the gash in his foot. Here we have that symbiotic relationship between writing and the body that has endured years of horrific violence and neglect. Despite years of trauma, Douglass was able to write and speak himself into existence. He published three autobiographies and became a national spokesman against the enslavement of black people. Young black and Latino males who have experienced trauma also have the ability to write and speak themselves into existence, if they have the proper guidance and encouragement.

According to Herman (1992), the ultimate goal in trauma recovery is to put the trauma story into words (p. 177). The study and documentary participants were provided emotionally safe spaces and given an opportunity to tell their counterstories. The young men were allowed to "come to voice" and to overcome what Ken Hardy (2011) called "learned voicelessness." Hardy asserted that it is a task of the subjugated to advocate for themselves; to challenge the belief that it is not worth speaking up; to unlearn the behavior from being taught to be silent and not to "speak unless spoken to."

The study revealed that writing about traumatic experiences as a way to get the pain on the paper can be an effective tool for recovery from trauma. Several participants came to the study by writing about their pain through personal narratives in the classroom setting. The following excerpts from the young men's writing suggest the power of these counterstories and their healing potential:

- "I'm getting healing through writing, because I'm venting it out. . . . I'm feeling better."—Michael

- "My story was like a rock in my heart that I had to break down and let all my feelings out on paper."—Stephan
- "If I didn't tell this story it [the trauma] would drag on in me and never let me go. I felt I had to tell this story so people may do the same thing I did. They will know how to overcome the situation."—Kami

Data from the study and documentary suggests that the writing of personal narratives for young men of color is a good way of broaching issues of trauma in the classroom and in the counseling setting. In *Engaging out of School Males in Learning*, an educational ethnography, Joan Schwartz (2010) explored the therapeutic nature of writing for young men of color in greater detail.

It is critically important that these young males see themselves in classroom texts and other materials that are used in the classroom. As Douglass did, these young black men can remember and mourn the tragedies and disappointments in their lives and move on. Richard Wright and Chester Bomar Himes are twentieth-century black male writers who had difficult childhoods but were able to write themselves into existence through both nonfiction and fiction.

It is also important for educators to understand the various ways young men cope with or *come to voice* about their trauma, and to whom they disclose their experiences. Of the 20 study participants, 16 had not sought out nor participated in formal counseling. They did not believe that counseling "would do any good," and they felt they just "have to bear it," or, "tough it out" for themselves—the "it" being traumatic experiences. Damien explained his mistrust of counseling: "We grew up self-healing. We can handle it." Jason concurred: "I have to handle this myself. I can stand up—not be a punk." However, the four young men who had participated in counseling thought it was helpful. Stephan, who went to counseling due to family loss and past school trauma, said issues of trust were crucial, "Statistically, counseling works . . . but, it's finding someone you trust."

Kami stated that before counseling he had not known how to process traumatic events in his school, neighborhood, and home. Both Stephan and Kami were apprehensive about counseling. Kami described his feelings going into counseling: "I had intense fear, anxiety, angry. I felt out of control. . . . I thought I was going crazy. I had lack of power and control but I saw that connection [counseling]."

Kami, whose young niece had been shot and killed during a children's birthday party and who had also lost his father, became very emotional when recalling these experiences during the interview. He engaged in counseling and spoke positively about its benefits.

Herman (1992) warned that telling the trauma story inevitably "plunges the survivor into profound grief." She wrote, "Reclaiming the ability to feel the range of emotions, including grief, must be understood as an act of resistance. . . . The survivor frequently resists mourning, not only out of fear but also out of pride" (p. 188). Herman's strategic approach to resistance seems especially fitting for young men, helping them to reframe mourning as "an act of courage rather than humiliation" (p. 202).

RECONNECTION

In the final stage of trauma recovery, reconnection occurs with self, with others, and often with God or a spiritual, greater-than-self reality. According to Herman (1992), after having safely confronted the reality of trauma in one's life and "mourned the old self that trauma destroyed," survivors must develop a new self, with new relationships, new beliefs, and new meaning since "helplessness and isolation are at the core experiences of psychological trauma" (Herman, 1992, pp. 196–97). Participants in the project were discovering their new selves during the interviews, focus groups, and member-checking activities. Although this was not formal group therapy, a therapeutic climate was created that provided "spaces" where healing could occur. The young men reconnected with self, acknowledging and validating their experiences as integrated into their lives, helping them reconnect and become whole.

Participants experienced reconnection with others. They encouraged each other, not only verbally, but also with their shared enthusiasm and willingness to work on the project. The intentional efforts from all who worked on the project conveyed hope, confidence, belief, and trust that counteracted the hurtful voices and contributed mightily to the participants' feeling empowered. Hearing each other's experiences and being able to name the formerly wordlessness of trauma helped the young men to know that they were not alone. They gave voice to unspoken fears.

Originally, groups were scheduled for one hour, but groups ran well over the time because the young men did not want to stop. Many participants commented that they enjoyed the group very much, felt open and willing to share their traumatic experiences, and felt "relieved" and very good after the group. They also said they were "grateful" to be a part of a group talking about their own lived experiences. Data suggest that these research groups were therapeutic to the young men because participants were all male; shared the same type of traumatic experiences; and felt that their experience as men of color was unique. They found that the group was confidential enough to allow them to share deep feelings. Many said they felt free to talk about traumatic experiences, especially as they related to education, and trauma's impact on current engagement in learning.

The participants also saw a purpose outside of themselves. They wanted their voices to help other young men and educators. The reciprocal nature of the relationships between participants and interviewers made the difference. This type of reciprocity and interaction can occur when helpers (adult educators, counselors, mentors, life coaches) genuinely and intentionally see and appreciate these young men and their experiences; believe in them; and draw out their strengths and abilities.

In the confrontation with the slave master Covey and in the final chapter of Douglass' (1845) narrative where Douglass relates his escape from slavery, we have the theme of reconnection. Covey is one of the most abusive slave masters to be found in the canon of slave narratives; he was always spying on his slaves and finding fault with them, whippings would often follow. Douglass relates his decisive fight: "This battle with Mr. Covey was the turning-point in my career as a slave. It rekindled the few expiring embers of freedom, and revived within me a sense of my own manhood. It recalled the departed self-confidence, and inspired me again with a determination to be free" (p. 104). As Douglass had his hands around Covey's throat, he experienced an epiphany of subjectivity: "My long-crushed spirit rose, cowardice departed, bold defiance took its place; and I now resolved that, however long I might remain a slave in fact, I did not hesitate to let it be known of me, that the white man who expected to succeed in whipping, must also succeed in killing me" (p. 105).

The transformation of Douglass is analogous to the metamorphic transformation that many black and Latino males can experience in the classroom. Despite how the dominant white society repeatedly criminalizes black males, the educational experience can empower them to change their lives and circumstances. Thus, the adult education setting can become a site of emancipatory transformative learning (Johnson-Bailey & Alfred, 2006) where young men of color can have positive experiences through honest dialogue, a caring environment, and an intentional minimizing of the power relationship between educator and learner. Michael Lapsley (2012) said the goal for trauma survivors is to acknowledge the past, and the pain, but not to be its prisoner (p. 162). In the final chapter, Douglass discussed the paradoxical nature of his escape: "The wretchedness of slavery, and the blessedness of freedom, were perpetually before me" (p. 142). Too many young black and Latino males who have been traumatized feel locked down and oppressed by the wretched conditions in which they live, but there are countless examples of men who have become free and blessed with possibilities that they could hardly imagine.

IMPLICATIONS FOR PRACTICE

We were encouraged by the enthusiasm of the young men in the study. This enthusiasm translates into genuine engagement with learning and can be inspired by practitioners through integration of the following principles into pedagogy and therapeutic intervention. First, utilize texts and classroom materials that young men can relate to such as reading topics that include traumatic experiences and historical and present-day racial violence and injustices. In career preparation and training settings, the materials and discussions might include the work experiences of men of color whose racial identities have historically limited access to employment. Including learner experiences not only promote engagement but provide resources for learning opportunities that enhance understanding and application. Second, encourage young men of color to voice their counterstories by writing. As research (Schwartz, 2010) has shown, this contemplative practice of expressing deeply significant experiences is a source of healing, and especially for adult basic education learners, also a means of enhancing the technical skills of writing. In addition, because the experiences of men of color have been ignored or marginalized, their stories challenge commonly held beliefs of the larger society, and practitioners in particular, about how the world works. Third, promote learners' active participation in class discussions and support groups that will allow their voices to be heard and valued. Fourth, foster active participation through meaningful classroom activity such as small groups and writing shares that facilitates trust and safety and lead to empowerment. As the participants in this study clearly convey, the creation of a safe space is critical to their engagement. This implies that practitioners may need to be intentional about helping young men of color to feel safe in their classrooms. Regardless of the educational context, the intersection of race, class, and gender influences learner experiences in the classroom; and for men of color connecting learning to lived experience is a necessary ingredient for engagement and transformation (Johnson-Bailey & Alfred, 2006; Sheared, 1999). The lessons learned and approaches presented here can benefit educators and counselors by increasing an understanding of and appreciation for their students, and their students' experience, which will often be very different from their own. If this society is truly to be a place of possibility, it is critical that young black and Latino males have the agency associated with a truly democratic and post-racial society.

This chapter was previously published in *New Directions in Adult and Continuing Education, Swimming Upstream: Black Males in Adult Education, no. 144, Winter 2014 © Wiley Periodicals, Inc.*

REFERENCES

Delgado, R., & Stephanic, J. (2001). *Critical race theory: An introduction.* New York: New York University Press.

Douglass, F. (1845). *Narrative of the life of Frederick Douglass, an American slave written by himself.* Boston, MA: Anti-Slavery Office, Elegant Ebooks.

Hardy, K. (2011, December 11). Insights from Dr. Kenneth Hardy [Web log post]. Retrieved from http://traumatreatment.blogspot.com/2011/12/insights-from-dr-kenneth-hardy.html.

Herman, J. (1992). *Trauma and recovery.* New York: Basic Books.

Johnson-Bailey, J., & Alfred, M. (2006). "Transformational Teaching and the Practices of Black Women Adult Educators." In E. W. Taylor (ed.), *Fostering Transformative Learning in the Classroom: Challenges and Innovations.* New Directions in Adult and Continuing Education, no 109. San Francisco, CA: Jossey-Bass, 2006.

Kroll, A. (2013, September 19). This is how private prison companies make millions even when crime rates fall. *Mother Jones.* Retrieved from http://www.motherjones.com/mojo/2013/09/private-prisons-occupancy-quota-cca-crime.

Lapsley, M. (2012). *Redeeming the past: My journey from freedom fighter to healer.* Maryknoll, NY: Orbis Books.

Mauer, M. (2006). *Race to incarcerate.* New York: The New Press.

McLaughlin, E. (2014, January 28). 2nd grand jury indicts officer in shooting of ex-FAMU football player. *CNN U.S.* Retrieved from http://www.cnn.com/2014/01/27/us/north-carolina-police-shooting/.

Noguera, P. (2003). *City schools and the American dream: Reclaiming the promise of public education.* New York: Teachers College Press.

Schwartz, J. (2010). *Engaging out of school males in learning* (Doctoral dissertation). Retrieved from http://hdl.rutgers.edu/1782.2/rucore10001500001.ETD.000052893.

Schwartz, J., Schwartz, P. (Producers), & Osborne, R. (Documentarian). (2012). *A New Normal: Young Men of Color, Trauma, & Engagement in Learning* [Documentary]. New York City: City University of New York. https://www.facebook.com/anewnormalyoungmenof-color.

Sheared, V. (1999). Giving voice: Inclusion of African American students' polyrhythmic realities in adult basic education. *New Directions for Adult and Continuing Education, 82,* 33–48.

Solórzano, D. (1998). Critical race theory, racial and gender microaggressions, and the experiences of Chicana and Chicano scholars. *International Journal of Qualitative Studies in Education, 11,* 121–36.

Wood, P. (2003). The rise of the Prison Industrial Complex in the United States. In A. Coyle, A. Campbell, & R. Neufeld (Eds.), *Capitalist punishment: Prison privatization and human rights.* Atlanta, GA: Clarity Press.

Chapter Ten

Epiphany of a Prodigal Son

An Autoethnography

John R. Chaney

As the final days of the semester begin to wind down, my criminal justice students anxiously await the appearance of a promised special guest. Each student is required to have read an article that highlights his rather robust criminal profile. They learn that he will arrive with a history of a quarter century of drug abuse, four felony convictions, and three periods of incarceration within the city, state, and federal prison systems. I promise they can ask whatever they desire. No one is particularly surprised that I, their professor, would actually include this unusual component to their curriculum. Video excerpts from television appearances billing me as an authority on reentry and evidence-based practices are strategically incorporated into several of the lessons. Students visiting my office peruse a wall adorned with diplomas, civic awards, and testimonials. The array includes a recent plaque containing my now retired badge, forever memorializing my tenure as an administrator with the Kings County District Attorney's Office. Throughout the semester my black students, especially the men, routinely approach me after class. They make a point of telling me how happy they are that they can look to me, one of their own, as a role model and possibly a mentor in their quest for academic and professional achievement.

On the day of the much-anticipated visit ten minutes pass by as I try my best to interest them in a conversation about current criminal justice news items. Soon their collective impatience begins to manifest itself in audible sighs and soft whispers. Eventually someone finally raises their hand, daring to voice the disappointing possibility that our guest is probably too irresponsible to even think of showing up. I then turn on the projector, smiling as the whispers morph into audible gasps of disbelief as the picture of men, obviously, prisoners in their jailhouse garb, comes into view. "Professor! That tall guy in the middle . . . that looks like you!"

Everyone loves a good second-chance success story. The end-of-semester ritual never fails to produce applause, wide eyes, and eagerly proffered questions that are always predicated upon the false assumption that post-release education paved my road to my salvation. Practically all my black students born in the United States have had friends or family members who've had some form of criminal justice involvement at some point in their lives. For this reason, several look to me, a black man who managed to successfully overcome the throes of addiction and incarceration, as a genuine source of inspiration and hope, further extolling the virtues of higher education. The rosy "second chance role model" persona they designed for me soon, however, becomes infinitely more complicated for them to digest upon learning the truth.

"So how long after getting out did you decide to go back to school, Professor?"

"Well, it didn't exactly happen that way."

RECONCILING TWO CONFLICTING PREMISES

Horace Mann's famous statement about education being "the great equalizer" begs new millennium introspection when considering the unique issues of the educated black professional who later becomes a consumer of correctional services (Mann, 1848). Considerable time, sacrifice, and often expense is invested in obtaining academic credentials that are supposed to lead the way to higher paying employment, higher intellectual status within the American and global community, and life-everlasting satisfaction. I followed this time-honored formula, received two degrees, and began practicing law at age 25. When I consider the many accepted precepts of critical race theory (CRT) in shedding light upon why I made those fateful choices that threw these universally expected outcomes horribly off track, two fundamental points become painfully clear. First of all, I'm all too aware of the madness of current policies that result in the disproportionate ratio of my fellow black males within the American prison system, nearly six times the rate of their white counterparts (Pew Research Center, 2013). My black male students work hard to use education as a traditional social and economic tool to avoid this unfortunate consequence, in addition to enhancing their overall quality of life. I have no immediate answers for them in explaining why this number includes people like me; individuals with advanced education who currently comprise roughly 4% of our prison population (Travis et al., p. 65), representing that unfortunate "1" in the 1 to 11 ratios of our nation's black males who found themselves in prison (Drake, 2013).

Second is the fact that my criminal lifestyle and three periods of incarceration are indelibly connected to a quarter-century addiction to hard drugs, including heroin. Does a former addict even dare reconcile former addictive and criminogenic behavioral patterns with legal and sociological concepts that are the accepted hallmarks of critical race theory (CRT)? Consider the fact that irrespective of one's demographic profile, best practices within the world of responsible addiction recovery mandate that no addict can develop the coping and self-efficacy skills necessary to lead a life of sobriety until he or she first accepts full and complete responsibility for their actions (Bonnie, 2002, p. 405). When one attempts to incorporate CRT concepts when exploring the root causes of criminal activity and incarceration of an educated black male, and when addiction is a factor, does one do so at the possible risk of diminishing the effectiveness of these recovery mechanisms? If one chooses not to consider CRT does this mean that we naively ignore the probability (some may say certainty) that many legal, political, social, and economic variables directly attributable to race may have a catalytic effect upon the development of addictive and criminogenic behavior patterns, patterns that may have a neutralizing effect upon the virtues of education?

In an attempt to explore a real-life example of how this tension between CRT and personal responsibility come into play, I respectfully offer myself as a test case for the reader's review. This evocative autoethnographic study is directed toward scholars seeking to analyze cases of formerly incarcerated individuals from both sides of the educational spectrum. During the second half of my incarceration, I had written a weekly journal that recorded my reflections as a recovering addict determined to reclaim his life. These memoirs, in addition to letters saved by my family, became extremely effective tools in writing this piece (Badenhorst et al., p. 6). They became invaluable as I respectfully offer this honest, occasionally raw overview of the life of an educated black male who later found himself a consumer of correctional services. You may well find that my recollections of significant life episodes and microaggressions merit the responsible application of a CRT yardstick (DeAngelis, 2009, p. 42). Ideally they will assist in generating more informed and intelligent discussions involving the effectiveness of education's role as it pertains to black males who have had criminal justice involvement. It may also provide arguments in support of the thesis that relying solely upon education to avoid a criminal lifestyle and resulting incarceration can be a naive and possibly dangerous proposition.

THE DEVELOPMENTAL YEARS

I grew up in a Harlem housing project during the civil rights era in an environment consisting almost entirely of black friends, classmates, and neighbors. There was very little interaction with white people, save for the nuns who taught at the Catholic school I attended until age thirteen. My father, John Sr., an army veteran who never made it past the eleventh grade, came to the big city from a small town in Virginia. A former amateur boxer who enjoyed his liquor, he was a good man with low expectations, and was a product of his time. My mother, Joyce, an amazing woman, was raised in a series of foster homes. She managed to graduate from high school, raise my sister Joanne and me, and along the way acquired a strong appreciation of the value of education for her children. A woman of uncommon grace, intelligence, and strength, her amazing sense of humor belied the realities of our daily existence in later years. Over time she watched my father's alcoholism slowly destroy any vestige of hope that our family would remain intact. She was the driving force for my sister, Joanne, and me to attend Catholic grammar school to ensure that we both receive top quality learning. Joanne became a poster child of how the educational formula was supposed to work. She eventually graduated from college, never got involved with drugs or the criminal justice system, and became a successful model citizen.

For a time both our parents provided us with a good life and lots of love. The climate within our household began to dramatically change for the worse when I was around 10 years old. Still very much into my books at the time, several of our school nights ended with episodes of domestic violence . . . sometimes physical, blood-on-the-floor violence. There were visits from the police, followed by next-day stares and head shakes from whispering neighbors. Joanne and I witnessed some really fierce battles between our parents during that time, later thanking God that no one had gotten seriously hurt or worse. We still marvel at how our mom somehow managed to handle our father's alcohol-fueled rages. I would sometimes hide the kitchen knives before he arrived home from work, all but one that I would keep handy in my back pocket. I fully intended to use it if he again put his powerful hands upon my mother intending to hurt her or worse. Interestingly, he and I would reconcile many years later, including a time when we lived together as dysfunctional adults, feeding our respective demons until I had to serve my final term of incarceration.

THE TROUBLED MAN-CHILD

At age 13 with my mother's encouragement and sacrifice, I began attending a predominantly white all-male Catholic high school in Manhattan. Here, for the very first time, I was very much in the minority. The civil rights struggle had become an increasingly hot topic, and for the first time I would begin to hear disparaging, racially driven comments from students and occasionally even from a few of the teachers. They generally questioned the need for a civil rights movement, even regarding icons like Martin Luther King Jr. as troublemakers.

During my senior year, my band was reluctantly hired by the school to entertain at the school's annual boat ride in response to a petition circulated among the school. It would be the first time the school had ever hired a black band. Our band was twice as large as the white band but only received half the pay. As we all happily boarded the boat, the school's dean of discipline ominously warned me, "I'm holding you personally responsible for anything they do!" (Henfeld, 2011, p. 141).

I continued to receive decent and sometimes great grades in high school, but resentment and rebelliousness has begun to build within me. I always felt better when, once school ended, I returned to the familiar flow of my block. Some colleges had begun to create Martin Luther King scholarships immediately after his assassination. I managed to receive full scholarship offers from four, accepting the one offered by NYU. By this time my father had permanently moved out, a cause for celebration for our stressed-out household. It also left me with a ton of confusion, insecurity, and more than a little resentment.

ACQUIRING THE CREDENTIALS

The 1970s provided a colorful, permissive atmosphere when I, now an insecure but very inquisitive college student, smoked my first joint. My father's violent behavior when drunk at home had killed any lingering curiosity I may have had for alcohol. Marijuana, though, was the amusing pastime of intellectuals, geniuses in the arts, and of course the rebels. I had a wealth of socially acceptable excuses to inhale with pride back then, but there was another deeper, more compelling reason why I took my first step into the netherworld of drugs one Friday evening on campus with a group of bored, "hip" classmates.

I had never felt completely accepted in either of the two worlds I had inhabited at the time, school and the streets. Unlike many of my college buddies who were raised with strong fathers or big brothers at home, I had no positive male role model to confide in, get advice from, or emulate. My parochial school upbringing had given me strong academic tools but if anything, probably exacerbated the normal teenage insecurities I had harbored within. It certainly offered no practical answers on how to deal with latent, occasionally blatant racism I began to encounter as I began navigating through predominantly white environs. On one such occasion I had been hired as a college aide by a city agency. My supervisor had given my white colleagues interesting field visit and writing assignments. My responsibility? Erasing the ink toner smudges from office documents!

Perhaps the answers to all my perceived troubles did lay within the innoc-
uous stick of paper-wrapped leaves that was offered me that Friday evening.
Then again, I might simply end up with a flaming ember on one end and a
flaming fool on the other! In retrospect, I now see that it was inevitable that
the fanciful illusion would win out that evening, as it did for many years to
follow. My slightly older, worldlier peers accepted me that night as a fledgling initiate into the drug-inspired world of the black urban intelligentsia.
Many members of that little college clique eventually outgrew the desire to
get high, becoming quite successful and happy in their respective professional and life choices. For me, it was the volatile combination of my early
experiences with my painfully fragile and scarred psychological makeup that
would cause me to travel the darker path.

By this time the nation's law schools had also undergone critical review
in terms of their enrollment numbers and minority student admissions policies. While my grades had been good but not great, it was a nice surprise
when I, now a confirmed daily user, was offered a full Martin Luther King Jr.
scholarship to Brooklyn Law School. In early July before our classes would
officially begin, I met a handful of other black and Hispanic fellow recipients
during a pre-orientation session. We soon learned that we would all be required to take special instructional classes in legal writing and research during the summer as a condition of maintaining our scholarships. It was the
school's way to ensure that their new minority students would be able to
keep up with our white classmates during the upcoming fall classes, irrespective of the quality of our undergraduate education or individual performance
while there.

Still living in the projects with my mom and sister, I began to occasionally add cocaine and later heroin to my arsenal of personal poisons. Both drugs
were as readily available in my Harlem neighborhood as bread and milk, and
my peers now regarded me as a brother on the move who knew how to work
hard and play hard. Had any of them even suggested that this seemingly
harmless dalliance would become the catalyst, installment style, to a life of
self-destruction, I would have dismissed the sentiment as a product of a
paranoid, possibly demented mind. While still maintaining my vices, I graduated law school, then passed the bar exam on my second try. My pastime had
not yet hit the stage where my drug use had completely dominated my
lifestyle, but it was definitely getting close. At age 25 when applying for
what would become my first job as an attorney, it became quite obvious
during my interview that my future boss, a likeable white middle-aged attorney, fancied himself a liberal who wanted to do his part for "the cause." It
was, therefore, a "win/win" as I was hired as the only black attorney for a
union offering legal services for its members. I scrupulously avoided drugs
while at the office and slowly developed a solid reputation. In time my boss
soon began offering me hits of cocaine in his office. Sometimes I would

proudly come with a girlfriend to his luxury home in midtown Manhattan to split large purchases of the drug that we would sample on a special platter. He was the first significant male figure I had in my life since my father. Amazingly, he too struggled with alcohol. Seeing him as a sort of role model and mentor, he served to validate my warped logic. I concluded that those of us who achieved higher education and professional status with its accompanying demands had earned the right to indulge in these types of pleasures.

Three years later I decided to strike out on my own, leaving the solid, predictable structure of my job. The lack of accountability to a schedule or to a superior became a recipe for disaster as getting high eventually became the top priority of my day. Never short of clients, some had begun to comment on changes in my appearance and behavior. Before long, I began spending retainer and escrow money on my heroin habit. In time, I would be facing arrests for forgery and mail theft, resulting in convictions that would sound the death knell for my career.

PLUNGING INTO OBLIVION

By the late 1990s I had become a three-time felon still trying hard as hell to keep the magic alive in my quarter-century love affair with hard drugs. My life now revolved around enjoying the sweetness and euphoria of the high. The fact that I had acquired a college and law school education some years back meant nothing when it came to what really counted to me. My entire day and eventually my entire life had evolved around scheming, "copping" (purchasing), sniffing, then nodding from heroin. In fact, virtually every acquaintance I had, whether male or female, were "dope fiends." I had no problem with that at all! Now in my forties, I had invested much energy into becoming an "old head," and had over time perceived myself to be the object of both affection and respect among the people who daily inhabited the street corner. My people: slingers (drug peddlers), boosters (professional shoplifters), creepers (office burglars), con artists, and closet-addict nine-to-fivers (as I once had been) who needed to have their feet firmly planted in two different worlds. I now lived with my mow invalid father who had gotten his own place in a Bronx housing project. Whenever I was lucky to have acquired a steady job I would wake up an hour early each day to cop my morning bags before heading to work.

When the paychecks stopped, I got into my "any means necessary" mode. Getting "dope sick" was no joke and honestly, I simply couldn't allow that to happen too often. It was the worst feeling in the world. If that meant conning a friend or family member out of a little cash, doing a little boosting, or maybe a daytime office burglary once in a while, then so be it. An equal-opportunity office thief who victimized irrespective of ethnic or racial considerations, I found myself often enjoying a perverse satisfaction when later realizing that the wallet I stole from a sports jacket pocket or purse had come from a white professional. It took me merely six months after my last short-term stay at Rikers to get arrested yet again, this time for a third-degree burglary trying to steal a woman's purse from her work desk.

Eventually I blew trial and began my three- to six-year sentence with stays at the Manhattan House of Detention (commonly known as the "Tombs"), Rikers Island, and medium-security New York State facilities. While upstate one of the officers accused me of an "act of aggression" after jerking my hand, broken and mending from a basketball injury, when he mashed it against the wall during a search. This resulted in three months in the box, followed by a trip to the infamous Attica prison.

It didn't take long for me to sense the palpable and very intense depression and danger of Attica, replete with officers who would just as soon smash your face in as look at you. During my second day there, waiting on line for processing, I felt eyes on me and realized that one officer was staring me down. When I deigned to look at his face he spat out the words, "Don't be eyeballing me, boy!" It was just the kind of atmosphere one would want to quickly forget about in any manner possible.

What fascinated me the most were the older, hard-core addicts I'd come to know who were serving seriously long sentences. Each had developed strong jailhouse hustles and lived under the hard and amoral code of the predator. They were practically always black men in their forties or fifties, always sizing up each new arrival as a possible victim of extortion, con artistry, or force. They had become my new companions; in essence men who, through their commitment to getting high in the most oppressive of conditions, had become animals. These were men who had at some point given up all hope of ever becoming anything else than what they had become. A realization began to slowly seep into my thoughts and began to haunt me as I continued to get high in the prison yard and in my cell.

THE EPIPHANY

It slowly dawned upon me that when looking at these men, I was actually looking at myself. They had simply taken our lifestyle to its logical next level in this netherworld we now lived in. Truth be told, there wasn't much difference between them and me, just a few errant legal circumstances and the fact that I had squandered the advantage of my education. I had lost so much in traveling my long road to ruin, and as I regarded the walking dead now around me, the grim reality hit me that I was in serious danger of losing my very soul. That observation, made during the summer of 2001 a few days after sharing a bag in the prison yard, scared the shit out of me. I had to scrounge up at least a vestige of hope that the balance of my life could have some meaning and purpose. My entire thinking pattern as well as my character had over time been shaped and distorted by choosing drugs as my convenient remedy in neutralizing the fears, insecurities, and social stresses that had invaded my psyche. I knew that I had to make a mission of slowly but surely acquiring new ways of thinking, new friends, new pastimes, and new reasons for living.

I then made a pact to always be honest with myself, to be courageous enough to deal with all my personal issues head on, and, upon my eventual release, to use every advantage my education offered. With less than two years before my release on parole, I was appointed a teacher's aide and assigned to Attica's GED class. It turned out to be an amazing experience. I found myself developing strategies to motivate lifers how to write essays, use fractions, decimals, and the Pythagorean theorem. Each day I joined the other prisoners as we were escorted from our cells to the prison classrooms, always under the watchful eye of a group of corrections officers, always all-white. While most silently observed this daily morning parade of mostly black male GED candidates, there were always one or two who would occasionally comment about their tax money being wasted. One proudly racist officer routinely interrupted the class instruction, always to order me to perform some menial janitorial task. "Hey, porter!" These intimidating onslaughts increased my appreciation for the value of learning, including learning more about myself and how strong I could be in the face of extreme adversity.

I stayed strong, true to myself, and began to acquire more confidence in applying my natural abilities. Before long I came to respect, even like, more of the person I saw in the mirror each day. I accepted, then tackled the fact that all my life, lack of confidence, often enhanced by subtle societal messages that cast clouds over my confidence in my abilities, had much to do with the drug abuse that hastened my spectacular downfall.

My prison epiphany opened my eyes to the fact that while building my socially acceptable academic and professional credentials, I had simultaneously contributed toward stunting my psychological and professional growth for over two decades. It was a saddening realization, but also one that fortified my resolve to make a serious mission of developing the building blocks leading to a successful and rewarding life. I realized that a key objective toward this end would be for me to achieve both success and lasting satisfaction in a career commensurate with my education.

RECOVERY, REINTEGRATION, AND TRANSFORMATION

My new resolve to live a successful drug- and crime-free lifestyle was soon to be tested by the death of my father three weeks before my release on parole, a yearlong stay in a shelter and transitional housing, and my frustrating efforts, now a middle-aged four-time felon, to secure a foothold in a depressing job market.

My initial efforts to obtain professional employment of any type were completely unsuccessful. Sometimes the three-year hole in my resume or eventual disclosure of my criminal record ended any serious discussion of hiring. CEO, a program for parolees, gave me a steady job paying $30 a day cutting weeds and emptying garbage from vacant lots, including a memorable week when I actually worked on the same NYU campus where once I was a naive, wide-eyed student. I later acquired my first full-time job as an outreach worker at Brooklyn Plaza Medical Center. Now deeply involved in volunteer work to help newly released men and women returning home, I began immersing myself in the world of program development, grant writing, and evidence-based reentry practices. Over time my newfound confidence in facing the world head-on, coupled with my enhanced skillset, enabled me to pry open some amazing doors in health services administration, academia, and even law enforcement.

As I accepted this challenge of a brutal introspection in revisiting some of the pivotal moments of my life, my emotional journey validated hypotheses often proffered in discussions involving addiction recovery as well as with critical race theory (Delgado & Stefanic, 2001, p. 2). These days, whenever I dare to raise the bar in pursuit of a new personal or professional milestone, I am thoroughly convinced that my actions are predicated upon knowing that my powerful, unadulterated mind is the gateway to achievement, both good and bad. Armed with this knowledge, I fully realize that a huge part of tapping into this power involves taking ownership of all that I do, good or bad, past or present. Whether my actions resulted in detectives' interrogations or community leaders' celebrations, I am responsible. That being said, I also clearly see that so many of my racially influenced life episodes occurred because of prevailing racial policies and attitudes. For this black male, whose system of support and confidence level was severely compromised, these incidents when added to these deficiencies, became a volatile mix. Even with the advantage of education, it was a deadly combination that significantly fueled many of my emotional and anger-driven responses, resulting in life choices that nearly destroyed me.

As I now applaud my graduating students, saying special prayers for my young black men when doing so, I pray that for each, their educational achievements are invigorated with a strong support network that will include solid role models and mentors. They are essential partners in nurturing a well-developed system of values, self-worth, and self-efficacy. Our best and brightest will then be better equipped in navigating through the hills and valleys of life, avoiding consequences that, in the absence of these qualities, can be enhanced through subtle racially driven practices and policies that lie embedded within our nation's political and social infrastructure.

REFERENCES

Badenhorst, C., H. McLeod, & Joy, R. (2012). "Becoming a researcher: Stories of self." *The Morning Watch*, Vol 40, Nos. 1–2.

Bonnie, Richard J., LLB. (2002). Responsibility for Addiction. *The Journal of the American Academy of Psychiatry and the Law*, Vol 30, No. 3.

DeAngelis, T. (2009). Unmasking 'racial micro aggression. *American Psychological Association*, Vol 40, No. 2.

Delgado, R., & Stefanic, J. (2001). *Critical Race Theory, an Introduction*. New York: New York University Press.

Drake, B. (2013, September 6). Incarceration gap widens between whites and blacks. http://www.pewresearch.org/fact-tank/2013/09/06/incarceration-gap-between-whites-and-blacks-widens/.

Henfeld, M. S. (2011). Black male adolescents navigating Microaggressions in a Traditionally White Middle School: A Qualitative Study. American Counseling Association, *Journal of Multicultural Counseling and Development*, Vol. 39.

Mann, H. (1848). Twelfth Annual Report to the Secretary of the Massachusetts State Board of Education.

Travis, J., Western, B., & Redburn, S. (eds.). (2014). *The Growth of Incarceration in the United States: Exploring Causes and Consequences*. Committee on Causes and Consequences of High Rates of Incarceration; Committee on Law and Justice; Division of Behavioral and Social Sciences and Education; National Research Council.

Part III

Counterspaces

Chapter Eleven

Returning to School after Incarceration

Policy, Prisoners, and the Classroom

Brian Miller, Joserichsen Mondesir,
Timothy Stater, and Joni Schwartz

War is hell, and war is an appropriate metaphor for the depressing state of formerly incarcerated men of color who return to adult education. These men might be called the collateral damage of a war caused by history and failed policies. They continue to be punished by barriers to reentry into society and education. Men who have been incarcerated need strong support to rebuild their lives; if denied education, they will become recidivists, not necessarily by choice, but because they cannot adjust to society.

In preparation for writing this chapter, the authors completed archival research, informally talked with men of color who were navigating the complicated minefield of the American educational system, and also drew on their own experiences. We considered three factors that determine the impact of the drug war on men of color and their access to education: Past and current policies of the war on drugs; the effects of these federal policies; and reentry into the classroom experienced by those exiting the detention system and entering and/or returning school.

As you reflect on our participants' experiences and thoughts, connect their voices to those of your own students and their struggle to find a classroom climate that is secure and affirming (Schwartz, 2014). Ponder as well your role in the war and in their lives.

PAST AND PRESENT POLICIES – A WAR OF SORTS

War on drug policies continue to depress the economic, social, and educational outcomes of men of color, who are overwhelmingly the victims and targets of these policies (vanden Heuvel, 2012). While the war on drugs is not an actual war, law enforcement tactics produce real casualties: prisoners. Since its inception in 1961, 45 million people have been arrested (NAACP, 2013). The effects of these arrests are lasting; the ripples affect both the arrestee and his community.

U.S. Bureau of Justice Statistics (BJS) defines drug abuse violations as state and/or local offenses relating to the unlawful possession, sale, use, growing, manufacturing, and making of narcotic drugs including opium or cocaine and their derivatives—marijuana being one of the derivatives (2013). Drug laws were designed to disrupt the flow of drugs to the United States; however, more than four-fifths of drug law violation arrests are for possession (BJS, 2013), not for trafficking or manufacturing. Taxpayers spend 70 billion dollars per year on corrections and incarceration, culminating in a price tag of one trillion dollars over the past 40 years (Armentano, 2010).

In addition, this war is fought in certain neighborhoods, particularly neighborhoods of lower socioeconomic status, not in places like Wall Street, where possession of drugs is also reported to be high (Alexander, 2010). It is not surprising, but no less troubling, that a study by the Sentencing Project and NAACP (2013) found that 38% of all people arrested on drug charges are African American. Of the 2.3 million people currently incarcerated, 25% are incarcerated for drug offenses, mainly possession, and in many cases for possession of marijuana (BJS, 2013).

Historically, presidents have used rhetoric to underscore their political interest or the interest of the constituents they represent, and it was President Nixon who initiated the language of war into the public conversation relating to the "war on drugs." Ronald Reagan would later add a heightened sense of urgency, declaring illegal drugs a threat to national security. In 1996, President Bill Clinton appointed an actual military general, Barry McCarthy, to the position of director of the Office of National Drug Control Policy (Associated Press, 2010). President Clinton did not select someone who understood the complexities and sensitivities of drug use in this country. Instead he chose a man of war, a choice that reflected both his views on drug control, and those of a large swath of the population who elected him. It is tempting but fallacious to see the war on drugs as an earnest attempt to curb the flow and the use of drugs. Drug control policies indicate that there was and is a war on men of color, particularly in poor urban neighborhoods (Alexander, 2010).

These policies and arrests resulted in the disruption of education for large numbers of men of color and the destabilization of their families. The welfare ban on drug felons is one example. In 1996, President Clinton signed into law the Temporary Assistance for Needy Families (TANF), a program which replaced the Aid to Families with Dependent Children (AFDC). The new program changed the amount of financial assistance available to formerly incarcerated individuals who have been convicted of drug crimes. The Welfare Reform Act (Section 115) states that persons convicted of a state or federal felony offense for using or selling drugs are subject to a lifetime ban on receiving cash assistance and food stamps. No other offenses result in losing benefits (The Sentencing Project, 2002). These policies seem targeted at those who need the most help.

Today, this ideology seems to remain, but the words have changed. President Obama's 2013 budget proposed cutting services and assistance for formerly incarcerated individuals. The budget did not include federal housing mandates, giving states discretion to decide the level of assistance. In addition, there are federal bans to Supplemental Nutrition Assistance Program (SNAP), which affect the formerly incarcerated individual and his family. Such adverse policies extend as well to federal funding for school-related expenses, and restrict federal aid to anyone who has been incarcerated, on probation, on parole, or residing in a halfway house (US Department of Education, 2013).

These restrictions encourage recidivism by limiting options and support, effectively forcing young men of color into the underground economy. Consider the experience of one man we will call (pseudonym) Jah:

> I ended up doing dirt kuz I ain't have no choice. It was either I hustle 'n feed my kids, or I try to go back to school and hope the system feed me 'n my kids! That ain't no life. So, I made a choice—the wrong choice, I know, but I did what I felt was best. Then I got caught. Now I'm a felon and it's almost impossible to get a legal gig. Now I can't get a job or help.

Jah's experience is common to formerly incarcerated men, particularly those newly released. They are members of communities that have lost generations of capable men to the war on drugs. A father is incarcerated, then his son.

Education is not an option for them. Whole communities of people of color view education as the white man's dream; the same communities that need to participate in the restoration of the formerly incarcerated. These men face social, mental, and economic exile promulgated by policies that stigmatize them after incarceration (Alexander, 2010). Economic and social hardships cause culture shock when an ex-prisoner reenters society and, if he can manage it, reentry to school.

CULTURE SHOCK: RETURNING TO SCHOOL

Exiting the prison system is as scary as going in. The world that was left behind has changed; the formerly incarcerated individual has likely failed to change with it, having acclimated to prison culture. Being out of touch is frustrating and confusing. Trauma suffered during incarceration leaves mental and emotional scars that burden an individual returning to GED or fast-paced college classes. The pressure can make for an outright terrifying experience—culture shock.

The effects of war do not end with incarceration. Zai was incarcerated in his early twenties, leaving behind a son. He was sentenced to 25 years to life. When he entered prison, there were no iPods or cell phones. Zai lacked access to computers or other technology, and he feared that he could not participate in this new world. During incarceration Zai achieved a GED, which he had not been able to do outside. He had never had a trade, but in prison he learned basic skills in carpentry, barbering, and manual labor. Once he was back in the community, however, Zai found that his skills were not suited to employment in the age of technology. Given his felony record and his limited training, he could not earn enough to meet minimum living expenses. Now he wants to return to school, but has neither the time nor the foundation. He initially stayed with relatives and received welfare assistance on the condition that he work 30 or more hours a week. He is granted less than $200 a month in cash and just over $200 from SNAP. He accepts any work, most of it on call, making attending school very difficult.

Obtaining a GED

If one can manage to attend school, obtaining a GED has become a viable alternative to a high school diploma. Unfortunately, funding for GED programs either outside or inside a correctional facility is limited (Spycher, Shkodriani, & Lee, 2012), even though research has demonstrated the efficacy of correctional education programs both in reducing recidivism and in gaining future employment (Davis, Bozick, Steele, Saunders, & Miles, 2013).Therefore, many prisoners do not have the opportunity to pursue a GED. Although many take the initiative to educate themselves, the majority become discouraged. Upon release, numerous formerly incarcerated individuals avoid pursuing higher education through a GED for fear of being behind socially and academically.

The location of the adult education program or college is another source of culture shock. Many former prisoners want to attend school away from home to get away from "bad blood" in their neighborhoods. Others fear for their lives and avoid their old neighborhoods altogether. Some take long bus routes or subway rides to bypass neighborhoods where gang activity makes them vulnerable. Yet, even with these fears, for the sake of their children some opt to remain near home.

Child Care and Employment

If basic needs of employment and housing are not met, it's hard to focus on school. Some students are also parents who have to feed children and, possibly, partners. Children may motivate or de-motivate a pursuit for education; one parent may believe that his own education will provide his children a better life and a good example. Another may be discouraged by child care expenses and opt to focus solely on a full-time job. Formerly incarcerated parents may need jobs to pay court-mandated child support. Some GED programs and many colleges offer employment assistance that prepares individuals with interview training, resume writing, job fairs, and searches. However, sometimes this feels like too little too late; the obstacles of housing, employment, and child care seem insurmountable.

Not Walking Alone: Advisement and Counseling in College

Counseling is different from advisement. Counseling is emotional assistance, and it is important that men have an opportunity to receive one-on-one counseling should they desire it. Something as simple as having a person to talk to, listen, and understand can make a world of difference. Friends and teachers are good to talk to, but in some cases professional help is needed. Trauma counselors are especially trained to address post traumatic stress disorder (PTSD) and to walk the formerly incarcerated through the shock of reentry and the pains of the past.

Ex-prisoners who are working on or have obtained a GED, and want to go to college will need to negotiate academia—another new culture. Many prospective students do not know which colleges or programs are shams that will take their money while promising lofty outcomes but delivering few. These men need coaching to identify legitimate institutions. The advising process should guide GED graduates through the process of applying for college and registering for classes (National Academic Advising Association, 2006). Good academic advisement will help men find majors that suit them. A skilled advisor will give them purpose for the present and confidence for their future, encouraging them to stay on top of things while in college.

The formerly incarcerated will need assistance with social constraints. The penal system limits a person on "extended supervision" in what social engagements he can engage in and with whom. It is at this stage that the new culture outside of prison becomes an obstacle, and counseling requisite for success. An individual may have been released with conditions such as curfew; social restraints forbidding association with any individual who has a felony (family member or other); or restrictions on travel and leaving the state. These restrictions limit academic and social flexibility for meetings with tutors, advisors, classmates, professors, or just socializing with a love interest, friend, or family member.

College and Financial Support

Contributing to the culture shock are the economic realities of entering higher education. "How will I pay for it?" is a hard question to answer. Ex-prisoners can become discouraged when they try to negotiate the maze of financial aid regulations, especially because their eligibility for federal funds may be limited by the nature of their offense (U.S. Department of Education, 2013). A financial advisor who is familiar with guidelines for financial aid to the formerly incarcerated, and who will take time to discuss options, is key to academic success for them.

After enrollment, college advisors should be aware of obstacles facing the formerly incarcerated. Many students must work as well as take classes, but a felony conviction limits or excludes the formerly incarcerated from employment (Alexander, 2010). Some colleges also require students to report criminal offenses on admission applications. Advisers need to be knowledgeable about legal rights and be able to advocate for students with potential employers and college admissions officers.

A Healthy Classroom Climate

Instructors create a healthy classroom (Wood, 2010). Students will be comfortable and ready to learn in an atmosphere of acceptance, respect, enthusiasm, and freedom of expression. The formerly incarcerated will need to adjust to a non-hostile climate. In prison, inmates had to be alert for danger; now they have to learn new behaviors. Their old behaviors may be misunderstood.

One particular behavior found special resonance with the authors and several formerly incarcerated individuals: refusing to sit with your back facing the door or a blind eye to the exits. This acute awareness of surroundings can be misconstrued as disobedience, but is actually an attempt to ensure safety or to preempt a perceived attack (Schwartz, 2014).

Formerly incarcerated students may have a problem with participation because of the fear of being wrong and the need to project an image of strength that protected them in prison. They may act in ways that appear awkward, absurd, guarded, or tough.

Some young men may act out when they sense a disparity in their level of skills compared to other students. They don't lack intelligence; they are trying to comprehend what is being taught (Wunderlich, Bell, & Ford, 2005).

In addition, the formerly incarcerated are often older than the other students; this age disparity is an additional barrier to fitting in. Their prison experiences plus the age difference makes it a challenge to relate to students just out of high school. The formerly incarcerated would be considered highly non-traditional students who experience a great degree of both cultural incongruence and dissonance (Ross-Gordon, 2005) upon entering academic environments.

An instructor needs to find creative solutions to bridge disparities between prison and school behavior. The classroom climate, coupled with the instructor's zeal for his craft along with compassion, helps the formerly incarcerated to engage while still challenging them at their current level. Schwartz, in her research on engagement of young men of color in GED programs, calls the creation of these classroom climates a type of counter-space (2014). This effort is anything but easy, but the reward is great.

Gender of Instructors

An instructor may have difficulty understanding a formerly incarcerated student who brings prison defenses to the classroom. Research by Einarsson and Granström (2002) and Rodriguez (2002) explores the relationship between the gender of the teacher and its impact on student engagement However, there is less research on how the gender of an adult educator may affect some formerly incarcerated males. It is the view of the authors that male instructors may be perceived as possible threats, due to a learner's previous interactions with male police officers, prison guards, and inmates. Poverty-stricken environments are frequently like police states, and males tend to respond with aggression. The same scenario applies in prison. Prisoners who are respected are not harmed. Showing innocence and submissiveness will cause problems. Male students will not feel so threatened by female instructors.

Structure and Support in the Classroom

A class with clear expectations and goals will provide necessary structure. Men coming from prison, a very predictable, extremely structured and controlled space need structure in their lives. Establishing a code of behavior is effective classroom management. Being able to recognize the effort of the students and praising them is important for a student's progress. This is true of all students but, again, particularly for the formerly incarcerated. Learners should not be judged for a wrong answer. Making it known that it's fine to participate without being right is an effective way of learning, especially for the struggling or guarded student. Being able to use affirmation in the class creates a great environment. Words matter. Positive language promotes respect. Respecting classmates' opinions and ideas serves to motivate and creates a classroom where students and teacher agree to put their egos to the side and to accept constructive criticism.

Relationship is key. Many young men do not have individual counselors with whom they can discuss their trials around reengagement in school. In this case, the instructor becomes the counselor; there is no better way to create a deep connection with your student than an individual private session after class. This will formulate a sense of trust. Mentors and supportive relationships with faculty are crucial for many non-traditional students (Kasworm, 2002) and even more so for the formerly incarcerated.

Peers can become another support system. Adult educators can incorporate group work so that classmates can form connections that resonate with being a family. For former gang members, a new family system is essential.

Prison inmates often turn to reading to keep occupied. Reading gives inmates the opportunity to find out their history, to understand the justice system, and, most of all, to learn about who they are as individuals. Adult educators can build on that habit developed in prison by encouraging learners to continue to structure their days with time for reading. Time can be carved out in the classroom for quiet and solitary reading.

Meaningful Curriculum

Some formerly incarcerated males choose not to attend higher learning after completing a GED or high school. One such young man explained his choice this way: "Some may say the lack of funding is the reason for not further pursuing an education, but in my situation it was both the lack of funding and my dislike with the current curriculum, which is geared to Eurocentric concepts." When it comes to the teaching of history, minorities generally find themselves marginalized. Not everyone has this view, but it does raise the point of how important it is to have a relevant curriculum for students to apply to life outside of school (Ross-Gordon & Brown-Haywood, 2000; Ross-Gordon, 1998; Ladson-Billings, 1994).

THE WAR CONTINUES: THE BATTLE CAN BE WON

Leonard Cohen (1974), the Canadian singer-songwriter, declared that "There is a war between the rich and the poor. . . . There is a war between the ones who say there is a war and the ones who say there isn't." In our current educational system, the poor are often minorities and are the victims of the war on drugs and the policies associated with it. Meanwhile, those who benefit from the policies (or are unaffected by them) either don't know there is a war or support it. This reality prompts first an acknowledgment of the war, its policies, and its casualties. Then the work toward a resolution can begin. There is no better starting point than the classroom, with support from the community and commitment from the individual. The process of healing is largely in the hands of the instructors who reeducate these individuals to find their place in society.

Educators who understand the signs and symptoms of culture shock in formerly incarcerated men will be able to assure them that they are not victims, but plausible future presidents. Ultimately, it is the adult educator who can impart the knowledge that is necessary to secure a lasting future and the greatest chance at success. Adult education programs can acknowledge the needs of formerly incarcerated students, not to give them special treatment, but to minimize the effects of culture shock. Formerly incarcerated men have been through war and back. Before these eager minds can excel in the classroom, they have to survive to make it there. For this, the war must end and policies must change.

This chapter was previously published in *New Directions in Adult and Continuing Education, Swimming Upstream: Black Males in Adult Education, no. 144, Winter 2014* © *Wiley Periodicals, Inc.*

REFERENCES

Alexander, M. (2010). *The new Jim Crow: Mass incarceration in the age of colorblindness.* New York: New Press.

Armentano, P. (2010, May 13). After 40 years, $1 trillion, US war on drugs has failed to meet any of its goals. [Associated Press] http://blog.norml.org/2010/05/13/associate-press-after-40-years-1-trillion-us-war-on-drugs-has-failed-to-meet-any-of-its-goals/.

Associated Press. (2010). AP IMPACT: After 40 years, $1 trillion, US War on Drugs has failed to meet any of its goals. http://www.foxnews.com/world/2010/05/13/ap-impact-years-trillion-war-drugs-failed-meet-goals/.

Bridegland, J., Dilulio, J., & Morrison, K. (2006). *The silent epidemic: Perspectives of high-school dropouts.* Washington, DC: Civic Enterprises.

Bureau of Justice Statistics (BJS), Office of Justice Programs. (2013). Drugs and crime facts. Retrieved from http://www.bjs.gov/content/dcf/enforce.cfm.

Cohen, L. (1974). There is a war. On new skin for the old ceremony. New York: Columbia Records.

Davis, L., Bozick, R., Steele, J., Saunders, J., & Miles, J. (2013). Evaluating the effectiveness of correctional education. Prepared for the Department of Justice. Retrieved from www.bja.gov/Publications/RAND_Correctional-Education-Meta-Analysis.pdf.

Einarsson, C., & Granström, K. (2002). Gender-biased Interaction in the Classroom: The influence of gender and age in the relationship between teacher and pupil. *Scandinavian Journal of Educational Research, 46,* 117–27.

Kasworm, C. (2002). African American adult undergraduates: Differing cultural realities. *The Journal of Continuing Higher Education, 50 (1),* 10–20.

Ladson-Billings, G. (1994). *The dreamkeepers: Successful teaching for African-American students.* San Francisco: Jossey-Bass.

National Academic Advising Association (NACADA). (2006). Concept of academic advising. Retrieved from http://www.nacada.ksu.edu/Resources/Clearinghouse/View-Articles/Concept-of-Academic-Advising-a598.aspx.

National Association for the Advancement of Colored People (NAACP). (2013). Criminal justice fact sheet. http://www.naacp.org/pages/criminal-justice-fact-sheet.

Rodriguez, N. (2002). Gender differences in disciplinary approaches. Retrieved from ERIC database ED 468 259.

Ross-Gordon, J. M. (1998). Investigating the needs, concerns, and utilization of services reported by minority adults at "Eastern University." *The Journal of Continuing Higher Education, 46 (3)*, 21–33.

Ross-Gordon, J., & Brown-Haywood, F. (2000). Keys to college success as seen through the eyes of African American adult students. *The Journal of Continuing Higher Education, 48 (3)*, 14–23.

Ross-Gordon, J. M. (2005). The adult learner of color: An overlooked college student population, *The Journal of Continuing Higher Education, 53(2)*, 2–11.

Schwartz, J. (2014). Classrooms of spatial justice: Counter-spaces and young men of color in a GED program. *Adult Education Quarterly, 64*(2), 110–27.

Spycher, D., Shkodriani, G., & Lee, J. (2012). The other pipeline: From prison to diploma. Prepared for the College Board Advocacy and Policy Center. Washington, D.C. Retrieved from youngmenofcolor.collegeboard.org.

The Sentencing Project. (2002). *Life Sentences: Denying Welfare Benefits To Women Convicted Of Drug Offenses.* Washington, D.C: Allard, P.

U.S. Department of Education. (2013). Federal student aid. Incarcerated individuals and eligibility for federal student aid. Retrieved from studentaid.ed.gov/.../aid-info-for incarcerated-individuals.pdf.

vanden Heuvel, K. (2012, November 20). It's time to end the war on drugs. [*The Nation*] http://www.thenation.com/blog/171383/its-time-end-war-drugs.

Welfare Reform Act of 1996 § 115, 42 U.S.C. § 1305 (1996). Personal Responsibility and Work Opportunity Reconciliation Act of 1996. Pub. L. No. 104–193, 110 Stat. 2105 (1996).

Wood, J. (2010). *Communication mosaics: An introduction to the field of communication.* Independence, KY: Cengage.

Wunderlich, K., Bell, A., & Ford, L. (2005). Improving learning through understanding of brain science research. *Learning Abstracts, 8*(1), 41–43.

Chapter Twelve

Infinite Space and Common Ground

The Humble Wisdom of Scholar-Allies

Norman Conti and Elaine Frantz

We are "white" people who for several years have collaborated weekly with six African-American men serving life sentences to develop and implement strategies to enable reintegration by forging meaningful understandings and productive conversation between incarcerated and free Pittsburghers.[1] We have been constantly aware that we are not only developing strategies but modeling collaborative interaction between incarcerated people and those on the outside who would like to be allies to them. We have long struggled over the terms of our own collaboration, and have come to believe that setting the terms of collaboration is not just a bureaucratic problem to work through on our way to developing strategies for reintegration, but rather that developing functional terms of collaboration is the key to successful reintegration. We have gained hard-won insight that we hope may open further discussion with those engaged in similar projects and be of use to currently or recently incarcerated men and women and those who hope to be their allies.

Our think tank operates under the Inside-Out program, and our dynamics and approach are shaped by that program's philosophy. Inside-Out focusses on shifting the consciousness of each student from contentious to collaborative. Through the program, non-incarcerated (*outside*) members go through several scripted informal interactions within incarcerated *inside* members which evolve into issue-based discussions structured so as to encourage and reward mutual participation and mutual respect. That is, *inside* and *outside* members learn to converse in a structural position of equality, which is meant to destigmatize and individualize the parties: incarcerated men and women no longer appear as misfits and monsters, but as people with lives and families beyond prison walls, while college students no longer seem the willfully blind children of privilege (Davis & Roswell, 2013).

Our group began with that structure and approach (all but one of us began this work participating in an Inside-Out class) and has developed it over the years for more long-term engagement which, by their nature, will have to be more loosely structured and less policed than interactions in the courses. In this longer term, higher stakes relationship, we have found that the racial assumptions and practices we might have been able to recognize and repress in shorter interactions tend to reemerge. Often, woven into the "explicit" business we are conducting is continued group sense-making (and un-making) in which we speak to the process of collaboration itself. While our prison group does not provide a representative sample of U.S. prisoners (the prisoners are all black and male, allowing us to elide issues faced by incarcerated women and non-black prisoners, and we are "white," so we have a different set of issues than might an ally of color), we have all been deeply moved by this process, which we believe models reintegration.

In addition to the powerful framework provided by Inside-Out, our understanding of the challenges faced by African American prisoners and their "white" allies in achieving meaningful integration is inspired by two thinkers: sociologist Erving Goffman, who decades ago theorized stigma and moral career, and Tony Gaskew, a scholar-activist who recently developed a "Humiliation to Humility" model for the identity self-transformation of incarcerated men and women.

STIGMA, MORAL CAREERS, AND HUMILITY

When we attempt to build and maintain a substantial collaboration, to "reintegrate" prisoners and allies into an egalitarian community, one of the key barriers we face is stigma. Stigma is a process "entirely contingent on access to social, economic, and political power that allows the identification of differentness, the construction of stereotypes, the separation of the labeled persons into distinctive categories, and the full execution of disapproval, rejection, and discrimination" (Link & Phelan, 2001, p. 367). Loury (2002) developed a conception of "racial stigma" that explains both the historic and present mistreatment of African Americans. Others have noted that stigmatic narratives are institutionalized within the social imagery that facilitates racism (Bloor, 1991, p. 5) and African Americans have to dismantle those belief systems within their own minds in order to establish positive identities (Howard, Flennaugh, & Terry, 2012, p. 93). Incarceration, of course, poses its own even stronger stigma, which, in our society, is closely interrelated with racial stigma.

Most unincarcerated people comfortably construct and maintain a racist belief system to which stigmatization is central. Some, however, either by choice or circumstance, have or develop personal ties to the stigmatized which force or enable them to identify with them. Goffman calls these *the wise*: "persons who are normal but whose special situation has made them intimately privy to the secret life of the stigmatized individual and sympathetic with it, and who find themselves accorded a measure of acceptance, a measure of courtesy membership in the clan" (1963, p. 28). Often, *wisdom* results from working and eventually identifying with and becoming conversant in the discourse of the stigmatized, thus allowing them to feel *normal* in their presence.

Failing to join in a common cultural stigmatization transforms the *normal's* identity. Goffman defines the process through which some *normal* become *wise* as a "moral career"—a series of changes "in the person's self and his framework of imagery for judging himself and others" (1961, p. 128). The *normals* who go through this process come to understand themselves, and gain the status of *the wise* through their apparent special knowledge of stigmatized people (1963, p. 28). Goffman cautions, however, that such well-meaning people "can in fact make both the stigmatized and the *normal* uncomfortable" by confronting them with seeming self-righteousness (1963, p. 30).

In *Rethinking Prison Reentry: Transforming Humiliation into Humility*, Tony Gaskew develops this idea in his critique of Inside-Out and its training program. As *normals* (in this case, "white" academics) enter into teaching roles, they often understand their work through the lens of their own moral growth and social capital, at the expense of focusing on the needs of the stigmatized population they are there to serve. Many people are fascinated by deviance and tend to impute to stigmatized people some special wisdom, so connection to those worlds offers us cache that can advance us in our social as well as professional lives. If hubris and opportunism drives us to position ourselves as experts or as moral examplars (i.e., using our connection to the stigmatized merely to elevate ourselves above other *normal*), we fall into the subcategory of *the hip*. Since *the hip* sees themselves as the heroes in a tale of intellectual or moral development, they must control the group's trajectory and meaning-making, interrupting the group's authentic conversation.

The self-focus of *the hip* shapes their expectations and behavior in interacting with *inside* students. Lacking a substantial and intentional orientation to the experience or contribution of *inside* students, such white would-be allies prevent the authentic voicing of "the multiple narratives of the collective lived black American experience" (Gaskew, 2014, p. 151). Too often, such encounters stink of "academicians hiding behind white privilege" (Gaskew, 2014, p. 154).

[White allies] subconsciously bring with them the pedagogical baggage of white privilege, playing the social "messiah" for everything that is wrong regarding incarcerated black men, the criminal justice system, and their relationship with the black American experience. Contributing to a modern day "white man's burden"—the urge of white Americans to "educate and civilize" incarcerated black students became an unwavering perceptual reality and one that I did not want to perpetuate. The quagmire becomes, "How can a white scholar who has never lived the collective black American experience become the *pedagogical authentic voice* of a post-secondary education experience or offer any advice of critical substance directed to incarcerated black student, without bringing with them the *socially constructed lie*, of four hundred years of white privilege?" (Gaskew, 2014, pp. 152–53)

Our path through Gaskew's quagmire is illuminated by an inversion of his Humiliation to Humility Perspective (HHP). According to Gaskew, in order to regain agency and authority in relationships with non-stigmatized people, incarcerated black Americans must move from "humiliation" to "humility." That is, they must consciously reject the structural denigration of their identity, and therefore, their worlds, and come to understand themselves as equally capable participants in meaning-making as their non-stigmatized peers.

Because of the dialogical relationship between the humiliation of African American men within our criminal justice system and the hubris of white *messiahs* seeking to educate and civilize them, *outside* members in conversation with *inside* members should go through a parallel process. We should contemplate and acknowledge that "a white scholar who has never lived the collective black American experience" *will* carry "the socially constructed lie, of four hundred years of white privilege," into our attempts at critical race activism. And we must further acknowledge that this devalues and corrupts our meaning-making, which can only be redeemed to the extent that our stigmatized colleagues are willing to authentically and critically engage and rework it in collaboration with us. Just as incarcerated individuals must move from humiliation to humility, so "white" allies must move from hubris to humility.

As Gaskew points out, the Inside/Out program itself is vulnerable to this privileging of whiteness: It constructs a carefully regulated egalitarian discursive space, but sets up (usually white) teachers, structurally positioned as though above and outside the process, to police the space. A better model, and one that our own think tank has found ourselves stumbling toward, is one in which the *outside* member is always in a state of radical interactive community-building and meaning-making with the *inside* members. Rather than *hip*, such a white ally is *humble* in Tony Gaskew's sense. If we approach our experiences with the stigmatized with humility, seeking to learn and work together as allies in the struggle for social justice, and acknowledging that we may not be most fit to understand where that struggle should go, then we rise to the level of *the humble*. This approach is fundamentally collaborative: *The humble* see themselves as one of many equal voices living the experiences with allies rather than imposing their own narrative on the situation.

NOTHING IS GOOD OR BAD, BUT THINKING MAKES IT SO

Our attempt to be white allies without falling into the traps of self-impor-tance or *hip* identity began with a series of Inside-Out courses offered behind the walls of State Correctional Institution Pittsburgh. The classes attracted 15 incarcerated men (i.e., *inside* students) selected to spend two semesters stud-ying criminal justice, philosophy, and sociology with university undergradu-ates (i.e., *outside* students). The following summer, we formed an Inside-Out think tank at the prison. Each of our incarcerated partners has been convicted of murder. The oldest two have been incarcerated since the 1970s and the youngest for a decade. While all of them passionately hope for eventual parole or commutation, none has concrete grounds to expect ever to be re-leased from prison. Nevertheless, they see one of their major functions (both as individual older, more experienced men living in the prison and as group members) as helping other incarcerated men to prepare to readjust to life outside prison. That the process of collaboration has never been easy is illustrated by the fact that over the years we have lost nine of these members, in part through disagreements that we failed to resolve. Yet the work contin-ued.

The challenge of collaboration was present from the start: inspired by the work of groups like *Shakespeare Behind Bars* and *Prison Performing Arts*, the first author wanted to call our group the *Elsinore Think Tank*. Illustrating the folly of revenge, *Hamlet* seemed to resonate for a group focused on restorative justice. However, in an early meeting, Malakki, one of our *inside* members, objected, pointing out that *Hamlet* is an artifact of European cul-ture and Elsinore was a castle, while most of our group is of African descent and—at least for him—the prison is nothing like a castle. Malakki offered suggestions for alternative names including "The Bennu" (i.e., a predecessor to the phoenix from Egyptian mythology). After some negotiation, we settled on *Elsinore Bennu Think Tank* (EBTT), as an intercontinental resolution. These early discussions were crucial in establishing our working relation-ship. We all had a stake in this group: whatever we built, we were going to build together.

As "white" allies coming from the privileged world of higher education, we saw our goal in creating the think tank as ethical and other-directed: we wanted to work with these men to establish a more sustainable model of civic engagement, but our incarcerated colleagues were keenly aware of all of our personal stakes in the project. Faruq, a member, describes himself as motivated by "the self-righteousness of proving *them* wrong, smirking while showing that *ah ha* look, I am more than you thought I am a decent human being worthy of consideration and capable of change and improvement" (private correspondence). Or, as Oscar put it, "The EBTT allows me to become human, Even if only on Fridays" (private correspondence).

As Malakki (a member), explains:

> A life sentence in the state of Pennsylvania means a social death. Because we have been found guilty of taking another life, we have lost the right to have a social life. But we still live. We breathe and love and hate and have OK days and better days. So my questions are: Is life without parole enough of a punishment? And should there be a more just sentence? . . . Now there is one thing I want you to consider: the power of human endurance. The victims' loved ones must carve a new meaning of life from what's left behind. Many refuse to let the perpetrator win. Physical death can cause the emotional death of others, so those that stand strong in defense of their dignity should be commended.
>
> But, we, the doomed, also endure. There are those of us that accept the call to darkness and inevitably flash and tumble into the jaws of oblivion. When this happens, we lose the few pieces of us that still keep us loosely defined as part of humanity and become the ultimate human hyenas. Others fight back. Incarcerated men who share our agenda use meager scraps of self-determination sewn together with shreds of dignity and inflated with hints of hope to float above the depths of the living dead.
>
> . . . It was wrong for me to take another's life and in my opinion, I deserve to suffer a social death. But what if I can stop the same anti-social, venal, monster that enticed me to a bad decision from possessing someone else? Shouldn't part of my sentence be to stand in defense against what I've done and act against it ever happening again?
>
> The inmates we mentor here have already committed crimes, and our goal is to prevent more damage to the social structure once they leave. But what if people like us serve as "medics" to the dispossessed *before* another trial, hospital visit, or funeral? Think about it? We can't just continue to follow the status quo and assume that handcuffs cure criminal hearts and continue to let the violent, greedy, and pushy cycle through the steps of their damage plan. For the Elsinore-Bennu, our resurrection comes at a cost, and our role in this think tank is our best attempt at restorative justice. That's what [Elsinore-Bennu] means to us.

These *inside* members illustrate what is at the heart of our alliance: in engaging in collaborative restorative justice, each member transforms him or herself. *Inside* members gain voice, agency, and effectiveness. They hunger for authorship and authority. For them, the very existence of the think tank, and its ability to move our ideas into the public discourse, is an end it itself. Making meaning remakes men, and remade men restore a broken outside society.

But how are *outside* members remade? As privileged white *normals,* we have the opposite problem from the *inside* members: our positions within a respected university allow us to take our voice for granted. We expect to be invited to weigh in on important social issues, and are accustomed to being listened to. Our danger is the constant urge to offer answers even when we have none. The group does not give us a rare opportunity to speak, but simultaneously gives us knowledge and reminds us to question the notion that we alone have something to say. Working with men whose daily experience of incarceration will not allow them to forget the consequences of crime and injustice perpetually re-centers us in our efforts to do more and make something better. The challenge, however, is to recognize that we will only satisfy our needs if we satisfy theirs: we will only have content to the extent that they have voice. As Khalifa, a member of our group, has written, we together aim to "establish a sincere vanguard for social justice through dialogue, research, and active partnerships" (Khalifa, Restorative Justice, 2016).

Our meetings have changed substantially due to the response of *inside* members, who have over time become more than willing to question our motivations, criticize the tone, content, or organization of the meeting, and simply exit with their feet when things are not going in a way that works for them. Over the years, after much of this trial, error, dissent, and critique, we have developed a system that empowers *inside* members as collaborators and discourages *outside* members from falling into ego traps. First, we put in the time. Collaboration is hard work: we meet for two always-intense hours every week. And we bring our authentic and vulnerable selves to the table. Both *inside* and *outside* members spend time at each meeting sharing information not only about our achievements and pleasures, but about our anxieties, shortcomings, and failures. *Inside* members then can take the role of consoling, encouraging, giving advice, and sharing victories.

Second, the meetings are generally unstructured, to allow for the group to find its own shape. Group members claim space within the meeting by raising their voices. Some bring writings to read aloud—they signal that they want to read them by pulling them out and placing them on the table. Often they simply jump in. Frequently, a group member will raise a concern about what we are or are not talking about in the meeting, and ask that we go in a different direction. From time to time, the group has asked one of its *inside* members, Fly, a particularly organized and pragmatic man, to serve as a timekeeper and agenda enforcer. The most productive, intellectually generative times in the group have often been when the group took off in a direction the *outside* members did not expect.

Third, to enable the *inside* members' authentic contributions, both of us had to change or let go of some of our own priorities. Collaboration is slow, so projects do not always move at the pace that would best fit the pace of our professional requirements. We have an "open floor" ethic of conversation: we do not take turns and we do not strive to allow each person equal time to speak. Rather, each person, once s/he gains the floor, speaks as long as he/she has something to say. At first, this could feel uncomfortable, as some men would speak at considerable length. But soon we noticed other *inside* members were having no problem patiently following long monologues: we realized that this structure of conversation was natural within the context of the prison, where time for discussion was abundant, and where men had things they were deeply committed to fully expressing. Key to the process of moving from "humiliated" to "humble" is to claim, and exercise, the right to speak, and to keep speaking.

Fourth, we learned to follow the lead of the *inside* members in determining who spoke when, as often happened, multiple people were angling to jump in. There are a few group members who are particularly charismatic, and oriented toward community-building. Shawn, in particular, will often intervene on behalf of both *inside* and *outside* members who seem to want to speak, pointing or gesturing toward them. Some members are more readily listened to than others, and sometimes tensions between members of the think tank will cause certain people's words to be more and others less welcome. *Outside* members have learned to use our own positions as equal individuals in the group to try to smooth over these (as *inside* members have done for *outside* members when we experienced tensions among ourselves), but we also respect that these structures and priorities are serving functions important to their internal culture, and individual personality needs that we do not always understand.

Fifth, we also work to remain cognizant of what *inside* members cannot or will not say. As men under the direct physical control of the prison system, and who live their daily lives among their fellow prisoners, they must be constantly aware of how their speech and meaning-making in the group impacts their relationship with fellow prisoners and also with prison guards and administrators. Tuned in to the power structures under which they live, they are best equipped to determine which battles are, and which are not worth fighting, to locate moments of structural opportunity for change, and to knowingly shake their heads when a given idea is simply not going to work. A guard is usually present to monitor our meetings. But we also recognize that they cannot, will not, and should not always entirely trust us as well-meaning allies with our own limitations, weaknesses, and failures of vision. Not infrequently, an *inside* member will announce that he chooses not to talk about something, or, less explicitly, will be obviously navigating around a subject he does not consider useful, or safe, to discuss. Part of their claim of agency is determining where, and where not, to collaborate.

Sixth, we humbly accept the fact that the men frequently kindly but firmly reject our ideas: initially, Norm wanted the men to become "convict criminologists" and document their personal transitions from the culture of street crime to their roles as incarcerated activists. However, he was unable to effectively organize the project or make it seem meaningful to the men, so they chose to pass on the opportunity. Elaine wanted the group to work on a history-themed project, but the men declined. *Outside* members acknowledge that we have interests and priorities of our own. We bring up, and *inside* members ask us, how the work we are doing in prison meets our own professional and personal agendas. We note when we have won grants or gained advantages or publicity due to our work with them, and are painfully conscious of the injustice in the fact that we have so many privileges and advantages that we cannot share with them. And all of us acknowledge one another as flawed individuals with whom we are in solidarity. We have a culture of teasing, in which all of us, inside and out, have particular quirks and shortcomings that other members nudge us about, but in a way that acknowledges our solidarity, interdependence, and common humanity.

The culture we have built is not perfect: we have lost members, had conflicts, missed opportunities. But we believe that it works remarkably well. And it works as it does only because the *outside* members are comfortable radically sharing control over both meaning-making and group priorities and *inside* members are willing to risk authentically investing themselves in the collaboration. Were *outside* members committed to the promotion of their own *hip* agendas or *inside* members unwilling to take the chance of investing in the group in the hope that their voice would be heard, the group would have failed.

Upon reading an earlier draft of this chapter, a few of our *inside* members took serious issue with our using the term "deviants" and asked if that is how we saw them. We explained that it was a term of art in sociology, and talked about its use in the field. They countered that, nevertheless, in using that label on them, we were defining them in a degrading way that would, in some way, adhere. The hour-long discussion that followed fundamentally called into question whether the project of making them subjects of academic inquiry served their ends, or only our own professional goals. In the end, the term "deviants" went.

BOUND IN A NUTSHELL

In conclusion, we reflect back on the initial naming of our group as part of our ongoing transition into "the humble wise." This early moment in our alliance illustrates how "white" allies may enter into a relationship with an incarcerated group and discard the stigmatic narrative imposed by the larger society, and seek to replace it with one of his/her own creation. Yet the process can still be problematic. The privileged intellectuals are imagining themselves as reverse-engineering the Stanford Prison Experiment in order to turn a prison into a university. While this is an admirable goal, it is hubris that places them in the starring role in a production imposed upon the other actors.

Hamlet argues that Denmark, and by extension the world, is a prison. A friend challenges him on this by arguing that he is more a prisoner to his own ambition than to Denmark. Hamlet replies that he could be "bound in a nutshell and still count [him]self king of infinite space" if it weren't for the bad dreams. We were discussing this line as a potential title for an edited volume we are building, when Malakki asked us if we understood how all space could be infinite. He explained that if you tried to move from wherever you were to the nearest wall in increments that were 50% of the total distance between you and the wall (i.e., half way at a time), you would never get there. Since we were a group of *white free* and *black incarcerated* sharing a dialogic space within a prison, there was a pause as we absorbed this idea. In that space, we could not help but recognize how solidly this idea holds for people living beyond the prison as well. If we imagine the chasm of race as a socially constructed barrier between human beings, it is easy to understand how even with perpetual fifty-percent closures along a more level playing field, when we are bound by the concept of race we can never fully join with one another. In all truth, the only way to shatter our socio-biological illusions and achieve meaningful unity is for people to abandon hubris and embrace the hard work of collaboration.

NOTE

1. We also work with Remi Annunziato, Maggie McGannon, and Steven Stept. Prison officials and guards are also necessary collaborators in this process, both in bureaucratically enabling it to go forward and in creating a safe atmosphere in which it could occur. We put "white" in quotation marks to point to the constructed nature of whiteness. Our African-American group members strongly prefer that the term "African American" not be put in quotation marks, as they feel that their racial reality is concrete indeed.

REFERENCES

Bloor, D. (1991). *Knowledge and social imagery*. Chicago: University of Chicago Press.

Conti, N., Morrison, L., & Pantaleo, K. (2013). "All the Wiser: Dialogic Space, Destigmatization and Teacher-Activist Recruitment." *The Prison Journal*, 93(2): 162–87.

Davis, S., & Roswell, B. (2013). *Turning teaching inside out: A pedagogy of transformation for community-based education*. New York: Palgrave MacMillan.

Gaskew, T. (2014). *Rethinking prison reentry: Transforming Humiliation into Humility*. Lanham, MD: Lexington Books.

Goffman, E. (1961). *Asylums: Essays on Mental Patients and other Inmates*. New York: Simon and Schuster.

Goffman, E. (1963). *Stigma: Notes on the Management of Spoiled Identity*. New York: Simon and Schuster.

Howard, T. C., Flennaugh, T. K., & Terry, C. L. (2012). "Black Males, Social Imagery, and The Disruption of Social Identities: Implications for Research and Training. "*Educational foundation* (Winter–Spring): 85–102.

Khalifa, Restorative Justice. (2016). Participants personal written communication.

Link, B. G., & Phelan, J. C. (2001). Conceptualizing Stigma. *Annual Review of Sociology*, 27: 363–85.

Loury, G. C. (2002). *The Anatomy of Racial Inequality*. Cambridge, MA: Harvard University Press.

Chapter Thirteen

A College Initiative Success Story

Terrance Coffie and John R. Chaney

One crisp February morning in 2006 I (John) was one of a half dozen graduates of the Rikers Island Fresh Start program (Wynn, 2001) privileged to take part in a memorable meeting with Benay Rubenstein, cofounder of the College Initiative (CI). Held in CI's original midtown Manhattan headquarters our small group, now members of a small reentry support group known as the Eagles Foundation, had heard from our reentry peers about this innovative new organization. Barely four years old, CI had earned recognition as a reliable reentry resource, offering returning citizens assistance navigating the bureaucratic and fiscal quagmire of college admissions. CI utilized a holistic approach to guide and support formerly incarcerated individuals in planning, preparing for, applying to, and financing a college education. Additionally, CI also develop a strong network of partners that assisted its students with wraparound services including access to job readiness training and employment, housing and health services, and even resources for the family. Some of us knew personally a number of the program's outstanding graduates and had begun to understand how CI had developed into a respected counterspace. We then met Benay Rubenstein, a leading prison educator for over 25 years who had designed and directed a number of college programs within the corrections system. She founded the CI in 2002, developing it as a user-friendly reentry education program for men and women in the New York City metropolitan area who wanted to begin or continue their higher education after release from prison or jail.

Over 60% of CI's students were black men, and the organization had made a special point of having its administrative and counseling staff reflect the population it served. Additionally, productive linkages had been made with responsible neighborhood organizations located in the very same areas where many of their students resided. The goal of our inexperienced but

143

*energetic group that day was to explore the possibility of the Eagles develop-
ing a permanent partnership with this organization. Unfortunately, such
would not be the case for our fledgling group that was enthusiastic and well-
meaning, but back then had precious little expertise to offer. A wonderful
consolation, however, would be our attendance and eager participation for
CI's class of 2006 graduation ceremony. The program continued to produce
some of the city's most outstanding college graduates, many who later became leading voices, advocating better access to even more educational
opportunities for men of color; graduates like Terrance Coffie. The following
narrative illustrates how CI has created a fertile counterspace that fostered
both the personal and professional growth for Mr. Coffie, one of the thousands of returning citizens determined to reverse the cycle of recidivism
through education.*

I earned my GED while in Florida's Gainesville Correctional Institution.
Until then, the only thing I had ever "achieved" was completing two prison
sentences. When I enrolled in the prison educational program, it wasn't because I had some internal belief that my life could improve. My introduction
to education had come from a career criminal, Chin. Chin was someone
young men refer to as an OG (Original Gangsta); he was from another era of
time, but had survived the street life and maintained the code of the streets. I
mention Chin because my relationship with him taught me the fundamental
concept of mentoring. He was someone I admired and respected, so when he
encouraged me to enroll in school, it was a catch twenty-two. On one hand, I
wanted to be like him, an OG, but at the same time the very man I sought to
emulate was encouraging me not to waste my life. A mentor need not have
any form of traditional education, per se, but he must have the ability to
connect with the individual and inspire action. His role in my life was somewhat of a surrogate father. This coincides with a report issued by the Association for Supervision and Curriculum Development's (ASCD) Empowering
Black Males Organization:

> The reality is, approximately 50 percent of black children in the United States
> live in households without a father figure present . . . Who is going to provide
> black male students with the proper male guidance, direction, leadership, and
> structure that they desperately need to fulfill their own potential and who are
> also committed to the growth and development of the younger generation? If
> students had men in their lives whom they could relate to and identify with,
> they would look at their education differently and the probability for their
> success would increase exponentially. (Kafele, 2012)

I never had the opportunity to thank my friend for his encouragement and
support. By the time I had earned my GED, Chin had been transferred to
another institution. His influence played a significant role in my future en-
deavors.

I dropped out of high school at age 17 and by age 18 I began selling drugs. Without a high school diploma my options for employment and educational opportunities were greatly affected as noted in an Alliance for Education article:

> Black men, in particular, face enormously dim prospects when they fail to complete high school. More than one-third (37 percent) of black male dropouts between the ages of 20 and 34 are currently behind bars. This exceeds the share of young black male dropouts who have a job (26 percent). Thus, as adults in their twenties and early thirties . . . black men without a high school diploma are more likely to be found in a cell than in the workplace. (Amos, 2010)

I knew nothing of statistical data that reflected the reality I was living. What I do remember is attempting to seek employment, but finding that most jobs required a high school diploma. My dilemma was not uncommon; the same report by Alliance for Education goes on to say, "the astronomical jobless rates for black men in inner-city neighborhoods are both mind-boggling and heartbreaking. There are many areas where virtually no one has a legitimate job" (Amos, 2010). Like many others, I had been taught the value of education and the idea that hard work leads to a promising life, but since I was a high school dropout, black and poor, that idea was just that, an idea.

When I learned I passed my GED test, there was a sense of disbelief, joy, and a hope of a promising life. On some level I accepted my life for what it was; I had dropped out of school, I did sell drugs, so this entire situation was my fault, right? Whether the statistical data I previously mentioned were confirmed or not I didn't know; what I did know was that I had earned my GED! And with that came the hope of a better life: a good job, college, and a future.

A NEW ERA

For any person being released from prison, the night prior to one's release is full of anticipation and anxiety. It is probably the most sleepless night you may have outside of your first night being incarcerated. For me, all those feelings applied, but I also possessed something else: hope. Malcolm X once said, "Education is the passport to tomorrow's future for those who prepare for it today." I relished in the fact that I had earned my GED, I savored the knowledge that I had used my time productively. I also relished in the fact that I had the key to a better life: education. During my last night in prison, I looked at my GED and believed I would never return to prison again. However, I did not take into consideration, but would learn later: I was an ex-felon. The first three days of my release I began going over my plan of action. I read somewhere that if you do not have a plan, then you are planning to fail. After my first two prior releases from prison, I had nothing to plan with or for. But having earned my GED this time opened doors of possibilities that no prison wall could contain. I don't mean to put such emphasis on how I felt in regards to earning my GED, but you must realize that for many years prior to earning my GED, I felt like a failure and feared my life would be doomed to a lifetime of disappointment, mediocrity, and incarceration. Earning my GED was like being exonerated from years of letdowns; all the opportunities that I was once locked out of seemed accessible.

I recall my first job interview. I have been happy about a lot of deviant things: copping my first ounce of cocaine, evading the police, waking up from a drunken stupor. But I must admit there was no greater joy than when I received that application. I vividly remember being excited to answer the question regarding my academic requirement for the position: Do you have a High School Diploma or GED? Yes. I also remember answering the question that asked "Have you ever been convicted of a crime?" To be perfectly honest, I really didn't give the question any thought, I answered yes to the question just as freely as I answered the others. I note this because up to this point the only barrier I encountered, or thought mattered, was that of my education. Besides, I had used my time constructively while incarcerated and if nothing else, I had earned my GED. After completing my application, I imagined discussing my future goals, my desire to enroll in college, I even thought about how firmly I would shake the hiring manager's hand to thank him for this opportunity. Before I could finish my thoughts, I was informed the manager would see me. I walked in, nervous, but confident. We greeted one another cordially but I was not prepared for what he said next: "I see you have been incarcerated, would you like to explain that?" I was really taken back. I wasn't prepared to answer his question, at least not as the first question. After I made a feeble attempt to explain my criminal conviction, he then said to me that due to company policy he would not be able to hire me but would keep my application on file. Not once did he ever ask me about my academic achievement.

The Equal Employment Opportunity Commission (EEOC) said that while employers may legally consider criminal records in hiring decisions, a policy that excludes all applicants with a conviction could violate employment discrimination laws because it could have a disparate impact on racial and ethnic minorities. In publishing its extended guidance to employers, the agency made clear that employers were prohibited from treating applicants with the same criminal records differently because of their race, color, religion, sex, or national origin (Greenhouse, 2012).

Years later in June 2016 I would actually testify at the signing of the Fair Chance Act making it illegal for New York City employers to ask potential job applicants about their criminal backgrounds. I wish I could say that when I began the transition process I possessed the same drive and determination that drives me today. Unfortunately, I did not; as I continued to encounter rejection after rejection, my determination began to dissolve. I had been taught my entire life that the key of education would open the doors of opportunity, but it was not available to me. A new unwritten sign had been posted: ex-felons not allowed. It would be another 14 years, numerous failures, homelessness, three more prison bids, and the election of this country's first black president before I would reengage in the academic arena.

By the time I was 39 years old, I had been sentenced to prison six times, was homeless and broken mentally, physically, and spiritually by the ravages of poverty, with no foreseeable means of escape. One jarring event would reignite my hope: the 2008 presidential election. I wish I could recall every detail that led up to his election on that night, but I do remember being in another correctional institution. I distinctly remember the announcement that Barack Obama had won the presidential election, becoming the forty-fourth president of the United States of America. I remember various news outlets from around the world broadcasting this historical event, seeing the faces of young blacks on college campuses cheering, the tears of older blacks reflecting on all the years of slavery, Jim Crow, the civil rights, witnessing a moment in time none of us ever thought we would see. And there I was sitting in a prison, crying in my own state of astonishment, disbelief, and regret because, like Chin had warned, I felt I had wasted my life. I knew on that night the world changed in a way that was quite evident, but another change had occurred that was not as evident sitting in that dayroom.

COLLEGE INITIATIVE: A STEPPING-STONE

Today I am a graduate student at New York University, as well as the College Pathways Advisor for The Doe Fund, a transitional housing program providing resources for the homeless and formerly incarcerated. The greatest influence on my academic journey has been my relationship with College Initiative (CI). CI creates pathways from criminal justice involvement to college careers. One of the most interesting aspects about CI is that nearly 70 percent of the staff are formerly incarcerated people who have achieved academic success, which is probably the most significant component of CI. My advisor was a beautiful woman named Cheryl Wilkins, who shared with me her journey. She spoke of the many challenges that I also felt, but, more importantly, she shared with me the measures she took to address them. Another important aspect of the CI program is how the organization walks you through each phase of the enrollment process, from financial aid and selecting a school, to making sure that you have all the necessary tools needed to have a successful academic experience, which included pairing you with a mentor. The mentorship component was integral. My mentor not only assisted me in my academic transition, but also consulted and advised me on personal matters unique to transitioning back into society. This pairing reminded me of my relationship with Chin. My mentor would contact me to see how I was doing, inquired about my enrollment process, and invited me to events. There were several occasions I attended academic conferences that highlighted academic achievements of formerly incarcerated individuals and the work they were doing to help others. These experiences, along with my involvement with CI, inspired me to believe that I could face life's challenges and succeed, which meant not going back to prison.

According to a Loyola University study, "recidivism rates in the United States are about 60%. The Bureau of Justice Statistics conducted a longitudinal study over a 5-year time span of inmates released in 2005 and found among the prisoners from the thirty states that participated, 67.8% were rearrested for a felony or serious misdemeanor within 3 years and 76.9% were rearrested within 5 years after release" (Hill, 2015).

Prior to my involvement with The Doe Fund and CI, I found myself rearrested constantly and sentenced to prison just as consistently. I don't deny my involvement in criminal activity that led to my numerous incarcerations, but neither do I deny the fact that economic and educational opportunities were being denied to me and countless others due to our criminal backgrounds. In a 2013 report by Rand Corporation, "researchers found that inmates who participate in educational programs have 43 percent lower odds of returning to prison than those who do not." The last thing I wanted to do again was to go back to prison. I applied and was accepted to Bronx Community College (BCC)(I still have the acceptance letter framed on my wall). In a study from the Center for Collaborative Classrooms, Dr. Eric Schaps writes, "that supportive schools and groups foster positive outcomes by promoting students' sense of "connectedness." College Initiative gave me the support and encouragement I needed to walk on that campus that first day. It was the most liberating moment I had in the last 20 years.

In 2009, the reins of College Initiative's executive leadership had been transferred to Michael Carey, an outstanding reentry educator who actually began his association with CI as a volunteer. Founder of the Interdependence Prison Project, Mr. Carey also facilitated the design of CI's innovative peer mentoring program that continues today. Trained CI peers with exceptional grades and firsthand knowledge of the criminal justice system are strategically paired with new students, with these personalized interventions giving highly individualized support. This mentoring component was a key factor leading to an increase in the first-to-second-year retention rates among CI students. Mr. Carey continued to nurture productive linkages with outstanding community-based organizations, including the Fortune Society and the Black Male Initiative, the City University of New York project directed by Elliot Dawes (see Foreword). He would form a lasting bond with Terrance Coffie that would result in professional collaborations and inspiring Mr. Coffie's development of the College Pathways program.

In December 2013 I (JC) was honored to moderate a panel consisting of distinguished College Initiative graduates entitled Education After Incarceration held at Medgar Evers College. Later in July 2015, CI merged with The Prisoner Reentry Institute at John Jay College of Criminal Justice under the college's Educational Initiatives program where it continues in operation today.

HOPES AND DREAMS

My academic career began at age 40. By the time I had completed my first two semesters, I had become more comfortable with my academic abilities. A great deal of my apprehension in regard to school was my lack of confidence; was I smart enough, bright enough, or anything enough? It was one of the reasons I was inspired when I earned my GED; but this was college. For me in all honesty doing well was very simple: don't fail any classes. I spoke with various members of CI and my mentor, who felt the field of social work would be a great place for me to build a career. The curriculum and my first semester were challenging; the idea of being a non-traditional student concerned me on many levels: being formerly incarcerated, working full time, and being nearly double the age of my fellow classmates was daunting. But these challenges also reflected the value of my relationship with CI, which prepared me to deal with these encounters as they arose. The most significant lesson I absorbed, which helped me tremendously, was embracing the value that my life lessons could bring to my classroom experiences. I established relationships with my classmates who were just as beneficial and helpful to me. Initially, I felt that they were so young that we would not have any common interest, but I soon learned we had more in common than differences. In those students, I saw a part of me that had gotten lost years ago: hope. I began to share with them the value of their lives and futures, and subsequently began to find the value of my own life. College Initiative provided me the opportunity to train in the capacity of a mentor. This opportunity was yet another pivotal point of my life. Helping traditional students was rewarding and beneficial, but to assist men coming from similar backgrounds of incarceration to reach their own level of success was truly a humbling moment. In my first year as a mentor I was assigned two mentees, and, like my mentor, I became very engaged with their lives and academic careers. The highlight of my mentorship career would be the semester that both my mentees and I made the Dean's List.

FINDING ME

Between work, school, and studying, I really can't remember anything else except finals and grades. Through the first semester I was learning a lot about myself, my study habits, and time management. After completing that semester and finals, I was just happy that I had completed the semester. I share this story as an indication of the influence that CI and my fellow peers had on my academic outcome. After my first semester, grades had not been posted as of yet. I felt I had done well enough to pass my classes, but was concerned. Throughout this time I drove my mentor, colleagues, and staff at CI crazy with my concerns and questions. I was fighting demons of failure from the past, but the support and encouragement that the CI gave me when I began this journey, was the same supportive encouragement they continued to give me at this point. When I learned that grades had been posted, I remember taking a deep breath, and opening the portal, A, A, B+, A. When I first saw my grades, I thought that Bronx Community College had somehow made a mistake. I wanted to call them to let them know, but somewhere during that semester year I had heard that if they make a mistake, they will catch it, and fix it. So, over those next 24 hours, I would check my Ossess account, literally 20 times, and even though they would catch the mistake, it was nice to just look at the grades, in a nostalgic hope. When I finally realized I had in fact scored my grades, there was a moment of utter gratitude and reflection over my entire life: things my mother had said to me, things teachers had said to me, things society had said to me, but also things CI had said to me. The main thing that stood out the most was Cheryl Wilkins, my intake specialist, who said, "I see you doing some great things." At the time she said this to me, I don't think I actually believed her, but I wanted to.

ALONG THE WAY

During my tenure at BCC I took an active role in my academic career, I became a member of CUNY's Black Male Initiative, a program designed to help young men of color succeed academically. I was awarded numerous awards such as: being selected to The Presidents' Roundtable Men of Color Student Leadership Institute 2012, 2013. I was selected to attend the International Study Program, held in Salzburg, Austria, and named a Global Fellow. I was later inducted into the Phi Theta Kappa Honor Society in 2013. I would then go on to be named to the 2013 Coca Cola and New York State All-Academic Team as a Gold Scholar, and in 2014 the NYACCE Student of the Year. My participation in CI would allow me the opportunity to participate in various venues such as the New York Reentry Network's, Transitional Talk, the Vera Institute of Justice Committee, and Columbia University's Transitional Study Committee. In May of 2014, I would graduate from Bronx Community College. I consider my graduation from BCC as my moment of self-actualization. When I think back on it today, I see it as a time of redemption for my own insolvencies in life. It can also become a time of absolution for those who believed in the value of education as a transformative means to alter one's life chances. Perhaps it can create an avenue that leads to success, a success not only defined by not returning to prison, but one in which the individual ascends to a level of academic attainment that renders oppressive ideas, research and theories, erroneous.

CI was the critical factor in my academic success. The fact that the organization's front-line representatives had once themselves been incarcerated challenged my deep-rooted beliefs that success was not possible. Being inundated with story after story of individuals who had achieved against all the stereotypical beliefs was my first step toward success. Secondly, the supportive network CI creates around the student seemingly insulates any counterproductive notions or ideas. In addition, I was deeply impacted by the ongoing support and acknowledgment by CI through events like the annual awards ceremonies, highlighting each member's academic successes. This builds a "communitive" spirit among the students themselves, which only enhanced the bonds being formed. The students become the greatest supporters of one another. Upon graduation, I was encouraged to apply to New York University. In spite of life-changing events and newfound academic success, when the idea of applying to New York University was broached, I think I moved forward more of a false bravado than confidence, to combat my internal fears. My greatest concern was not the idea of not being accepted, but giving into the fear of not applying. So, against all my own fears and doubts, I applied. I met with members of CI who were pursuing their academic careers at some of this country's most prestigious institutions, and again, their optimism outweighed my pessimism. Each time I would leave those conversations thinking, just maybe, and that shot of optimism would sustain me long enough to make the next step. I can't remember how long my acceptance process took, but similar to my experience at BCC, I found myself waiting to learn of my acceptance to New York University. In June 2014, the email confirmation finally came, informing me that my application to NYU was accepted. During my first semester there I spent a great deal of that time just relishing in the fact that I was completing my undergraduate studies there, even though I did not allow myself to get lost in the euphoria for long. I began to apply the same principles that I had utilized while at BCC, and in May of 2016, I earned my Bachelor's in Social Work.

As a senior at NYU I was honored with the distinguished 2016 President's Service Award and the Excellence in Leadership Award for my development of College Pathways, a program founded in the framework of College Initiative. My academic career and development of the College Pathways Program was highlighted in NYU's American Story. This fall I am slated to begin graduate school, where I will intern at the Mc Silver Institute for Research and Poverty. Having seen the cycle of poverty, substance abuse, unemployment, homelessness, and incarceration firsthand, I am committed to promoting educational and criminal justice reform. I am still an active member of CI, currently mentoring one student.

The greatest influence that CI has had on my life is expressed in the work I now do as the College Pathways Advisor for The Doe Fund. There I have established other networks to assist students with educational opportunities, but 90 percent of my students are referred to CI. My belief and support of the program is my guiding force today. I am grateful to College Initiative for their work and commitment not only for opening the door to higher educational opportunities, but for their unflagging belief in the human spirit: that everyone, even those beset with life challenges, possesses the capacity to succeed.

REFERENCES

Amos, J. (2010). *New PEW Report: Young Black Men without a High School Diploma Are More Likely to Be Found in a Cell than in the Workplace*. Alliance For Excellent Education New PEW Report Young Black Men without a High School Diploma Are More Likely to Be Found in a Cell than in the Workplace Comments. N.p., n.d. Web. 28 Oct. 2016.

Greenhouse, S. (2012, April 25). Equal Opportunity Panel Updates Hiring Policy. *New York Times*. Retrieved September 29, 2016, from http://www.nytimes.com/2012/04/26/business/equal-opportunity-panel-updates-hiring-policy.html.

Hill, A. (2015). *Education Reduces Recidivism-Loyola University Chicago*. Retrieved 29 September 2016, from http://luc.edu/media/lecedu/law/centers/childlaw/childed/pdfs/2015studentpaper.

Kafele, B. K. (2012, October). *Empowering Young Black Males*. Association for Supervision and Curriculum Development. Retrieved September 25, 2016, from http://www.ascd.org/publications/educational-leadership/oct12/vol70/num02/Empowering-Young-Black-Males.aspx.

Minton, T. D., & Zeng, Z. (2015, June). *Jail Inmates at Midyear 2014*. Bureau of Justice. Retrieved 25 September, 2016, from http://www.bjs.gov/content/pub/pdf/jim14.pdf.

Schaps, E. (n.d.). *The Role of Supportive School Environments in Promoting Collaborative Classrooms*. Retrieved September 25, 2016, from https://www.collaborativeclassroom.org/research-articles-and-papers-the-role-of-supportive school-environments-in-promoting-academic success.

Tag, B. (n.d.). A quote by Malcolm X. Retrieved September 25, 2016, from http://www.goodreads.com/quotes/788-education-is-our-passport-to-the-future-for-tomorrow-belongs.

Wynn, J. (2001). *Inside Rikers: Stories from the World's Largest Penal Colony*. New York: St. Martin's Press.

Chapter Fourteen

High School Equivalency as Counterspace

Joni Schwartz

GED preparation courses and examinations continue to be a significant focus of adult basic education in the United States, despite efforts to retain high school students; the 2014 redesign of the test; and the now for-profit status of the GED Testing Service. For many marginalized African American males and other young men of color who have not had the privilege of attending a quality high school, the GED is a reasonable alternative to high school completion (Tuck & Neofotistos, 2013). Collectively, African-American and Hispanic men are the least likely to graduate from high school or college. According to recommendations from a recent national report, "policy makers must make improving outcomes for young men of color a national priority" (College Board Advocacy & Policy Center, 2013, p. 70).

While policy makers hopefully work to make systemic changes to address racial inequities that have historically haunted public and higher education, African-American and other young men of color are entering adult education for GED preparation. In fact, during the 1990s there was an actual "adolescentizing" of the GED (Rachal & Bingham, 2004). In this past decade, nearly half of GED test-takers were under 21 years of age (Zhang, Han & Patterson, 2009). We know from talking to adult educators, and can infer from demographic data on high school completion (Schott Foundation for Public Education, 2012) that many of these adolescents and young adults are men of color.

The GED is sometimes considered a lesser alternative to or second chance for high school, and in some instances it is. However, for some young men who had few alternatives but to attend violent, chaotic, and toxic high schools, the GED may be a good choice. The purpose of this chapter is to do what Tuck calls "reclaim the GED" (2012) and to position GED programs not as an alternative to high school, but as a counterspace in response and opposition to young men's previous school experiences. This chapter is based on an ethnography of one community-based urban GED program and looks at the elements that make a GED program a potential counterspace.

COUNTERSPACE DEFINED

The concept of counterspace derives from critical race theory (CRT), which originated in legal studies (Delgado & Stefancic, 2012), but is now utilized across academic disciplines. CRT postulates that race is prevalent in any discussion of education and cannot be separated from a larger social context. The issue of race is full of contradiction and complexity, particularly as it is institutionalized. CRT further holds that the disparity in educational opportunity is an issue of civil rights and social justice (Heaney, 2000; Ladson-Billings, 2005; Closson, 2010).

Using this CRT framework, Solórzano and colleagues defined counterspace as a regenerating space that black students created in white universities to escape discrimination. Counterspaces are often created in same-race settings to acknowledge a marginalized group's life experiences (Solórzano, Ceja, & Yosso, 2000). They may be actual physical places of meeting or emotional spaces of voice, resistance, and healing. Carter (2007) calls these spaces "identity affirming counterspaces" (p. 542).

Case and Hunter (2012) expand the definition of counterspace to include settings that promote emotional and psychological health for individuals who have experienced marginalization and oppression. Counterspaces challenge deficit perspectives, creating interior and external spaces of resistance (hooks, 1989) which are characterized by counterstorytelling and solidarity.

This chapter expands the concept of counterspace to include GED programs. These programs can serve as a space in response and opposition to young men's previous school experiences. Both CRT as the prevailing paradigm and counterspace as an operational concept are relevant, because the participants are African Americans and Hispanics attending schools of color but within the United States where racial marginalizing is institutionalized and the prevailing cultural pedagogy is "white" (Grant, 1992, p. 112).

THE ETHNOGRAPHIC STUDY—THE YOUNG MEN AND PRIOR SCHOOLING

Javier, Dustin, Jamal, David, and Shaw and eleven other African-American and Hispanic males ages 16–25 were GED students and participants in an ethnography of an Adult Basic Education (ABE) program in a large urban northeastern city. Note that all names and all names that accompany quotations are pseudonyms throughout this chapter. The program served 700 students annually in GED, English for Speakers of Other Languages (ESOL), and literacy classes. The remainder of this chapter is based on the findings of this research (Schwartz, 2010; Schwartz, 2014).

The young men reported that their previous schools were unsafe or unjust spaces marked by frequent violence, abuse, excessive rules, drab surroundings, and what students perceived to be ethics violations. At best, their schools were nondescript and unpleasant spaces where neither teachers nor students wanted to be. These previous settings were not predominantly white schools, but racially diverse or predominantly black schools with a racially diverse staff. The atmosphere was chaotic and tense, with frequent gang activity and bullying. Gun-related violence permeated many of the high schools, and the young men reported feeling unsafe both physically and emotionally. Abuse ranged from mild teasing and bullying to physical violation, from neglect to psychological mistreatment. Learners reported that inappropriate special education placement, racial profiling, and low expectations resulted in boredom. The young men stated that such an environment was normal to them.

THE GED PROGRAM AS COUNTERSPACE

In contrast to the toxic schools that the young men had left, the GED program was a space of physical safety, voice, silence, emotional healing, and relationship. The young men viewed the GED as a counterspace embodied in physical, ideological, and experiential dimensions (see figure 14.1).

Physical Place and the Circle

The physical layout of a classroom elicited powerful feelings the moment students walked in. For Javier, Dustin, Jamal, David, and Shawn, the space did not "communicate" public school. They reported feeling safer because the physical configuration of furniture and dimensions of the room were in contrast to public schools with isolated classrooms, drab walls, police security, and barred windows. The GED program was housed in two gymnasium-size rooms with high ceilings and no walls between study groups. Learners perceived these open classrooms as spaces safe from the threat of violence. The rooms felt unconfined and not cramped. Javier said that the space allowed him to see what was going on. Dustin scoped the room before taking a seat; scanning brought a feeling of safety because he could "eye" the three wide doors for easy egress.

Within these large rooms, eight to twelve small groups met around their own table. There was no physical separation between tables. Each circle was self-contained and intimate. There could be as many as twelve circles with twelve different activities. Participants spoke about the comfort of "my group" or "my space" in contrast to traditional classrooms of 30 students in rows and desks. Similar learning circles have deep roots in this country, reaching from Native American culture to adult education practice best exemplified at Highlander Folk School, where the open circle and rocking chair configuration are historic (Horton, 1998, p.150).

The relationship between race and classroom architecture was not explicitly explored in this ethnography, but the significance of the physical setting and the learning circle was prevalent in the findings, especially as the space counters and looks different than past learning spaces.

Space for Voice

What does it mean to make room for voice within a program? Black feminists were among the first to articulate "coming to voice" and to use voice as resistance to oppression and marginalization. hooks (1989) describes this speaking up, speaking out, telling your story, whether it be through writing, dissenting, discussion, public speaking, rap, or poetry. She wrote: "oppressed groups who have contained so many feelings—despair, rage, anguish—who do not speak for fear they won't be heard [for them] coming to voice is an act of resistance" (p. 12). This need to speak about the different dimensions of one's life begins the "process of education for critical consciousness" (p. 13).

In the same vein, the GED program fostered spaces where the men could use this liberatory voice: in student councils, speaker forums, and discussion circles as well as in writing and in writing-sharing groups. These are democratic forums for dialogue and dissension, listening and speaking. Again, these spaces are not new to adult education, but speak to the very history of the field. Past examples are best epitomized by Danish Folk Schools, the Antigonish Movement and Highlander (Jorgensen & Schwartz, 2012).

Among the most valued experiences of space for the men was writing. This was dedicated writing time within each small group; the goals of these 20-minute intensive sessions were to write for GED practice and for their own "coming to voice" for healing. Writing created space to say what might not be spoken, and the men were often very candid and frequently wrote their pain. The young men began by writing personal narratives about past educational experiences and trauma (Schwartz, Schwartz, & Osborne, 2012), often using journaling, poetry, and sometimes rap.

Writing seems a less risky initial approach to sharing pain—an opportunity to get the pain on paper, to examine, share, and sometimes ease it. Learners' journals frequently mentioned hardship, feelings of invisibility, and how "it feels in the heart of a man." The men wrote about their "pops being always locked up" and "mom's never being around" and the impact that such events had on their progress in school. They wrote about daily racial microaggressions (Sue, 2010) that they experienced as black males in a racialized society.

After writing, learning circles frequently engaged in what the program called "knees knocking": another space where students and tutors read the writing. Knees knocking was voluntary. Writers sat in a circle of chairs with no physical barrier between them, aiding listening and intimacy. The space is guarded, meaning that once the group starts no one new can enter.

Total respect for the reader was expected, and responding to the content of the writing was primary. Field note:

> Six young men sit in a circle of chairs with their knees almost touching. Justice reads his personal narrative. The other five listen, bending into the center trying to catch every word. The piece is about the writer's betrayal and brutal gang initiation. Fortunately, the beating was intercepted, and the writer got away with minor bruises. Yet the emotional trauma was evident. Once the writer finished reading, someone whispered, "That's OK, man, it happens to the best of us." The others nodded in agreement.

The goal of knees knocking was to understand the writer's experience, to acknowledge and affirm his voice, and to assist the writer in moving forward through his pain, as well as to grow as a writer. These spaces are not explicitly therapy; however, they do seem palliative.

In addition to sharing their writing, the learning circles discussed newspaper articles and history readings from the GED book and other sources, attempting to make connections between the present and history—a space of intergenerational knowledge and voice. Mills (2000) calls this space "the sociological imagination" where an individual's problems are understood in relation to larger social and economic contexts.

After reading about for-profit prisons, one circle discussed the connection between past physical slavery and current mental slavery precipitated by re-segregation of public education. Outside of school, stop and frisk policies and the mass incarceration of black men continue to oppress. The group viewed this as a whole system set up for failure. While accepting responsibility for their own contributing behaviors, group members were invigorated when reflecting on the possibility that their own school failure may have been part of these larger systemic failures and institutionalized racism.

Research participants spoke about microaggressions on the job, in public places, in the church. They agreed that discussions of race were crucial, because there are few spaces to talk honestly about the "hard issues," and race is a hard issue "that everyone tries to avoid." Although the topic of race is often uncomfortable and complex, if it is not addressed "another negative message is sent to these young men that this is another place where racism is avoided" stated Shawn. Shawn then went on to straightforwardly voice,

"Yes, you are black and you are starting the race from somewhere in the back" because race was never completely uprooted or addressed.

Space for Silence

Coming from crowded urban neighborhoods and chaotic schools, the men expressed appreciation for spaces to be quiet, to think, and to feel. In the GED program, favorite spaces were the intentional silence during reading and writing that provided solitude with others. Thirty minutes of sustained silent reading (SSR) in each class was one such space. SSR is not unusual to K–12, but it may be less frequent in adult education. Typically, SSR is a designated period of silent reading when a whole class or school reads. The activity normally includes administrators, staff, teachers, and students, and in this GED program, such was the case. Thirty minutes each session were spent in SSR when often hundreds of learners in two large rooms were silently reading material of their choosing. Fieldwork notes record the following dialogue and observation. "Take out your favorite book, sit back, relax, and begin reading"—a voice from the microphone announces. David takes out a paperback with no cover; he reads with his tutor and his small group for 30 minutes—no moving, in complete silence.

This quiet space was counter to the constant chatter of many classrooms. Javier described SSR as "peace," giving him a sense of relaxation and focus. Knowing that to pass the GED exam they needed to read often, participants reported SSR as a primary space that engaged them. Quiet was so rare in their lives—separated from cell phones, texting, the Internet, and television, this counterspace made room for self-reflection.

Silence is also healing. "A safe place" is free from physical and emotional harm or potential violence, but "a healing place" is where emotional residue rises to the surface where it can then be addressed. According to John Rich (2009), we have underestimated the impact of all types of violence in and out of school and the "persistent psychological wounds" they cause to men in our inner cities (p. 12). Wounded individuals full of fear of failure and carrying unresolved pain cannot achieve a GED until healing is addressed (Schwartz, Schwartz, & Osborne, 2012). The young men reported that they wanted to learn, but often were carrying so much pain underneath seemingly hard exteriors that concentration was impossible. The silent spaces of reading time proved palliative.

Both the silent reading and writing spaces provided think-time. Neurological science has posited writing as a vehicle for thinking and a tool for cognitive restructuring (Menary, 2007). Thus the combination of silence and writing provides potentially cognitive and therapeutic benefits. Silence is in a sense countercultural, and in that respect, was a type of counterspace which was highly valued by the young men.

Mentoring Space

Mentoring is a recognized strategy for addressing the educational success of disengaged youth (Jekielek, Moore, Hair, & Scarupa, 2002; Miller, 2008). All five key informants reported that their mentors in the program were responsible for their reengagement. These relationships were emotionally intense, beginning at the GED program, but sometimes extending outside into their personal lives. The men reported having strong positive feelings for their mentor (who could be a tutor, staff member, or a peer) and believed the relationship was instrumental in their development of self-esteem and mental health.

These affective relationships were a type of counterspace as places of openness and trust, as opposed to previous school experiences where trust was almost always absent. The term "affective relationship" is adapted from the term "affective talent" and emphasizes the connection between the affective and cognitive aspects in learning (Astin, 1984) as well as the spiritual domain (Palmer, 1998). This mentoring relationship is characterized by its holistic, reciprocal nature as well as by the absence of color/race blindness (Bonilla-Silva, 2003).

Holistic

These relationships are holistic in that they address the totality of the person. For example, Shawn and his tutor studied math and science (cognitive) but also discussed the pain of being placed in special education and fears of failure (emotional). Because the program was housed in a church, they both felt comfortable praying together about both the GED and Shawn's fears (spiritual).

Emotional attachment is at the core of this mentoring relationship. The young men reported feeling and discussing a whole range of emotions while engaged in cognitive work. This is not surprising, as neurological research has determined that the brain does not separate emotions from cognition (Caine & Caine, 1994).

Javier described his relationship with Ms. Y, an internship coordinator, as one where he not only learned filing, computer, and appropriate workplace communication, but also learned to "release stress and pressure and absorb the love" from her. The data were permeated with affective language; the men were not afraid to use phrases like "I got mad love for [my tutor]," "that's what I call love," and "he's on my back but that's because he cares."

It seems that the formation of affective relationships was in part a result of the mentors' affective talent (Astin, 1984) for empathetic communication. A mentor's expectation that the young men take personal responsibility for their learning is balanced by sensitivity to the social context that has played a critical role in inhibiting progress in the first place.

In addition to the emotional and cognitive, there was often a spiritual dimension to the mentoring relationship not uncommon in adult education (Tisdell, 2008). As part of a faith-based initiative, the program was connected to a church; this connection made spiritual relationships not only commonplace but acceptable. For purposes of this discussion, spiritual relationships are defined as relationships that focus on the development of a religious faith, a spiritual inner life, and a relationship with God. Because prayer, Bible study, and worship through the church were voluntarily available, and the mentors were often members of the church, they frequently become spiritual guides and supports for the young men. This aspect of the affective relationship was culturally familiar to the young men, with the exception of David, who were all raised in the church and were open to and very accepting of spiritual support.

Reciprocal

In addition to being holistic, the relationships were reciprocal. These are adult-to-adult partnerships, sometimes of the same race and gender but also of mixed race and gender. Communication was characterized by dialogue, choice, autonomy, learner-centeredness, mutual respect, and equalitarianism—characteristics that define adult relationships (Knowles, 1970). Both participants in the relationship appeared to "share power." Often it was difficult to differentiate between tutors and students; all were together, sharing books they were reading, conversing and debating on current events, and negotiating the goals for the session.

Students provided emotional support to tutors, as well. Dustin's mentor had a death in his family, and Dustin organized the sending of cards and gifts. Other men exchanged phone calls and text messages when a mentor was sick. They prayed for each other. David helped his tutor move to a new apartment.

Sometimes these relationships extended long beyond the program and included multiple mentoring roles: parent, older sibling, teacher, guidance counselor, career or college consultant, therapist, friend, co-learner, spiritual advisor, and coworker.

Tutors helped with college tuition, rent, carfare, food, and clothes. They talked about getting sufficient sleep, about the importance of completing homework, avoiding potentially harmful sexual activity, how to respond when approached by the police, and choosing the right friends. Shawn's mentor addressed Shawn's drug use and entrance to college. The tutor contacted drug programs, made follow-up phone calls to reengage Shawn, and finally paid his college entrance fee.

Sometimes the mentor advised about colleges and the admission process, college fairs, and financial aid. Mentors and learners attended college open houses. Intense emotional health issues also were sometimes broached—issues of loss, gangs, bullying, and reentry from prison. Mentors appeared to keep good boundaries, and connected to professional therapists and guidance counselors when appropriate.

Absence of Color/Race Blindness

Although the research participants were black and Hispanic males and the majority of the tutors black and Hispanic as well, the data were clear that the gender or race of the mentor in an affective relationship was not a salient concern to the young men. Gender and race were much less important than their mentor's expressions of care (Ladson-Billings, 1997).

However, what did seem to matter, and what speaks to counterspace, is that the mentor did not engage in color-blind or race-blind discourse. Color or race blindness is the paradigm held by many whites, and some blacks, that race and racism are no longer issues in America and that they no longer have the power they once held. It is also the negation of white privilege (Bonilla-Silva, 2003; Doob, 2013).

Whether white or black, the mentor's capacity to address race and to open spaces for dialogue around race's impact on learning and equality of opportunity was necessary for counterspace development. The ability to avoid color-blind discourse that allows for the easy negation of racism and neither challenges nor examines current racism seemed to be more crucial in a mentor than gender or race.

GED tutors with this color-blind schema appear to have difficulty creating counterspaces that are emotionally safe for dialogue that engages issues around racial micro- and macro-aggressions that impact black men in America and their educational pursuit. Counterspaces do not deny individual responsibility or excuse lack of effort and lackadaisical intellectual engagement, but the concept does recognize the systemic forces of marginalization and oppression that still exist. Therefore, effective counterspaces must have mentors who recognize and can verbalize the impact that racism continues to have on African Americans and other young men of color.

CONCLUSION

In view of these findings, what recommendations can be made for GED programs as they engage African-American males and young men of color? First, be intentional about creating counterspaces and strategically plan with young men. Elicit their ideas and partner with them in designing or rethinking learning spaces. Don't underestimate the impact that past schooling experiences—violence before, after, and during school—has had on the young men. Think about ways to make learning spaces emotionally as well as physically safe. Encourage young men to talk and write about prior school experiences and their hopes for a different experience in your adult education program.

Second, do not underestimate the power of physical space. Within the financial and spatial limitations you have, think "outside the box" about how your physical space can be counterspace to previous schools. Simply re-arrange the tables, desks, or chairs to create small groups with a classroom—the less the space looks like school the better. Third, create experiential spaces like SSR and knees-knocking as well as discussion circles that make room for small-group learning and embrace both voice and silence.

Fourth, with your staff and volunteers, encourage critical reflexivity that examines schemas toward race and racism and examines how these schemas help or hinder the establishment of counterspaces that are holistic, reciprocal, and are absent of color/race blindness. Engage your staff and volunteers in the hard conversations—communication around race. Especially if your group is predominantly white, it will be necessary to explore white privilege and how it manifests in relationships with men of color. It will be important to explore biases, stereotypes, and colorblind thinking with the ultimate goal of transformative learning for all. Finally, actively work toward creating counterspace through physical, ideological, and experiential dimensions with the goal of engaging previously marginalized GED populations.

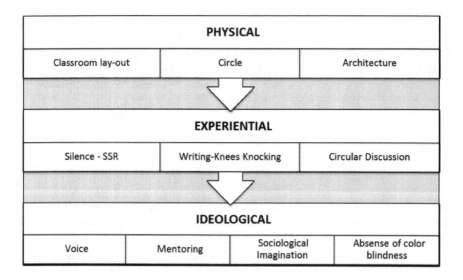

Figure 14.1.   Dimensions of GED Counterspace. *Figure created by Joni Schwartz.*

This chapter was previously published in *New Directions in Adult and Continuing Education, Swimming Upstream: Black Males in Adult Education, no. 144, Winter 2014 © Wiley Periodicals, Inc.*

REFERENCES

Astin, A. W. (1984). Student involvement: A developmental theory for higher education. *Journal of College Student Personnel, 25*, 297–308.

Bonilla-Silva, E. (2003). *Racism without racists: Color-blind racism and the persistence of racial inequality in the United States.* Lanham, MD: Rowman & Littlefield.

Caine, R., & Caine, G. (1994). *Making connections: Teaching and the human brain.* Menlo Park, CA: Innovative Learning Publications.

Carter, D. J. (2007). Why the black kids sit together at the stairs: The role of identity-affirming counter-space in a predominantly white high school. *The Journal of Negro Education, 76(4)*, 542–55.

Case, A. & Hunter, C. (2012). Counter-spaces: A unit of analysis for understanding the role of settings in marginalized individuals' adaptive responses to oppression. *American Journal of Community Psychology* (1–2): 257–70.

Closson, R. (2010). Critical race theory and adult education. *Adult Education Quarterly, 60*(3), 261–83.

College Board Advocacy & Policy Center. (2013). *The educational experience of young men of color.* New York. Retrieved from http://youngmenofcolor.collegeboard.org.

Delgado, R., & Stefancic, J. (2012). *Critical race theory: An introduction* (2nd ed.). New York: NYU Publications.

Doob, C. (2013*). Social inequality and social stratification in US society.* Upper Saddle River, NJ: Pearson.

Grant, C. (1992). *Research in multicultural education: From the margins to the mainstream.* London: Falmer Press.

Heaney, T. (2000). Adult education and society. In A. L. Wilson & E. R. Hayes (Eds.), *Handbook of adult and continuing education* (pp. 559–72). San Francisco: Jossey-Bass.

hooks, b. (1989). *Talking back: Thinking feminist, thinking black.* Cambridge, MA: South End Press.

Horton, M. (1998). *The Long Haul.* New York: Teachers College Press.

Jekielek, S., Moore, K., Hair, E., & Scarupa, H. (2002). Mentoring: A promising strategy for youth development. Washington, DC: Child Trends Research Brief.

Jorgensen, S., & Schwartz, J. (2012). Continuing the legacy: Democracy and education practice. *Journal of Research and Practice for Adult Literacy, Secondary and Basic Education, 1*(3), 179–84.

Knowles, M. S. (1970). *The modern practice of adult education.* Englewood Cliffs, NJ: Cambridge Adult Education/Prentice-Hall Regents.

Ladson-Billings, G. (1997). *Dreamkeepers: Successful teachers of African-American children.* Hoboken, NJ: John Wiley & Sons.

Ladson-Billings, G. (2005). The evolving role of critical race theory in educational scholarship. *Race Ethnicity and Education, 8*(1), 115–19.

Menary, R. (2007). Writing as thinking. *Language Sciences, 29*, 621–32.

Miller, D. (2008). *Man Up: Recruiting and Retaining African-American Male Mentors: Executive Summary.* Baltimore, MD: National Urban League.

Mills, C. W. (2000). *The Sociological Imagination* (40th Ed.). New York: Oxford University Press.

Palmer, P. (1998). *The Courage to Teach.* San Francisco: Jossey-Bass.

Rachal, J., & Bingham, M. (2004). The Adolescentizing of the GED, *Adult Basic Education: An Interdisciplinary Journal for Adult Literacy Educational Planning*, 14:1, 32–44.

Rich, J. (2009). *Wrong Place, Wrong Time.* Baltimore: John Hopkins University Press.

Schott Foundation for Public Education. (2012). *The Urgency of Now: The Schott 50 State Report on Public Education and Black Males.*

Schwartz, J. (2010). *Engaging out of school males in learning.* Ann Arbor, MI: ProQuest. Published Ph.D. dissertation.

Schwartz, J. (2014). Classrooms of spatial justice: Counter-spaces and young men of color in a GED program. *Adult Education Quarterly, 64(2),* 110–27.

Schwartz, J., Schwartz, P. (Producers), & Osborne, R. (Documentarian). (2012). *A New Normal: Young Men of Color, Trauma, & Engagement in Learning* [Documentary]. New York City: City University of New York. https://www.facebook.com/anewnormalyoungmenof-color.

Solórzano, D., Ceja, M., & Yosso, T. (2000). Critical race theory, racial microaggressions, and campus racial climate: The experiences of African-American college students. *The Journal of Negro Education*, 69(1/2), 60–73.

Sue, D. W. (2010). *Microaggressions in Everyday Life.* Hoboken, NJ: Wiley, Inc.

Tisdell, E. (2008). Spirituality and adult learning. In S. B. Merriam (Ed.), *New directions for adult and continuing education* (27–36). San Francisco: Jossey-Bass.

Tuck, E., & Neofotistos, T. (Eds.) (2013). Youth to Youth Guide to the GED. http://sites.newpaltz.edu/youthguideged/wp-content/uploads/sites/9/2013/04/Youth-to-Youth-Guide-to-the-GED-Final.pdf.

Tuck, E. (2012). *Urban Youth and School Pushout: Gateways, Get-aways, and the GED.* New York: Routledge.

Yosso, T., Ceja, M., Smith, W., & Solórzano, D. (2009). Critical race theory, racial microaggressions, and campus racial climate for latina/o undergraduates. *Harvard Educational Review*, 79, 659–90.dropus

Zhang, J., Han, M. Y., & Patterson, M. (2009). Young GED Examinees and Their Performance on the GED Tests. *GED Testing Services Report.* Washington, DC: American Council on Education.

Chapter Fifteen

Creating Counterspaces in College

LaGuardia Community College's
Correctional Education Initiative

Jane MacKillop

As has been seen in earlier chapters, City University of New York's LaGuardia Community College has always had a strong sense of social justice and has a history of serving vulnerable, first-generation students such as immigrants, minorities, and those involved in the criminal justice system or at risk. This chapter lays out the processes involved in researching the needs of this last group and most especially what formerly incarcerated students have to say about their own hopes and aspirations. This is done with the hope of enabling other colleges to learn from LaGuardia's experience at conceiving of and creating counter-spaces. The definition of counterspaces used in this chapter is from the *American Journal of Community Psychology*. It describes the settings (lounges, offices, rooms), which are considered safe and have the potential to promote well-being and liberatory responses to oppression (McConnell, Todd, Odahl-Ruan, & Shattell, 2016). It was through an action research project entitled the "Correctional Education Initiative" that LaGuardia faculty and staff came to understand how the college is already meeting the needs of this group and what could be done to enhance our efforts. This chapter describes the findings and recommendations of the initiative, many of which uncover and explore the need for counterspaces to promote the well-being of marginalized groups such as formerly incarcerated people. The findings and recommendations were based on interviews with formerly incarcerated students, community-based organizations (CBO), local agencies and colleges, and other extensive research. The most important source of information was the students themselves, both those who had reentered the community and those who had family members who were involved in the criminal justice system.

INITIATIVE BACKGROUND

LaGuardia's long history of involvement with correctional education started in 1983 with educational programs for inmates and detainees in New York City's prisons and jails. Over the following 12 years, faculty and staff at the college created and implemented a variety of programs for men and women both on-site at the college and in the correctional facilities themselves. These came to a halt in June 1995 with the enactment of lengthy mandatory minimum sentences, a consequence of the "Three strikes and you're out" laws. This refers to *de facto* sentences of life imprisonment after a person is convicted of three violent or serious felonies although sometimes a "strike" can include a non-violent and petty crime (Western & Petitt, 2010). At the same time, federal Pell grants for inmates were discontinued and after 1995 only the grant-funded educational program for youthful offenders remained at LaGuardia. This program provided an opportunity for more than 700 young men and women annually to prepare for college, employment, or high school equivalency at Rikers Island jail, one of the world's largest correctional facilities, and at the college following release.

A COLLEGE-WIDE RESPONSE TO THE IMPACT OF MASS INCARCERATION

In fall 2015 LaGuardia's president, Gail Mellow, called a college-wide meeting to find out what was happening on campus, both officially and unofficially, for formerly incarcerated students. At that meeting, attended by over 30 faculty and staff, she heard that there were isolated pockets of support and mentorship provided by people who often had direct experience of the criminal justice system themselves and had informally become "go to" resources for those whose experience was similar. It was also noted that there were a number of grant-funded programs for youth at risk of being, or actually who were involved with the criminal justice system as well as one program at a local jail and several training programs which by nature of their target population served people who had been formerly incarcerated. Out of that meeting with President Mellow in fall 2015 came the Correctional Education Initiative, the mission of which was to "explore the reentry landscape, evaluate how LaGuardia Community College currently serves youth and adults who are incarcerated, formerly incarcerated or at risk, and their families and recommend how the College can improve those services and educational opportunities."

The Initiative took place over a seven-month period, from December 2015 through June 2016, and involved many of the upper-level administrators of the college and a working group of 14 faculty, staff, and administrators from each of the college's main divisions, including Student Affairs, Academic Affairs, Adult & Continuing Education, Institutional Advancement, and the President's Office itself.

FINDINGS OF LAGUARDIA CORRECTIONAL EDUCATION INITIATIVES WORKING GROUP

While some of the findings of the initiative are unique to LaGuardia, the majority have wide application to all colleges seeking to support people reentering the community post incarceration. The first questions we asked were: *Who are the justice-involved LaGuardia students and How do formerly incarcerated prospective students enroll in the college?*

The working group discovered that there is no single conduit through which they enroll in college. Some have heard about the college during outreach sessions at local correctional facilities or at the Rikers Island jail; they may apply in the usual way through LaGuardia's Admissions or the University Application Processing Center. They may also enroll as a result of successful experiences in one of the Adult & Continuing Education training and pre-college programs. Some formerly incarcerated students enroll at La-Guardia through programs such as the Bard College Prison Initiative or John Jay College's College Initiative. The Bard Prison Initiative (BPI) offers the opportunity for incarcerated men and women to earn a Bard College degree while serving their sentences. It currently enrolls nearly 300 women and men pursuing either associate's or bachelor's degrees in six prisons across New York State each year. When they are released, Bard students transfer to local, mostly City University colleges. The College Initiative is part of John Jay College's Prisoner Reentry Institute and is an innovative reentry program linking formerly incarcerated men and women with college programs, primarily at the City University. But there is currently no single place at La-Guardia Community College where formerly incarcerated students can "land"; there is no "landing strip" available for them to alight on when they enroll.

JUSTICE-INVOLVED STUDENTS

Another question was: *How big is the universe of formerly incarcerated students at the college?* The working group learned that there is no readily available answer to this question; there is no way to know which LaGuardia students have been or are currently involved in the criminal justice system, if for no other reason than the question, quite properly, is not required on the CUNY application form. As part of the Correctional Education Initiative an attempt was made to estimate the number in the following way: Using incarceration data from the website *justice.com* and poverty data from the census, a list of the zip codes with the highest poverty/incarceration rates in NYC was created. (Poverty levels and incarceration rates are closely related.) The college's Institutional Research office then ran a search in the LaGuardia/ CUNY student database for all male students from those zip codes who enrolled at the college in credit courses, which totaled 4,805. Omitting students under age 25 from this estimate resulted in 1,015 first-time male students, of whom 40% may have been formerly incarcerated (Western & Pettit, 2010), that is, approximately 406. This number is a conservative estimate of formerly incarcerated credit students at LaGuardia, and using the same methodology we estimated that 622 non-credit students participating in Adult & Continuing Education training and pre-college programs may have been in prison or jail prior to coming to the college, giving a total for the college of 1,028. Note that this number does not include students from other zip codes or women or students under the age of 25 and is therefore likely to be on the low side.

We also tried to ascertain how many students have family members who are or have been incarcerated. And again, this had to be a rough estimate. Since LaGuardia students are predominantly immigrants (60% are foreign born, the largest groups are from South America and from India, Pakistan, and China, much smaller numbers are from Europe and Africa) the native-born estimates may not apply because immigrants are less likely to be incarcerated. Given that, it is estimated that the families of about a third of LaGuardia students include members who have been involved with the criminal justice system.

STUDENT DISCUSSION GROUPS

Members of the working group convened five student discussion groups as part of the evaluation of how well LaGuardia Community College currently serves youth and adults who are incarcerated, formerly incarcerated, or at risk. The college had never before reached out to this group specifically and that by itself sent a strong message to the college community. Recruitment for the discussion groups was done by means of flyers, announcements in class, and word of mouth. Participants were compensated with gift cards and Metro cards. Faculty and staff from the working group moderated, recorded, and transcribed the discussions. Seventeen formerly incarcerated current or former students (three groups) and 12 students (two groups) who have family members involved in the criminal justice system (incarcerated in prison or jail) discussed their experiences and made recommendations, each group meeting for a minimum of two hours.

The decision to have discussion groups of family members was based on the knowledge that more than five million children nationally have an incarcerated parent. There is a vicious cycle of poverty, incarceration, and school failure that is reproduced from one generation to the next. The LaGuardia students in the two family groups (all women) talked about "everyone losing," that is, incarceration not only affecting those incarcerated but also those left behind. One student said: "My father had left me when I was a baby. He was locked up and that really hurt me a lot." Another summed up the entire sad situation saying, "There's an effect that the families on the outside experience as well as those who are incarcerated. Everyone loses, not just the inmate himself."

It is impossible to exaggerate the impact of mass incarceration on families and family life, not only while the relative is incarcerated but also after he (it is most often "he") is released and is looking for work and trying to renew relationships.

Communities of color have been disproportionately affected by imprisonment policies and lengthy sentences and these are the communities from which LaGuardia Community College draws the majority of its students.

The students who had themselves been formerly incarcerated spoke in their discussion groups of the need to "create a new you," that is, figuratively to leave behind the person who got into trouble and made wrong decisions and become another person altogether. Students who have been involved with the criminal justice system described how churches and other religious organizations are able to help by providing a supportive community with clear expectations and a new self-image, for example, as a Christian or a Muslim. Another means to a new self-image is through education: by enrolling in college and becoming a student. Many of the most successful transitions into society are the result of forging "new selves" by completing a college degree. Enrolling in college allows a formerly incarcerated person to start over, to set new goals, and to begin with a clean slate. The success of such efforts is demonstrated by the fact that the recidivism rate for students in the College Initiative program is just 3%, compared to the national recidivism rate for all former prisoners, which ranges from 33% for women to between 43–60% for men.

The 17 students (all men) in the discussion groups of those who had been formerly incarcerated spoke of being significantly helped by different organizations such as community-based social service organizations, LaGuardia College programs such as the Black Male Empowerment Cooperative (BMEC), and the pre-college remediation program, CUNY Start. It is important to note that the students who participated in the discussion groups are successful students who have made it thus far, and in some cases have graduated from the college. There is no way to hear from those who never applied or who "melted away" after applying but before ever getting to the college or left halfway through their first semester. Those we met with were already "persisters." They talked a lot about the choices they had made:

"I got locked up and I didn't like the decisions that led me there."—Male, 25

"At the time, when I came here, I had a choice—I was on probation, right? I was still caught up in some stuff that I shouldn't be doing, so the choice was either go back to school or go back to prison. So, I chose school."—Male, 35

They described the impact of coming to college:

"I think coming to school changed me in more ways than one, not just furthering my education, but it gave me more of a purpose."—Male, 22

The students also talked about the excitement of learning, the joy of expanding their educational horizons, and the surprise at their own intellectual success:

> So, I decided I was going to go to college and basically when I got on that road, the more I started to learn the more I started feeling like things could actually go my way if I just accept this path. So, that got me way more interested in college.

But they also talked about the critical lack of information when they were released:

> When an inmate, ex-con, or whatever gets out of jail they don't have the right information, you know? So, they just go back to the community and they have nothing and they just fall right back into the system. So, information is just not available to them at the time when he really needs it.

This was in keeping with the working group's findings that students at LaGuardia who had been involved in the criminal justice system have interacted with many agencies and services. For example, the NYC Department of Correction, for students coming from NYC jails; the NYS Department of Corrections and Community Supervision, for those returning from NY State prisons; the U.S. Bureau of Prisons, for those returning from federal prisons. While we refer to the "criminal justice system" it is actually 18,000 different systems, nationwide, diffuse and unconnected (WNYC, 2016). Justice-involved youth also interact with the Department of Youth and Community Development, while the departments of Justice, Veterans Administration, Probation and Parole have direct responsibility for people who are or have been incarcerated.

In addition to these city, state, and federal agencies, the working group discovered that various services are provided by a wide variety of agencies and organizations: non-profit community-based organizations, the public library system, religious groups (mosques, churches, synagogues, and interfaith), professional associations, colleges and universities. Community-based organizations range in size and scope from the long-established, multi-service linchpins of the system, providing housing, training, employment, health services, and referrals, to smaller CBOs that specialize in serving women, or former substance abusers, or young adults as well as churches, mosques, and interfaith groups, which reach out to people reentering the community as part of their mission.

There are many services and resources for those reentering the community, but the working group at LaGuardia was most struck by how access to those supports sometimes seemed haphazard and required a recently released man or woman to navigate complex systems to obtain needed services, education, and training. New York State's Division of Criminal Justice Services (DCJS) has a reentry strategy to reduce recidivism and promote community safety by means of county reentry task forces that coordinate and strengthen community program services to help moderate to high-risk offenders remain crime-free as they transition from prison back to the community. County reentry task forces function to reduce recidivism and increase public safety through the coordination of services provided to individuals released from prison (Division of Criminal Justice Services, 2017).

RECOMMENDATIONS 1

Given this plethora of service providers, it was not surprising that the students wanted the college to act as a coordinator.

"LaGuardia could have some kind of contact with the probation and parole office."—Male, 35

They wanted a person who would help them navigate the college bureaucracy and who understood where they were coming from.

"I didn't have anybody to talk to who understood the process."—Male, 53

They even envisaged a separate reentry program, in which formerly incarcerated students could play the role of mentor.

"I really think there needs to be a reentry program for students that are already in school and also for students coming in. And those of us who have experience and have knowledge would be able to be more of a counsel than somebody with just book knowledge who's never been to prison."—Male, 25

They wanted separate services.

"For individuals that are formerly incarcerated one of the things that is necessary is that there's a liaison here that understand the process, somebody that understands the space."

But simultaneously they were afraid of seeming different, of being singled out, and they were anxious not to be stigmatized.

"It's been somewhat demoralizing and it needs to get better. It still continues to linger over me and I don't understand how millions of dollars are
being thrown into the reentry program but there's still stigma."

The students made a number of specific recommendations, beginning
with a pre-release outreach program with jails and prisons in New York City
and upstate and stronger connections with local CBOs and agencies. Specifically, they said that:

"LaGuardia could have some kind of contact with the probation and
parole office." —Male, 35

But at the same time, they were ambivalent about having an office like the
Veterans Office where they would be identified and stigmatized simply by
crossing the threshold. Like the community-based organizations, the students
recommended that the college start early by connecting with reentering students directly through staff at local jails as well as local and upstate prisons.
It was clear from the student discussion groups that the college should raise
awareness to better understand and elevate the concerns and challenges of
reentering students, and those students with relatives involved in the criminal
justice system. This ranges from faculty arranging office hours at flexible
times for those who might have curfews or meetings with parole officers, to
ensuring that admissions and financial aid counselors know the "work-
arounds" for students who might not have financial information, tax records
(or parents' tax records), a mailing address, earnings record, Social Security
card, or high school diploma.

RECOMMENDATIONS 2

The working group, at a number of roundtables and meetings, also surveyed
the correctional education landscape in New York City to discover what the
college's role could and should be. At two roundtable meetings in April
2016, representatives from 22 community-based organizations, religious organizations, and prison reentry associations discussed their understanding of
the role of the college. During the course of the roundtables, the community-
based organizations made a number of suggestions. They, like some of the
students, recommended that LaGuardia have a presence at correctional facilities upstate for pre-release engagement, because although sending flyers and
written materials to jails and prisons is helpful, it cannot replace a real person
able to answer questions and encourage potential students. They also recommended partnering with reentry organizations, connecting even more closely
with John Jay's College Initiative and with government agencies in order to
deliver shared programs, secure funding, and shape policy. They urged the

college to be mindful of the particular issues of mothers. They recommended creating the role of "navigator" and assigning it to at least one person whose responsibility would be to ensure that people who identified as having been previously incarcerated knew where to go for help and were properly served. Finally, they suggested having a centralized location where formerly incarcerated students could meet, but not be labeled.

The CBOs warned against having a deficit-based perspective and creating any sort of stigma. Reentry is a stage rather than a permanent condition and many people who have been incarcerated want to move on. Finally, the CBOs urged the college to know its niche, which is education and advocacy, rather than trying to be all things.

As we have seen, the feedback and the recommendations from the CBOs, the agencies, and other institutions of higher education were clear and unequivocal: Start working with potential students before they leave jail or prison, collaborate with all the other organizations, and keep to our core mission. But the response from the students was more complicated. On the one hand, they wanted some special services and sensitive treatment, on the other they did not want to be singled out. Much of what they highlighted in current college practice as less than satisfactory is unsatisfactory for all students, not just those who are formerly incarcerated; the intelligent, thoughtful treatment they expected from counselors and advisors is appropriate for all students; flexible faculty office hours are valued by all students, not just those who have curfews or need to meet with their parole officer.

As a result of the feedback from the CBOs, but especially from the students, the college is looking to integrate and align its services and schedules more closely and provide professional development for frontline staff (including the "work-arounds" needed for students who may not have the necessary documentation, remembering that they may not all be formerly incarcerated, they could be refugees, undocumented, or estranged from their parents). The college also recognizes that jail and prison can be so traumatizing that there is a need for specialist counselors or "navigators" to provide practical support and a safe space for people reentering the community. The safe space can be within another existing student space and the navigator can be one of a team of advisors and counselors, but there needs to be an actual location for formerly incarcerated people to regroup and where trained support is available.

GOING FORWARD

LaGuardia Community College's mission to "educate and graduate one of the most diverse student populations in the country to become critical thinkers and socially responsible citizens who help to shape a rapidly evolving society" moves the college's faculty to tackle the moral imperatives of racism awareness and action.

When the Correctional Education Initiative working group examined the college's capacity and resources to serve people reentering the community, they noted the wide variety of training and education programs available either through pre-college training or Associates degree programs. LaGuardia's Division of Adult & Continuing Education (ACE) offers many non-credit academic, professional training, and business programs for adults and youth in New York City. These include free (to the student, grant-funded) and tuition-based certification in a wide variety of health areas, computer applications, and support and training in the "Green" industries, as well as programs specifically targeting young fathers, approximately 50% of whom have been involved in the criminal justice system. In addition to assisting young men with obtaining a high school equivalency diploma and getting into college, the counselors work with them to navigate and complete parole or probation requirements. Two academic programs, the paralegal program and the criminal justice major, provide the foundation for careers in law, police, corrections, and social services related to community supervision and reentry.

Importantly, in addition to programs for the health, development, and overall well-being of LaGuardia's students sponsored by the Division of Student Affairs, the Black Male Empowerment Cooperative Program (BMEC) offers particular supports for those at-risk of involvement with the criminal justice system and those with criminal justice histories. It is a retention program designed to engage and empower young men (and women) to be lifelong learners and active participants in their own educations. BMEC is a community of students connected to each other and the college through academic support services and mentorship, networking opportunities, mentoring, personal guidance and academic tutoring, and Real Talk sessions. Its recently expanded and renovated space potentially provides a "landing strip" for students who are or have been involved in the criminal justice system.

The well-established paths from non-credit training courses to credit programs at LaGuardia also facilitate reentry. For example, some Adult & Continuing Education non-credit training programs are eligible for credit when students enroll in degree programs (e.g., the Community Health worker and Emergency Medical Technician certificates).

It is this combination of mission, broad academic offerings, and location that has made LaGuardia Community College an excellent provider of education and training on-site at correctional facilities and an ideal place for people who are formerly incarcerated to reenter the community. It is intrinsically a safe space.

As a result of the Correctional Education Initiative the college has a much clearer sense of how to proceed in raising awareness of the needs of students who have been involved in the criminal justice system and responding to those needs. This year the Carnegie Seminar for the Scholarship of Teaching and Learning offered by The Center for Teaching and Learning at the college is on "Incarceration in Daily Life" and the next issue of the college publication, *In Transit*, will focus on issues of criminal justice and mass incarceration. Other initiatives in Academic Affairs include modifying the First Year Seminar to reference the needs of formerly incarcerated students, including a reentry component in the current New To College Seminar for new faculty and staff and developing a cluster of interdisciplinary classes to focus on the factors that contribute to mass incarceration, highlighting careers in psychology, criminal justice, human services, counseling, and therapy. The college and the theater company Ping Chong + Company will seek funding to together create a performance giving voice to the stories of people involved with the criminal justice system.

LaGuardia rolled out a new program in fall 2016, the Second Chance Pell pilot program, which offers courses for college credits and industry-recognized certification in partnership with John Jay and Hostos Community College at two New York State prisons: Otisville and Queensboro Correctional Facility. The U.S. Department of Education has implemented experiments to allow colleges and universities to test alternative methods for administering the federal student aid programs under Title IV of the Higher Education Act (U.S. Department of Education, 2017). It is to be hoped that this will open the door to more on-site credit and non-credit education and training programs funded through Pell grants in state and city correctional facilities.

The college is also seeking funding for college-wide professional development in this area and has already self-funded the "navigator" position. The navigator, who is located in the Black Male Empowerment Cooperative space, will facilitate communication and optimize resources for students early in the reentry process, manage partnerships, facilitate information-sharing across departments, present LaGuardia's programs to policy makers and potential funders, and serve as a resource to provide information about correctional education opportunities. As partners with reentry organizations and the university faculty senate committees on Higher Education in the Prisons, we are already engaged with other like-minded agencies, organizations, and institutions to improve outcomes for the formerly incarcerated members of our community.

The final word on counterspaces belongs to our students:

> I would rather (the space) be a gathering. Instead of people feeling like they need help, more just like let's reach out and go somewhere. Like not feeling like there's obstacles in front of us that we have to already overcome. There needs to be some sort of liaison that can bridge the gap for us so we can feel more comfortable and more easily get accustomed to getting back in school.

Specifically, for people who have been incarcerated. Or maybe there can be an office specifically for people who have been incarcerated.

This expression of a desire for a safe space describes a place to regroup, catch your breath, and move ahead. It is fundamental to the effective reintegration of people who have been formerly incarcerated, a space in which they can come home.

REFERENCES

Division of Criminal Justice Services. DCJS County Re-entry Task Force Initiative. (2017, February 17). Retrieved from http://www.criminaljustice.ny.gov/crimnet/ojsa/initiatives/offender_reentry.htm.

McConnell, E. A., Todd, N. R., Odahl-Ruan, C., & Shattell, M. (2016). Complicating counterspaces: Intersectionality and the Michigan women's music festival. *American Journal of Community Psychology*, 57: 473–88. doi:10.1002/ajcp.12051.

U.S. Department of Education. U.S. Department of Education Launches Second Chance Pell Pilot Program for Incarcerated Individuals. Program will build on existing research to examine effects of restoring Pell eligibility (2017, February 17). Retrieved from: https://www.ed.gov/news/press-releases/us-department-education-launches-second-chance-pell-pilot-program-incarcerated-individuals.

Western, B., & Pettit, B. (2010). Incarceration & social inequality. Daeulus–American Academy of Arts & Sciences, pp. 8–19. http://www.amacad.org/publications/daedalus/10_summer_western.pdf.

WNYC (Producer). (2016, October 12). Brian Lehrer Show [Radio show]. NewYork City: National Public Radio. http://www.amacad.org/publications/daedalus/10_summer_western.pdf.

Index

About the Contributors

John R. Chaney, J.D., is widely recognized as a leading authority in developing effective agency partnerships that deliver essential transitional services for returning citizens. Currently a full-time criminal justice faculty member at the City University of New York (CUNY) LaGuardia Community College, he is perhaps best known for his notable appointment as an administrative manager for the high-profile Brooklyn District Attorney's Office, an unprecedented post-release accomplishment for a formerly incarcerated individual. Between 2009 and 2014 he served as the agency's executive director for the nationally acclaimed ComALERT (Community and Law Enforcement Resources Together) reentry program and as the New York State–appointed coordinator for the Kings County Reentry Task Force. A frequent media guest and expert panelist, John R. Chaney has provided technical assistance to the criminal justice section for the American Bar Association, the ACCES-VR (Adult Career and Continuing Education Services-Vocational Rehabilitation) division for the New York State Department of Education, Nevada Workforce Connections, and the New York State Division of Criminal Justice Services. His work has received formal recognition from the New York City and State legislature, and he has received civic awards from several community organizations. Born and raised in Harlem, New York, he received his Bachelor of Arts degree from New York University and a Juris Doctorate with honors from Brooklyn Law School.

Joni Schwartz, Ed.D., is a social activist scholar and founder of three adult education centers in New York City: Turning Point Brooklyn, the Brooklyn Tabernacle Downtown Learning Center, and Bethlehem GED as well as the former education director for Literacy Partners, Inc. As research coordinator for the Black Male Initiative (BMI) at New York City College of Technology, her research focused on men of color in STEM as well as high school push-outs. A recipient of a BMI Outstanding Academic Service Award and the NYC Literacy Assistance Center Outstanding Literacy Practitioner Award, she co-produced the documentary *A New Normal: Young Men of Color, Trauma & Engagement in Learning* through a CUNY Cultural Diversity Grant and is working on a second documentary about incarceration and education. Currently she is an Associate Professor of Humanities at LaGuardia Community College. Her work is published in the *Adult Education Quarterly, Science Education, International Journal of Science in Society, Adult Learning Journal,* and *Journal of Research and Practice for Adult Literacy, Secondary, and Basic Education.* She is coeditor of two volumes of New Directions in the Jossey-Bass series *Swimming Upstream* and general editor for *Dialogues in Social Justice: An Adult Education Journal.* Dr. Schwartz has degrees from the University of Minnesota, New York University, and Rutgers University.

* * *

Tiheba Bain is a student at City College, City University of New York, and was featured in the film *After Incarceration and Engagement in Learning.*

Michael Baston, Ed.D., J.D., is vice president for Student Affairs and Campus Life at LaGuardia Community College, City University of New York.

Michael Carey, MA, is director of the Prison Video Project for the Brooklyn Public Library; former director of College Initiative, a New York–based organization that helps formerly incarcerated and court-involved men and women enroll and succeed in college; and founder of the InterDependence Prison Project created in 2008.

Terrance Coffie is a graduate of Bronx Community College, the NYU Silver School of School of Social Work, and cofounder of "The Pathways Program," providing young men in need with educational opportunities.

Norman Conti, PhD, is associate professor at Duquesne University. He has published ethnographies of recruitment, socialization, masculinity, and ethics training in policing as well as two analyses of the social networks that develop within cohorts. His writing has appeared in *Policing & Society, Journal of Contemporary Ethnography, Police Practice & Research, Social Networks,* and *Prison Journal.*

Elliott Dawes, LL.M., J.D., is chief diversity officer for Institutional Equity and Inclusion at Empire State College, State University of New York; former developer and director of The City University of New York Black Male Initiative (CUNY BMI), as well as a former trial attorney in the Educational Opportunities Litigation Section, Civil Rights Division of the U.S. Department of Justice.

Colleen P. Eren, PhD, is associate professor in the criminal justice program at LaGuardia Community College, City University of New York. Her book, *Bernie Madoff and the Crisis: The Public Trial of Capitalism* (2017), is available through Stanford University Press.

Cory Feldman, PhD, is assistant professor in the criminal justice program at LaGuardia Community College, City University of New York.

Elaine Frantz is associate professor in the history department at Duquesne University. She is a member of the Elsinore Bennu Think Tank. She is currently working with Norm Conti and Amber Epps to edit a collection of writings on identity, transformation, and incarceration written by inside members of the think tank.

Tony Gaskew, PhD, is series chief editor and director, Criminal Justice Program, and associate professor of Criminal Justice Division of Behavioral and Social Sciences at the University of Pittsburgh-Bradford.

Joshua Halberstam, PhD, is a faculty member at Bronx Community College and Columbia University and author of *Everyday Ethics: Inspired Solutions to Real Life Dilemmas and The Community College Guide: The Essential Reference from Application to Graduation.*

Davon T. Harris is a student at LaGuardia Community College, City University of New York.

Michael Holzman, PhD, is an independent researcher and author of *The Chains of Black America, The Black Poverty Cycle and How to End It, Minority Students and Public Education*, and the Schott Foundation's report series on Black Males and Public Education.

Jane MacKillop, PhD, is interim dean of the School of Continuing and Professional Studies at Lehman College. Dr. MacKillop has worked in adult education in the United Kingdom and the United States for over 30 years, including 10 years as associate dean at LaGuardia Community College and senior consultant for the Correctional Education Initiative. Author of several books, white papers, and articles in adult education, she serves on the board of the Continuing Education Association of New York State, where she is co-chair of the professional development committee.

Brian Miller is a master's degree student at City University of New York and former coordinator for the Black Male Empowerment Cooperative at LaGuardia; chapter author of "Returning to School after Incarceration: Policy, Prisoners and the Classroom," in *Swimming Upstream: Black Males in Adult Education and The Intersection of Black Lives Matter and Adult Education: One Community College Initiative.*

Joserichsen Mondesir is a student at LaGuardia Community College and coauthor of "Returning to School after Incarceration: Policy, Prisoners and the Classroom," in *Swimming Upstream: Black Males in Adult Education.*

Paul J. Schwartz, LCSW, MSW, is faculty crisis counselor at New York City College of Technology and adjunct professor in the Graduate Center Counseling Program at NYACK College, and coauthor of *A New Normal: Young Men of Color, Trauma and Engagement in Learning.*

Dwayne Simpson, MSW, CASAC, is Offender Reentry Counselor for New York State Department of Corrections and Community Supervision, and Certified Alcohol and Substance Abuse Counselor.

Timothy Stater is a student at Brooklyn College and coauthor of "Returning to School after Incarceration: Policy, Prisoners and the Classroom," in *Swimming Upstream: Black Males in Adult Education.*

Carlyle Van Thompson, PhD, is a faculty member with the English Department at Medgar Evers College and author of numerous books, including *Black Outlaws: Race, Law, and Male Subjectivity in African American Literature and Culture, Eating the Black Body: Miscegenation as Sexual Consumption,* and *The Tragic Black Buck: Racial Masquerading in the American Literary Imagination.*